THE GOLDEN HOUSE OF NERO

Some Aspects of Roman Architecture

JEROME LECTURES

FIFTH SERIES

THE GOLDEN HOUSE OF NERO

Some Aspects of Roman Architecture

by AXEL BOËTHIUS

THE UNIVERSITY OF MICHIGAN PRESS   ANN ARBOR

Copyright © by The University of Michigan 1960
Library of Congress Catalog Card No. 57–9137
Published in the United States of America by
The University of Michigan Press and simultaneously
in Toronto, Canada, by Ambassador Books Limited
Manufactured in the United States of America

PREFACE

The lectures of which this book is a revised edition were delivered at the American Academy in Rome in December 1953 and at the University of Michigan in April 1954. My lectures at Ann Arbor were combined with teaching. In December 1953 and January 1954 Professor Lily Ross Taylor and I conducted weekly lectures and excursions for the classical group of the American Academy in Rome. I shall always remember the associations of those two months as among my pleasantest experiences of academic teaching. As I send out this book I hope it will reach some of my former students and remind them of the happy days we had together.

First of all, I wish to express my sincere thanks to the committee of the Jerome Foundation for the honor of being appointed Jerome lecturer. I regard Thomas Spencer Jerome as a great benefactor of mine and have with much interest come to know his classical research, his enthusiasm for his old University and for American studies in Rome, and his contributions to the American scholarly tradition in Italy. Warmest thanks go also to the director of the American Academy in Rome and to Mrs. Laurance P. Roberts for friendship and hospitality in the Villa Aurelia. I am deeply indebted to Mr. Roberts, to the American Academy, and to my friends here for inspiration, facilities for work, and congenial company, with rich exchanges of ideas and results in the library, where Mrs. Inez Longobardi is so competent and friendly a help, and in the delightful cortile and old Roman garden of the Academy from 1953 and onward to the present day. Many friends and colleagues are connected with my recollections of my work as a Jerome lecturer ever since I started to discuss my English with Dr. and Mrs. C. L. Barber and Mrs. Claire Elmqvist in 1953 in Göteborg. Professor Arthur E. R. Boak belongs to the friends from memorable weeks in Ann Arbor. He has further given me invaluable help in revising my English and in discussing the questions raised by my book. In that connection I remember also with special gratitude Messrs. Robert Broughton, Spencer Corbett, Mason Hammond, Paul Mac Kendrick, John Ward Perkins, Erik Sjöqvist, Miss Gisela Richter, and one of my oldest friends in Rome, Mr. A. W. Van Buren. I have been provided with photographs through the kindness of H. M. the King of Sweden and of a number of museums and friends, among whom I wish to mention especially Dr. Ernest Nash, director of the Photoreference Collection of Roman Architecture and Topography (Fototeca Unione).

The manuscript of this book was ready in February 1958. Important contributions to the problems discussed in my four chapters have appeared since then. I have been able to refer to some of them in the notes and in an Addendum. Of great importance in the revision of my public and private lectures have been two books which appeared after the lectures were delivered: Ferdinando Castagnoli, *Ippodamo di Mileto e l'urbanistica a pianta ortogonale*, and G. Lugli's monumental *La tecnica edilizia romana* (1957). Castagnoli has been able by pioneer work with air photographs to put the study of regular town planning on a new and better base than before, though in many respects the principles are the same as those which I tentatively laid out in my lectures and in my article, "Die hellenisierte italische Stadt der römischen Republik" (*Acta Athen. Suec.*, II, 1953). Lugli's *magnum opus* is for me connected with some thirty years of friendship and joint research with Italian colleagues, who have been actively present to my mind from beginning to end as I wrote the present lectures. Warmly remembered too are my first teachers in the field of Roman architecture—Thomas Ashby, Guido Calza, Tenney Frank, Esther B. Van Deman, Eugenia Strong, and Armin von Gerkan.

CONTENTS

ILLUSTRATIONS

THE GOLDEN HOUSE OF NERO

Some Aspects of Roman Architecture

FIG. 1. Hut urn, dolium, and models of
household implements (10 is a cooking
stand) from a tomb in the cemetery
along the Via Sacra in Rome (tomb 4,
period II A).

After E. Gjerstad, *Early Rome*, II (1956).

CHAPTER I

FROM EARLIEST ROMAN VILLAGES
TO ETRUSCAN URBANIZATION

There is no Homer or Hesiod to tell us what men, their dwellings, and their altars were like in early Iron Age Italy. Italy as a part of a primitive western Europe had no legacy from a splendid Bronze Age like the Minoan and Mycenaean period in Greece and had none of that wonderful richness and creative strength which characterized Homeric and geometric Greece even when compared with the Oriental empires in their late Babylonian, Assyrian, and Saitic renaissance.

When we take up the problems of Roman architecture we must begin with shepherds' huts resembling those found on green hills of the Roman campagna through the ages (Figs. 1–3). In Rome itself the admirable work of Giacomo Boni and in the last few years the excavations and research of Pietro Romanelli, Riccardo Gamberini, Salvatore M. Puglisi, Marella Vianello, Gianfilippo Carettoni,[1] and Einar Gjer-

1. P. Romanelli, G. Carettoni, E. Gjerstad, and S. M. Puglisi, "Nuove indagini su Roma antichissima," *B.P.I.*, n.s. 9, LXIV (1954). Among earlier publications see especially Puglisi, "Gli abitatori primitivi del Palatino," *Mon. ant.*, XLI (1951), 3 ff.; P. Mingazzini, *Bull. Comm.*, LXXIII (1949–50), 261; Romanelli, Puglisi, and A. Davico, *Rivista di antropologia*, XXXVIII (1950–51), 19 ff.; and articles, reports, and reviews in *Antichità, Fascicoli di studi e notizie sul mondo classico diretti da M. Marella Vianello*, I (1947); II (1950).

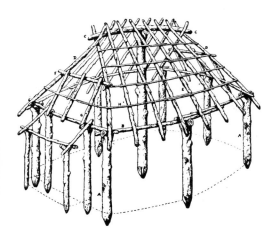

FIG. 2. Hut on the Palatine. Reconstruction by A. Davico. *Rivista di antropologia*, XXXVIII (1950–51).

stad[2] have given us a vivid picture of these villages on the Palatine of the eighth and seventh centuries B.C., with their burial tombs for cremation as well as inhumation (*pozzo* or "pit" and *fossa* or "trench" tombs). Scattered huts seem also to have been built on the other hills. The tradition of a hostile Sabine village on the Quirinal may be based on fact. In any case it is quite clear that the habitation on the Palatine (with extensions in the Via Sacra Valley and on the Forum) was in the seventh century already a large and well-organized settlement, whether one prefers to call it village or town.

2. Hut urns[3] and other urns for the remains of cremated bodies, models of the implements common in those villages, various ornaments, and so-called impasto pottery with incised geometric designs (partly earlier but closely related to the famous Villanova pottery from the hill towns of Tuscany) illustrate the life of the hut dwellers. Remains from the southwestern corner of the Palatine and beneath the peristyle and Aula regia of the Domus Augustiana (the palace of the Emperor Domitian) show rectangular huts with curved corners and a fairly wide entrance door at one short side. These huts were sometimes provided with flanking columns carrying a roof to form a covered approach to the entrance. They had no central hearth. Portable cooking stands of a type well

2. Gjerstad, "Early Rome. I. Stratigraphical Researches in the Forum Romanum and Along the Via Sacra," and "II. The Tombs," *Acta Rom. Suec.*, XVII (1953, 1956). See also A. von Gerkan's article "Zur Frühgeschichte Roms," *Rh. M.*, C (1957), 82 ff., with critical discussion of the historical conclusions and dates suggested by Gjerstad and by K. Hanell in his "Das altrömische eponyme Amt," *Acta Rom. Suec.*, 8:0, II (1946). Important reviews of Gjerstad's work in *Latomus*, XIV (1955), 506 f.; and by I. Scott Ryberg, *J.R.S.* XLVIII (1958), 208; *A.J.A.*, LX (1956), 78 ff.; by F. Castagnoli, *Arch. Cl.*, IX (1957), 134 f. Gjerstad himself has summarized his results in an article entitled "Per strata ad data," *Arkeologiska forskningar och fynd, Studier utg. m. anl. av H.M. Konung Gustaf VI Adolfs sjuttioårsdag* (Stockholm, 1952), 108 ff.

3. The material has been collected by J. Sundwall. See his "Die italischen Hütturnen," *Acta academiae aboensis. Humaniora*, IV (Åbo, 1925); and W. R. Bryan, "Italic Hut Urns and Hut Urn Cemeteries," *P.A.A.R.*, IV (1925). Cf. also the bronze hut urn in the Metropolitan Museum of New York, *B.M.M.A.*, XXXIV (March 1939), 60 f. The *Casae Romuli* on the Palatine and Capitoline suggest that the shape of the old huts was remembered *per saecula*; *Eranos*, XLI (1943), 174.

known from models in the tombs and remains in the huts were used for preparing food and for heating. The walls and roofs were of wattle daubed with clay and were supported by uprights. As the hut urns of the tombs show, the walls might be decorated with incised and painted geometric design. The urns also show that the columns at the entrance might be carved and that outlets for smoke were made above the entrance door, sometimes at both gables. Recent discoveries have added to the picture of the Palatine village not only a tomb of a child but also (at the so-called Villa di Livia) a tomb of an adult man, a cremation tomb with an ash urn of a type known from the cemetery in the Roman Forum,[4] and a portable cooking stand and other typical Iron Age implements. These finds suggest that the clusters of huts in the southwest corner of the Palatine and below the Flavian palace were independent villages divided by a cemetery.

To the old huts on the Palatine belonged the famous cemetery, the cemetery (*Sepulcretum*) which lies in the valley of the Via Sacra and extends westward to the fora of Nerva and Augustus. It was discovered by Boni, and has been studied more recently by Gamberini, Gjerstad, and Puglisi. They have shown that, in the seventh century B.C., huts like those on the Palatine, interspersed with children's tombs (*suggrundaria*), were built over the southern parts of the old necropolis from the temple of Vesta and the borders of the tufa plateau of the valley (the Velia) westward toward the swamp that originally filled the western part of the Forum in the area where the equestrian statue of the Emperor Domitian was later erected. The cult of Vesta probably goes back to this seventh-century village. Remains of cooking stands, spools and spindle whorls, pottery, grains of emmer, einkorn, and barley, horse beans, and fragments of animal bones constitute all the evidence that we have of the activities of its inhabitants. Here we see well-developed, clearly established types of dwellings, but these, like the culture of the villages as a whole, belong to the characteristic restricted and limited creations of prehistoric life.

4. See Carettoni's report in *B.P.I.*, n.s. 9, LXIV (1954), 261 f.

FIG. 3. Swineherds' huts. Gian Felice between Rosarno and Mileto in Calabria.
Photo Brita Wikström 1955.

3. Remains of the same kind of life have also been found on the Oppian hill, on the Viminal, the Quirinal, and in Satricum, in Veii, on the Alban Hills, and so on. Nowhere does there appear any trace of regular planning. The old theories about a Roma Quadrata (not to speak of a terramara village) on the Palatine seem to be completely unfounded.5 All the same the Palatine village obviously was a quite large municipal body and may even have extended its power to habitations on the other hills before Rome was reshaped, about 600 B.C., into a city under Etruscan and Greek influence. The legends about the Palatine—"*hoc primum condita Roma loco est*" (Ovid *Trist.* iii. 1. 32)—may well contain recollections of the role of the inhabitants of that hill in such political endeavors. On the other hand the testimony about the Lupercalia

5. In my opinion Castagnoli proves this in his article entitled "Roma Quadrata," *Studies Presented to D. M. Robinson* (St. Louis, Mo., 1951), 389 ff. S. Ferri has recently tried to interpret the frail tradition in a new way in the *Studi Classici e Orientali* of the Università degli Studi di Pisa, VII (1958), 189 ff.

and the route (*discursus*) of the Luperci and about the religious festival called Septimontium does not prove anything about what Gjerstad calls pre-urban Rome, about its extension, or about the pomerium of the Palatine.[6]

Whatever deep-rooted traditions of community life and cult may have survived from these old villages, they led to nothing from the point of view of formative culture in the field of architecture and town planning. We have, so far at least, not a scrap of evidence which permits us to assert that architectural traditions from the early Iron Age huts had any importance for later Roman architecture. They were simply superseded by the architecture and civic organization that Greeks and Etruscans brought to Italy. Earlier achievements in Italy can perhaps reveal something about pre-existing spiritual tendencies and home traditions, but from the point of view of architectural forms, when a higher culture came from the East, the break was fundamental. Attempts to figure out a coherent typological development from Italic prehistoric art and architecture to mature archaic creations in those fields seem to be completely fallacious. All that the early beginnings can reveal is the local spirit as it was before it was expressed by foreign art.

It seems clear that this early culture of Latium belonged to Indo-European tribes, which very likely invaded Italy—together with the Villanova people of Tuscany—probably already during the Bronze Age and ultimately about 1000 B.C.[7]

6. I refer to the critical analysis of the sources by Agnes Kirsopp Michels, "The Topography and Interpretation of the Lupercalia," *T.A.P.A.*, LXXXIV (1953), 35 ff.; and by Louise Adams Holland, "Septimontium or Saeptimontium?" *T.A.P.A.*, LXXXIV (1953), 16 ff. Cf. also A. von Gerkan, *Rh.M.*, XCVI (1953), 27 ff.; and M. P. Nilsson's "Les Luperques," *Latomus*, XV (1956), 133 ff.

7. Here I to a great extent agree with the opinions recently presented by M. Pallottino in "Le origini storiche dei popoli italici," *Relazioni, Congresso internazionale di scienze storiche in Roma 1955*, II, 1 f., and in his *Etruscologia* (4th ed.; Milan, 1957), Pt. 1, Chaps. 1 and 2. Among older contributions see especially G. Säflund, "Bemerkungen zur Vorgeschichte Etruriens," *St. Etr.*, XII (1938), 17 ff. Pallottino, "Sulle facies culturali arcaiche dell'Etruria," *St. Etr.*, XIII (1939), 85 ff., and *L'origine degli Etruschi* (Rome, 1947); C. F. Hawkes, *The Prehistoric Foundations of Europe* (London, 1940), pp. 303 ff.; A. Furumark, *Det äldsta Italien* (Uppsala, 1947) and L. Polacco, "Rapporti culturali di tre sculture villanoviane di Bologna," *St. Etr.*, XXI (1950), 59.

But did these early ancestors of the Latins, the Sabine and Sabellic tribes, the Faliscans, the Umbrians, and other Indo-European peoples of Roman history have any racial and cultural relationship to their Bronze Age predecessors in Italy and to the so-called Apennine (or *extraterramaricoli*) Bronze Age culture? To me it seems clear that Indo-Europeans mixed with the Bronze Age people, but this has yet to be proved. However, it seems evident that such connections, if any, had not the slightest importance for the architecture and town planning of historic Italy.

Just as clear as the picture of the early Iron Age huts on the Roman hills and other similar settlements are the next basic facts in Italian prehistory, facts that illuminate the darkness of primitive western European culture and usher in the historic ages of western Europe. I mean, first, the beginning of the importation of geometric pottery from Greece into south Italy, Ischia, and southwestern Tuscany somewhat before 700 B.C.;[8] second, the strong Oriental influence at a slightly later period; and, third, the foundation of the great Etruscan and Greek towns in Italy and the influence of Greek archaic culture. But here again problems appear as soon as we try to account for the basic facts of archaeological discovery.

Who brought the geometric pottery from Greece to Italy? Was it Greek pioneers following in the tracks of Odysseus, the Phoenicians, or the Etruscans? The answer inevitably bears on the Etruscan question, although it is, as I see it, more important for the present to characterize the culture of the Etruscans in Italy and visualize it in its historical relationships than to discuss their origins—even though the Oriental features which are so evident in early Etruscan life may have

---

8. Most important are G. Buchner's finds from Ischia. See his communications in *Atti M. Grecia*, n.s. I (1954), 11 ff.; *M.d.I.R.*, LX–LXI (1953–54), 37 ff.; *Rend. Linc.*, s. 8, X (1955), 215 ff. For a general discussion see T. J. Dunbabin, *The Western Greeks* (Oxford, 1948), pp. 3 and 466 f.; Å. Åkerström, "Der geometrische Stil in Italien," *Acta Rom. Suec.*, IX (1943), 88 ff.; see also E. Frézouls "La fondation de Carthage," *B.C.H.*, LXXIX (1955), 170 ff.; and Furumark, *op. cit.*, pp. 82, 93, and 101; and the discussion about Urartu: K. R. Maxwell-Hyslop, "Urartian Bronzes in Etruscan Tombs," *Iraq*, XVIII, 2 (1956), 150 ff.; Pallottino, "Urartu, Greece and Etruria," *East and West*, n.s., IX (1958), 29–52.

been partly the result of an Oriental origin of the people and not merely of the commercial influence that reached the Etruscans in Italy. We must ask ourselves in any case whether the Etruscans were a people who had long lived in Italy and who, in the latter part of the eighth century B.C., were reached by the flow of late geometric pottery from Greece, and later by the Oriental trade. Dionysius of Halicarnassus believed so (i. 30. 2), and Massimo Pallottino and the majority of Italian scholars today agree. Or were Hellanicus and Herodotus (i. 94) right in maintaining that the Etruscans were among the Eastern immigrants who in those early days swarmed westward from Tyre, from Greece, and from Asia Minor?[9] Did they come simultaneously with the Greek and Oriental trade? Did they settle down on the hills in Tuscany where were flourishing already the so-called Villanovan villages with their stately Iron Age? Gösta Säflund has recently suggested that the inhabitants of these Villanovan villages were already Etruscans, on the assumption that they had lived in Italy together with the Indo-European tribes of Latium two or three centuries before the imposition of Greek geometric ware began in the eighth century B.C. and Oriental influences began to be felt.[10] This theory is very attractive, but to me it still seems more likely that the Latin tribes and the Villanovan people of Tuscany were Indo-Europeans and that the Etruscans immigrated in the eighth century.

Another question is: did the long story of successive waves of dominant Greek influence begin with the geometric designs of the Villanovan potters and artisans? Should the

9. In addition to the literature already cited in note 7, see A. Piganiol, "Les etrusques," *Cah. Hist. Mon.*, I (1953), 328 f. Did the old tales about Aeneas belong perhaps to the legends about the arrival of the Etruscans? See V. Georgiev, "Die Träger der Kretisch-mykenischen Kultur, ihre herkunft und ihre Sprache," *Annuaire* (University of Sofia), I (1937), II (1938); and Rhys Carpenter, *Folk Tale, Fiction and Saga in the Homeric Epics* (Berkeley, Calif., 1946), pp. 63 ff. Furumark has suggested (*op. cit.*, pp. 161 f.) that the Etruscans may have been Tyrsenians from Lemnos with Greek geometric culture and that the earliest Greek pottery in southwestern Etruria reveals their arrival. Among F. Altheim's inspiring studies I refer especially to: *Der Ursprung der Etrusker* (Baden Baden, 1950) and *Römische Geschichte*, I (Frankfurt a. M., 1951).

10. Säflund, "Uber den Ursprung der Etrusker," *Historia*, VI (1957), 10 ff.

Villanovan culture consequently be dated to the eighth century B.C., when we can begin to trace the importation of Greek geometric ware into Italy, as Åke Åkerström has suggested?[11] To me it seems obvious that Villanovan decoration was originally independent of Greek art. The early Iron Age culture, as we see it in the oldest tombs of the Forum and other places in Latium and in the oldest Villanovan culture in Tuscany, represents the culture that the Greeks, the Etruscans (if they were eighth-century immigrants), and the Phoenician traders encountered in Italy in the eighth century B.C. To my mind Åkerström has by no means been able to prove that Villanovan art was from its beginnings a conservative local style which was inspired by Greek geometric art but resisted the imported culture of the Etruscans. But I am inclined to maintain with him and with Arne Furumark and Pallottino that Greek influence is visible in the later, rich and fully developed Villanovan decoration, especially that of the metalware.[12]

For the architectural problems discussed here the question of the origin of the Italic peoples is in a way peripheral because all their architecture of any importance for the future starts with imported basic forms. We must accept them as already perfected importations when they appear in Italy, whether they were brought from other lands by immigrants or whether they resulted from the influence of the Phoenician trade. Whatever the date and the racial connections of the importers of Greek geometric pottery and the earliest Oriental products may have been, *in Italy* the Etruscans evidently developed what we call Etruscan culture under the influence of geometric Greece, the Phoenician trade, and the aristocracy of archaic Greece. It is evident—and splendidly proved by the treasures of the famous Etruscan tombs—that the

---

11. *Op. cit.*, 131 ff.
12. Furumark, *op. cit.*, p. 96; Pallottino, *Rend. Pont.*, XXII (1946–47), 31 f.; A. Boëthius, *Eranos*, XLI (1943), 169 f. Excavations in Ardea have revealed bottom layers without Oriental or Greek influence. They illustrate the situation before foreign culture reached the early Iron Age population of Italy; see E. Holmberg, *Boll. St. M.*, III, 3 (1932–33), 6 ff.; A. Andrén, *Acta Rom. Suec.*, XVIII (=*Opus Rom.*, I, 1954), 1 ff., XXI (=*Opus Rom.*, III, 1959), 39–47.

FIG. 4.
Etruscan barrow at Caere
(Cerveteri). Sixth century.
Photo A. B. 1953.

great Etruscan towns in southwestern Etruria came into being in the seventh and sixth centuries B.C. under the influence,
primarily, of Phoenician trade that was attracted by the met-
alliferous deposits of south Tuscany. The culture that we call
Etruscan was created under these conditions. The same commerce is described over and over again in a most vivid way
by Homer and later writers from Herodotus (i. 1) onward.
The parallel Oriental influence in Greece is proved by archaeological evidence of the same kind as is found in Latium and
Tuscany.[13] In Greece it inspired a highly original archaic culture, which also dominated the upper classes of Italy in the
sixth century B.C.

To sum up: about 600 B.C., villages like the one on the
Palatine were associated with neighbors such as Veii, Tar-

13. The Greek material is conveniently collected in Winter's *Kunstgeschichte in
Bildern*, I, pp. 97–117 ("Die Kunst der Homerischen Zeit"). An archaeological
commentary on the Homeric poems with a collection of clearly identified objects from the eighth and seventh centuries B.C. would provide obvious parallels
to the Oriental influence in Italy. See W. Schadewald, *Von Homers Welt und
Werk* (2d ed.; Stuttgart, 1951), pp. 87 f. and 352 f.; and H. Lorimer, *Homer and
the Monuments* (London, 1950), which has a full bibliography.

FIG. 5. Interior of Etruscan tomb. The so-called Tomba della Cornice at Caere (Cerveteri). Figures 5 and 6 no doubt give an idea of Etruscan patrician houses and also of the models for the domus of kings and patricians in Rome in the sixth and fifth centuries B.C. Typical for several of these tombs are the three doors leading from the main halls to chambers behind.
Photo Jan Mark 1956.

quinii, and Caere, which had Tuscan temples, rich chamber tombs beneath mighty barrows, and luxurious halls of the aristocratic families (Figs. 4–8). Farther north the princely families built mound tombs, domes vaulted with overlapping horizontal courses of stones. In the southern towns the Latins and their Italic neighbors encountered chamber tombs like the Tomba Campana in Veii—and no doubt halls—that were painted in Greek fashion with Greek mythological representations and, later, with funeral banquets. They also encountered Greek aristocratic modes and manners and Greek city organization; in short, a cultural life without creative literature but externally with Greek form and organization. The Corinthian pottery and the imitations of Greek vases which have been found in the Roman Forum and the surrounding hills, and also in tombs and strata with remains of habitation elsewhere in Latium, show that the culture of the Etruscan towns influenced their southern neighbors in the seventh century B.C.[14]

As I will point out in the next chapter, nothing in our literary and archaeological material indicates that the old Etruscan towns had any regular plan or shape. They were, no doubt, as crowded and irregular as early Athens and early Rome. But it seems likely that the Etruscans, as a legacy from the traditions of their native land—if they were immigrants —or by influence from the Orient, had certain architectural ideas which were alien to Greek architecture and which had no real background in what we know about primitive architectural attempts in Italy. The predilection for symmetrical and axial planning of public squares and temple courts seems to have been as characteristic of the Etruscans (and of the monumental architecture of the Orient) as it was alien to the Greeks

14. This is clearly shown in Ardea (Holmberg, *op. cit.*, p. 6 ff.). The Roman material has been collected by Inez Scott Ryberg in "An Archaeological Record of Rome from the Seventh to the Second Century B.C.," in *Studies and Documents ed. by Kirsopp Lake and Silva Lake*, XIII (1940). See also Gjerstad, "Early Rome," I and II. For the Etruscan tholos tombs, see Åkerström, "Studien über die etruskischen Gräber," *Acta Rom. Suec.*, III (1934), 134 f., 141, 146, 158, and 163; and Pallottino, *Etruscologia*, p. 100.

in classical and early Hellenistic times.[15] This predilection is probably linked with the basic ideas of the so-called Tuscan temple which displays the *tuscanicae dispositiones* known to us from the dogmatic systematization of Vitruvius[16] with orientation toward the front, a large vestibule, and a closed back wall with one or three cellas built against it (Figs. 7–8). To the old Etruscan features I also venture to assign tombs with tablinum and side rooms behind the main hall, like the Tomba dei Vasi Greci or the Tomba della Cornice (Fig. 5), the Tomba degli Scudi e delle Sedie, and others in Caere (Cerveteri), and the *cava aedium tuscanica* with the same basic disposition and planning. In analyzing this we must remember that the so-called Tuscan architectural types in their late Republican form—as Vitruvius described them and as we see them in Pompeii and Herculaneum—were the result of a long development to which Etruscans, Latins, and other Italic peoples contributed, even though we acknowledge that the Etruscans had an important position down to the second century B.C. within the cultural *koinē* which they had started in the seventh century. But if we stick to the main lines of development, it seems to me that Gjerstad is correct in deriving the plan with a main hall (or court) and tablinum and side rooms on its upper side from the Oriental liwan architecture.[17]

Whatever the derivation and earlier history of these architectural forms may have been, the temple of Jupiter on

15. Cf. on this subject Castagnoli, *Ippodamo di Mileto e l'urbanistica a pianta ortogonale* (Rome, 1956), pp. 65, 72, 103, with very sound conclusions regarding the axial symmetry of Etruscan temples and houses and the late Etruscan town planning and its connections with the regular town planning of the Greeks, which in the fifth century replaced the old irregularity.

16. Vitruvius' chapter about the Tuscan temple (iv. 6 f.) can be compared with the late, final versions of the Etruscan Libri Haruspicini, Fulgurales, and Rituales; see Pallottino, *Etruscologia*, pp. 232 f.; *Studi in onore di Calderini a Paribeni*, III (1956), 223–34; Polacco, *Tuscanicae dispositiones* (Padua, 1952); and my review in *Gnomon*, XXV (1953), 411 ff.; also my remarks in *St. Etr.*, XXIV (1955–56), 137 ff. For the Tuscan temple in general, see Andrén, "Architectural Terracottas from Etrusco-italic Temples," *Acta Rom. Suec.*, VI (1940), pp. 1 ff.

17. Gjerstad, *The Swedish Cyprus Expedition*, IV (Stockholm, 1948), 242; Piganiol, *op. cit.*, pp. 346 f.

FIG. 6. Tomba delle Leonesse. Tarquinii (Tarquinia). End of the sixth century. The great mixing bowl reminds one of the colossal crater of Vix (France) and also of the fame which the Etruscans had as metalworkers among the Greeks in the fifth century.
Photo Alinari.

the Capitoline hill in Rome, which in the sixth century B.C. replaced the altars of old shadowy demons (Dion. H. iii. 69. 4), proves in one case that cannot be disputed that large standardized types of architecture were part of the overwhelming influence of the Etruscan towns in old Latium. Here, in addition to what we know about the building itself, what Pliny (xxxv. 157) and Livy (i. 56. 1) tell about Etruscan workers and about the sculptor Vulca from Veii and the terracotta sculptures which he made for the Capitoline temple clearly shows that a great foreign art was introduced. The famous finds from Veii and from towns like Satricum, Falerii Veteres, Caere, and Rome itself show us what these revolutionary novelties in the center of Rome were like (Fig. 9).

From the fully developed Etruscan art and architecture of the sixth century B.C., we may now, once more, return to the old villages on the Roman hills and all over central Italy. The late Roman authors and artists often with obvious anachronism attributed the origins of their later architecture, temples, city walls, and so on, to a time as far back as that of Romulus. The town of Latinus in the *Aeneid* and the historic frieze of the Basilica Aemilia will serve as illustrations of these anachronistic fancies. But on the other hand the Romans were aware that as late as the beginning of the sixth century B.C., they had no personified images, not even wooden shrines (*kaliades*) for their idols, but only altars of turf.[18] Splendid is Livy's story (i. 10. 5) about the holy oak on the Capitoline hill to which in olden times the spoils of the enemy were carried at the triumphs of the shepherd soldiers. With Rome in their time at its noisiest, the poets of the age of Augustus indulged in descriptions of peasants, happy green valleys, rivulets, and shapeless wooden idols.[19] Above the remains of the Iron Age village, in the southwest corner of the Palatine hill and on the Capitoline, the Romans kept ancestral huts of straw with thatched roofs (*casae Romuli*). These were always rebuilt in the old primitive style,[20] and the traditions connected with them show that recollections of the old villages which existed before the organization of Rome after the model of Greek and Etruscan towns (*poleis*) were also alive. This conception of prehistoric villages might, of course, have been suggested by analogy with contemporary shepherds' huts of the type shown on Roman sarcophagi that has lived on in unbroken succession to the present time, but the archaeological evidence already referred to makes it clear that some real knowledge remained about the prehistoric settlements of

18. Augustine *De civitate dei* iv. 31; Plutarch *Numa* 8. 8; Tertullian *Apologeticus* 25, 12.
19. Propertius iv. 1 and 4; Tibullus I. 10, 17; ii. 5, 55; Ovid *Ars amatoria* iii. 113 ff.; Ovid *Fasti* i. 199 ff. and *passim*; Columella *De re rustica* x. 31 f.; Cicero *De republica* II. 2 (4).
20. Dionysius of Halicarnassus i. 79; Plut. *Romulus* 20; Dio Cassius xlviii. 43, liv. 29; Vitr. ii. 1, 5; Conon *Diegeseis* 48, *F.H.G.*, I, p. 210; Seneca *Controversiae* ii. 1, 5; Vergil *Aeneid* viii. 654.

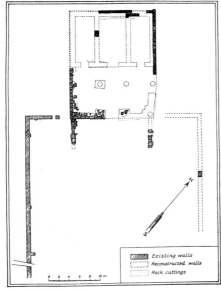

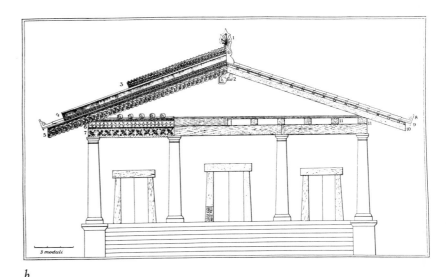

a

b

c

huts scattered without any regular plan. I agree with Romanelli that the site of the Casa Romuli on the Palatine, directly on the top of the early Iron Age village on the southwestern part of the hill, probably demonstrates that the Romans retained a memory of a village of this kind in this place. Contrary to the romantic tales about great luxurious towns there is no doubt real historical not to say archaeological knowledge in Vergil's charming words (*Georgics* ii. 532 ff.) in which he contrasts the old rustic Rome of the Sabines, Romulus, and Remus with the grandeur to come:

This was the life which once the ancient Sabines led,
And Remus and his brother; this made Etruria strong;
Through this, Rome became the fairest thing on earth
And walled her seven hills into a single city.

(translated by Gilbert Highet)

In revising Boni's results and in checking them by his own excavations at the equestrian statue of Domitian (*Equus Domitiani*), around the temple of Caesar, and at the Rostra, Gjerstad has made admirably clear the transition to a town in the Greek and Etruscan sense. At a date which I would assign to the decades about 600 B.C., the huts and tombs in the Forum

d

e

valley were demolished.[21] Above their remains is a floor of gravel and pebbles, the type of paving which may have been in Cato's mind when instead of the paving of his time he wished for a forum paved with *murices* (Pliny xix. 24). Gradually, this civic center was surrounded by buildings with foundations or even entire walls of square-cut stone. This is the Greek and Etruscan urban system that suddenly transformed life in Rome and in towns like Satricum and Ardea all over Latium. A Greek-Etruscan common culture, a cultural *koinē*, spread through central Italy. Directing his attention to Rome only, Gjerstad calls this process "the founding," since he wishes to make it clear that the town of Rome in the

FIG. 7. The so-called Tuscan temple and atrium.

a) Reconstruction of an Etruscan temple with three cellas, closed rear wall and eight columns in front of the cella walls (the cellas right and left of the central cella can have been open alae). Orvieto.

b) Schematic reconstruction of a triple cella, based on Vitruvius and on actual terracotta remains.
After A. Andrén, *Architectural Terracottas from Etrusco-Italic Temples* (1940).

c) Old-fashioned closed façade. Etruscan ash urn. Florence.
Courtesy of the Cabinetto fotografico della Soprintendenza alle antichità di Etruria.

d) Plan of the Casa del Chirurgo, Pompeii. The final shape, with one taberna opened toward the street and with impluvium.

e) A typical old-fashioned atrium.
Photo Tatiana Warscher.

21. Gjerstad dates it 575 B.C. See references to Romanelli, Davico, Puglisi, Vianello, Gjerstad, von Gerkan, and Ryberg in notes 1, 2, and 14. For the rostra see Gjerstad, *Acta Rom. Suec.*, 8:0 1 (*Dragma Martino P. Nilsson dedicatum 1939*), 206 ff. and *Acta Rom. Suec.*, v (=*Opus. Arch.*, II, 1941), 97 f. It must be emphasized that Gjerstad's study is based on his own and Boni's research around the area with the so-called Sepulcrum Romuli and the forum inscription. Excavations made by Romanelli in 1955–56 seem to show that these monuments rest on a hill or outcrop of the Capitoline with different stratification.

Greek sense of the word was founded only in connection
with this archaic cultural *koinē* and to stress what a revolution
this meant in the life on the Roman hills.

It is most important to realize that town life of the Greek
and Etruscan type was an importation which, as I have already
said of the Capitoline temple, was introduced in an already
developed form. That temple was, as far as we know, the
largest of its kind in Italy, and yet it was built only some
ninety years after 600 B.C. It is obvious that in sixth-century
Rome there was no place for a gradual local development of
the chief characteristics of old Latin culture. There may have
been some remolding due to obscure and tantalizing indigenous traditions from centuries of primitive life,[22] but the imported formal culture swiftly changed the whole aspect of
town life, architecture, art, and religion. From an external
and formal point of view Rome now appeared as an Etruscan
town (*polis Tyrrhenis*) or was considered by Aristotle and his
followers as a Greek town (*polis Hellenis*) far away on the
western coasts.[23] Famous monuments, the forum inscription,
the *fibula* from Praeneste (Palestrina) show that the Latin language remained, but—in addition to the overwhelming cultural influences—we have to remember that Rome got Etruscan kings before 509 B.C., and that bucchero pots with Etruscan inscriptions have been found on the Capitolium and on
the Palatine.[24]

In his masterly article "Il grande acroterio femminile di
Veii" Massimo Pallottino[25] has pointed out that archaic art

22.   For instance when the old shrines of Terminus and Juventus were incorporated in the new temple (Dion. H. iii. 69) and an opening in the roof was made
above the shrine of Terminus in the cella of Jupiter himself (Ovid *Fasti* ii.671).
23.   Dion. H. i. 29, 2; Plut. *Camillus* 22; E. Wikén, *Die Kunde der Hellenen von
dem Lande und den Völkern der Apenninenhalbinsel bis 300 v. Chr.* (Lund, 1937),
pp. 171 f.
24.   As a matter of fact these Etruscan inscriptions rank among the oldest inscriptions found in Rome (whilst in Praeneste the famous fibula inscription at-
tests Latin language from the earliest age of Etruscan influence). For the Etruscan
graffiti from Rome see the following publications by Pallottino: *Bull. Comm.,*
LXIX (1941), pp. 101–7; *St. Etr.,* XIII (1939), 427 ff.; *St. Etr.,* XXII (1952–53),
309 ff. *Etruscologia,* p. 118, Pl. X; cf. also *Glotta,* XXXIV (1954), 47 f.
25.   *Arch. Cl.,* II (1950), 122 ff.

had many capitals. It had acquired new and original centers in the far west in the sixth century B.C. This is evident for both art and architecture not only in Etruria, but also in Latium and Rome. Whether Etruscans (like Vulca from Veii), Greeks, or Italiote adepts were the masters, wherever they started to decorate temples and other monumental buildings the archaic Greek style found new centers. In the towns of Asia Minor, and especially in Aeolis, decoration with architectural terracottas persisted as in Italy, even at a time when marble architecture prevailed in the leading centers. It is interesting to learn from Åkerström's studies[26] how dependent on the Greek mainland styles were the terracotta artists of Asia Minor, and how deficient their art grew at the eastern periphery in contrast to the flourishing terracotta art in Italy.

What happened in Rome and the neighboring Latin towns in the sixth century gives us our first instance of a local Roman civilization—that of old villages—being abandoned for more developed, imported cultural forms. On much higher levels the same kind of sudden change appears when archaic style yields to the classical Greek style, and when Ennius gives up the saturnine verses and the national style of the old *Fauni vatesque*,[27] of the old funeral orations,[28] and even of Naevius. Ennius felt it his task as a reborn Homer to interpret the legacy of Rome and give it its true place in the international life of the Mediterranean world. In spite of all the differences of period and cultural situation, one might say that Vulca was, in his field, a predecessor of Ennius.[29]

As I have already pointed out, the Romans loved to dramatize their primitive prehistory after the Greek pattern,

26. Åkerström, "Untersuchungen über die figürlichen Terrakottafriese aus Etrurien und Latium," *Acta Rom. Suec.*, XVIII (=*Opus Rom.*, I, 1954), 191 ff.; "Arkitektonische Terrakottaplatten in Stockholm," *Acta Athen. Suec.*, I (1951); "Die arkitektonischen Terrakotten in Klein-Asien," *Acta Athen. Suec.*, in course of publication.

27. Ennius *Annales* 213 ff.; Cicero *Brutus* 18 (71).

28. Cicero *Brutus* 15 (61); Livy viii. 40, 4.

29. See G. de Sanctis' splendid pages about Naevius and Ennius, *Storia dei Romani* (Florence, 1953), IV, 2. 1, pp. 7 ff.; and also my article "Romerskt och grekiskt," in *Arkeologiska forskningar och fynd, Studier utg. m. anl. av H. M. Konung Gustaf VI Adolfs sjuttioårsdag* (Stockholm, 1952), pp. 92 ff.

but they also loved the charm of the *agreste Latium*, which they knew was behind them, and the *"tetrica ac tristis disciplina"* of the old Sabines, *"quo genere nullum quondam incorruptius fuit"* (Livy 1. 18, 4). In addition to holding these conflicting conceptions of their own prehistory, the Romans—we must also recognize—had very clear notions of the revolution in Italic life caused by Greek and Etruscan influences in the seventh and sixth centuries B.C. In connection with almost all the larger Latin towns we hear about Greek founders, Greek cults, Greek divinities, and Greek festival days. Ovid, speaking of Greek terminology and Greek heroes in Italy, summarized this in his *Fasti* (iv. 63 f.): *"Nec tibi sit mirum Graeco rem nomine dici: / Itala nam tellus Graecia maior erat."*

And Cicero, who elsewhere emphasizes the importance of the Roman character, says in *De republica* (ii. 19. 34) that it was no little rivulet that flowed from Greece to Rome in archaic times (sixth century), but a mighty river (*abundantissimus amnis*) of culture and learning (*n.b.*: through Etruria and the Greek towns of South Italy).

These old stories are basically relevant, quite apart from the testimony about continuous Greek influence in historic times. They may contain memories of Greek Mycenaean or Iron Age adventurers, but obviously are very often only etiological legends of the usual Greek type explaining the archaic Greek cultural influence in old patrician Rome and other towns of central Italy, which the fiercely Republican generation of the fourth and following centuries did not understand.[30] Modern archaeology has explained the context.

As for Etruscan influence, the evidence is less ambiguous and contaminated, which is quite natural since it is based on real events and not merely on legendary explanations. It is

---

30. Boëthius, "Ardeatina," in *Apophoreta Gotoburgensia Vilelmo Lundström oblata* (Göteborg, 1936), p. 368; Pallottino believes more than I in the stories about Greek pioneers behind the finds of Greek ceramics and so forth in Italy from the Bronze Age and the early Iron Age (see his "Le origini storiche dei popoli italici"). In substance, we mean the same; that these stories reveal strong Greek influence. In many instances Pallottino may be right, but I maintain that we must be very careful in attempting to discriminate between vague memories and etiological legends.

evident that in the sixth century B.C. kings of Rome and of the Latin cities were of Etruscan origin and that the aristocracy was imbued with the archaic Greek and Etruscan culture. The great authority which the patricians wielded was obviously connected with the fact that they—in contrast to the plebs—shared in the culture of the Greek and Etruscan nobility. The situation may be characterized by Livy's words about Evander and his primitive subjects: "*Auctoritate regebat loca, venerabilis vir miraculo litterarum, rei novae inter rudes artium homines*" (i. 7, 8). That Vulca from Veii and artisans from all Etruria (Livy i. 56, 1) were summoned to Rome when the last kings started to build the temple of the Capitoline Jupiter is a most significant fact. I have pointed out that at the time it was dedicated in 509 B.C. this shrine seems to have been the largest monumental building of central Italy. In the severe days of the early Republic the Romans needed an explanation for this archaic grandeur, and they interpreted it as proving that the kings had a presentiment of the future greatness of Rome (Livy 1. 38). To us the whole situation is quite clear. The important artistic life in Veii as well as the rich aristocratic culture of the sixth and fifth centuries in central Italy, as we see it even in small sixth-century towns around great centers like Caere, explains the great temple in Rome. In the Etruscan chamber tombs we also get a notion of what the domus of the Roman patricians were like. It contrasts strongly with the *disciplina et continentia* of the harsh Rome of Manius Curius Dentatus and Appius Claudius Caecus, which Cato the Elder exalted as truly Roman in style and which Cicero recalled when speaking of his grandfather's homestead, below Arpinum, as small and like that of Curius in the Sabine country.[31]

The testimony concerning Etruscan influence upon Roman political and religious institutions, ceremonies, and emblems is as clear as it is abundant. In spite of details that are still in dispute, it seems most probable to me that the Roman calendar was introduced at the dedication of the Capitoline

---

31. Cicero *Cato Maior* 16 (55); Ennius 373; Cicero *De legibus* ii. 1 (3). See G. Forni, *Athenaeum*, XLI (1953), 172 f.

FIG. 8. Gable of a temple of Tuscan type, ash urn lid from Chiusi. Sixth century B.C.
Courtesy of the Museo Nationale, Palermo.

temple in 509 B.C. and that it is one outstanding instance of this early Oriental-Greek-Etruscan influence in Italy.[32] In discussing this evidence a general observation has to be advanced. We must remember that the Etruscan influence was by no means confined to the Archaic Age, when the Etruscans were evidently the givers and the Romans the receivers. Exchange between the Etruscans and the Romans continued to the first century B.C., and Etruria remained important throughout this period. Cicero still in *De legibus* (ii. 9. 21), giving the gist of the laws concerning religion, says that according to them prodigies and portents should be referred to Etruscan soothsayers, if the Senate so decreed: "*Etruria principis disciplinam doceto.*"

On the other hand those responsible for the great interest in the Etruscan heritage (the *etruscheria* of late Republican and Augustan times) underrated the importance of Rome's share in the cultural *koinē* of the sixth and fifth centuries B.C.[33] The Romans no doubt even de-emphasized their pre-Hellenistic culture because of the conception which they held of an old, virtuous, and simple Rome—a concept that was already cherished in the days of Cato the Elder and which was summarized by Livy in the preface to his first book (par. 11). The censors tried no doubt to substantiate this conception. In contrast to these tendencies in Rome after 400 B.C., Etruria, like Campania and towns such as Pompeii and Capua, had a period of rich Hellenized culture under the sway of victorious Rome in its mighty fourth-century fortification. The Etruscan production of works of art, *sigilla* and *signa*, remained famous.[34] In spite of their disdain for *obesi Etrusci*, for *Graeculi*,

---

32.   This seems to me to be one of the many valuable results of Hanell's analysis of the sources for the oldest Roman history in "Das altrömische eponyme Amt," *Acta Rom. Suec.*, 8:0, II (1946).

33.   Polacco has made important observations on this subject in his *Tuscanicae dispositiones*, referred to in note 16. See also *Gnomon* XXV (1953), 407 ff., and Raymond Bloch's fine remarks in *Revue de Philologie*, XXVI (1952), 179 f., and in his books *The Etruscans* (London, 1958), *L'art et la civilisation étrusque* (Paris: Plon, 1955), and *Le mystère étrusque* (Paris, 1956).

34.   Horace *Epistulae* ii, 2. 180; Pliny XXXIV. 34; Aeschylus *Eumenides* 567 (*diatoros tyrsenike*); E. Kunze, "Etruskische Bronzen in Griechenland," *Studies Presented to D. M. Robinson*, I, 736 f. and 745. Probably, the *cratera aurea* which the

and for luxurious Capua the Romans continued to learn from both Tuscany and Campania. The well-known Roman contempt for the Etruscans and Livy's famous description of degenerate Capua (xxiii. 2 ff.) give us glimpses of the situation, which has now become quite intelligible thanks to the archaeological evidence from the so-called tufa period of Pompeii and the contemporary prosperity of the Etruscans during the first period of Roman dominion. There was a continuous exchange between Rome and its more luxurious, less disciplined Etruscan, Campanian, and Greek subjects. In Rome there even arose a love for their more easy-going life,[35] a love which proved fatal to the Roman style of the fourth and following centuries.

It is important to remember all this when we try to analyze the authority of the term *tuscanicus* (Etruscan). It is evident that the main reason for the importance of this term was that the Etruscans were the first people in Italy to adopt Greek and Oriental cultures and to spread them to other Italic peoples. The constant use of this word and the weight attached to it would be inexplicable otherwise. As far as this goes, it confirms the priority of Etruscan culture. But it would nevertheless be a serious mistake to accept all the attributions to Etruscan masters made by late Republican and Augustan authors, especially where not only basic features but complete architectural achievements such as the Tuscan temple and the Tuscan atrium of the last centuries B.C. are concerned. As we see them, they were a result of a common Italic development through at least three centuries. It is obvious that the word *tuscanicus* means three different things. Sometimes it means no more than "old."[36] Often it has the more specific sense of

---

Romans dedicated to Apollo in Delphi after the victory over Veii (Livy v. 23, 11; v. 25, 10) was Etruscan. In size this bowl must have equaled that of Vix, the bowl depicted in the Tomba delle Leonesse in Tarquinii and on the silver vase from Chiusi in the Museo Archeologico at Florence. See Inez Scott Ryberg, "Rites of the State Religion in Roman Art," *M.A.A.R.*, XXII (1955), Fig. 3.

35. From Scipio onward. See Strabo v. 4, 7; Plut. *Pyrrhus* 16; Dio C. fragment 57. 62; Livy xxix. 19, 11 f.

36. As used, for instance, in Juvenal's satire xi. 108, in which the spelt (*farrata*) is served "*Tusco catino.*" The same meaning ("old and simple") occurs in Persius' satire ii. 59 f. ("*Tuscum fictile*").

archaic style in art, Greek as well as Etruscan.[37] And, finally, there are many instances in which the word implies actual knowledge of the Etruscan origins of institutions, religion, architectural and artistic features, and so on—or at least familiarity with the basic tendencies alive in them. In reading Vitruvius and in reading Strabo, Livy, and other writers who claim Etruscan origins for Roman traditions,[38] we must always ask ourselves whether they had real evidence (as in the case of the Capitoline temple) or whether they only present conclusions which were fashionable in Augustan times. In addition, it may be true in many instances that borrowed Etruscan forms take us back only to the Hellenistic and Republican times and not to the archaic period of the sixth century B.C., when the center and melting pot for the common culture of the aristocracy of central Italy was still mainly the *litus Etruscum* (Etruscan coast) from Veii to Tarquinii and even farther north—the region to which the origins of Roman architecture belong.

In short, we can trace three conflicting elements in the picture of the early history of Rome that we see in our literary sources. The Romans in late Republican days tried to reconstruct their early history, its heroes, towns, and art, in imitation of the rich historical legends of the Greeks. On the other hand they also loved the old, simple agricultural Rome and its Campagna. Their admiration for its *disciplina* made them underrate the share which Rome no doubt got in the cultural *koinē* of central Italy after about 600 B.C. The third and most important element in old Roman life was the influence from the great archaic Greek and Etruscan towns and the continued exchange with them through Republican times. Those responsible for the *etruscheria* of late Republican and Augus-

37. "Etruscan" is obviously taken as a *terminus technicus* for all that is preclassic in Italy; by Quintilian, for instance, in *Institutio oratoria* xii. 10, 1 ("*differunt . . . ut graecis tuscanicae statuae*") and xii. 10, 7 ("*duriora et tuscanicis proxima Callon et Hegesias*"); Pliny xxxv. 154 (=Varro), "*Tuscanica omnia in aedibus fuisse*"; Pliny xxxiv. 43; Fronto to Marcus Antoninus (=Verus?), Loeb ed., II, p. 48.
38. Pliny xxxv. 157, xxxiv. 34; Livy i. 8, 3; Strabo v. 2, 2; Prop. *Elegiae* iv. 2, 1f. For the romantic *etruscheria* of the Augustan Age the material is abundant, e.g., Horace *Carmina* iii. 29, 1 and 35.

tan days tended to attribute everything to the Etruscans and to forget that Romans had contributed to the development of the common culture which Oriental and Greek influences created in the Etruscan towns of the seventh and sixth centuries B.C.

These three tendencies, taken together, rightly emphasize the three main elements in the culture of early Rome and its Latin neighbors—the Greek influence as evidenced by the presence of late geometric pottery and as lavishly described and freely elaborated by the poets and historians of late Republican Rome; the anonymous legacy of old Italic life, which indeed makes it expedient to regard the eighth-century shepherds on the Palatine as founders of Rome and to realize that Cicero, in spite of freely admitting foreign influences, had reasons to assert (*De republica* ii. 15. 29) that he was not sorry the Romans got their culture from the native excellence of the people (*genuinis domesticisque virtutibus*); and, finally, the overwhelming impact of the archaic Etruscan cities that started Rome as a town in the Greek sense of that word, and the continued exchange between them and their Latin offspring.

With the stories about civilized intruders in early, primitive Italy also belong the famous tales about Aeneas and his Trojans. As Strabo tells in a charming chapter about the southern parts of the Campagna (v. 3, 5), they belonged to the old tales told at the temples of Lavinium and Ardea. They are akin to the stories about Greeks and Etruscans and were—like many of those—Hellenized and expanded by the poets of the last centuries B.C. Perhaps they contained—as Rhys Carpenter suggests[39]—scraps of authentic tradition about the arrival of the Etruscans. In any case, the Trojan sagas add nothing appreciable to what has been said about the Greek, the indigenous, and—above all—the Etruscan factors in our survey of the origins of formal influences in early Italic architecture.

FIG. 9. Archaic acroteria from a shrine at the church of S. Omobono, south of the Capitoline on the Forum Boarium in Rome. The huge acroteria were probably placed as decorations right and left of the ridgepole like the top ends of the rafters on Villanova huts.
Courtesy the Antiquario of the Palazzo dei Conservatori on the Capitolium.

39. *Op. cit.*, p. 64. See note 9 and A. Alföldi, *Die trojanischen Urahnen der Römer* (Basle, 1957).

CHAPTER II

THE HELLENIZED ITALIC TOWN
AND ITS LEGACY TO IMPERIAL ROME

There has long been a tendency among modern writers either to regard Italic and Roman architecture as an outgrowth of prehistoric and archaic Etruscan developments or to date it to the Sullan Age or later and to connect it with the Hellenistic architecture of that period. The most important centuries in the history of the Roman Republic have been left out of the discussion. Today there is a heartening reaction against this. In the field of architecture this corresponds to what Gaetano de Sanctis in a masterly manner has said about the Hellenistic cultural influence in Rome and its most significant transformation by the Romans in the third and following centuries B.C.[1] A new kind of Hellenism was created in Rome under the influence of local traditions and the demands of the historical development of the Roman state. Pierre Grimal,[2] in a brilliant analysis of early Roman poetry, of Ennius and Naevius, their originality and their relations with early Hel-

[1]. *Storia dei Romani* (Firenze, 1953), IV, 2, 1. Among the latest contributions to the rich literature about the Hellenization of Rome I wish especially to emphasize what A. Alföldi, in *Die trojanischen Urahnen der Römer* (Basle, 1957), pp. 26 ff., states about the old Etruscan and Roman tales and how they were transformed after Greek fashion in obvious connection with the Roman political orientation towards the Hellenistic world. Very enlightening is E. Fraenkel's description of how an old Roman ceremony (Livy xxvii. 37; xxxi. 12, 9) was modernized by a procession song of Livius Andronicus, who obviously depended to a large extent on Hellenistic cult songs (Horace—Oxford, 1957, pp. 379 f.).

[2]. *Le siècle des Scipions* (Paris, 1953).

lenistic literature, has shown us at what an early date Hellenistic thoughts imported in the last centuries B.C., and often
mistakenly thought to form part of the Greek and Oriental
influence of the Imperial Age, began to affect life in Rome.

It is against this background of Rome's eager ("*dociles
vires,*" as Pliny put it, xxxvi. 101) attempts to learn—in spite
of traditional and censorial conservatism—that we must understand the Hellenization of her architecture. We may trace
the origins of this awakening back to the centuries in which
the Romans created their first fleets by using captured Car-
thaginian and Greek ships as their models (Polybius i. 20 and
59), but themselves added important features required by
their own practice. Giorgio Gullini has attempted some of
this research and rejects the generally accepted Sullan dates in
the conclusions of the important study of Palestrina in which
he collaborates with Furio Fasolo.[3] Another significant contribution is Karl Schefold's study "Pompejis Tuffzeit als
Zeuge für die Begründung römischer Kunst,"[4] in which the

FIG. 10. The fortifications of the acrop-
olis of Aletrium (Alatri) in Latium.
Probably *ca.* 300 B.C.
Photo G. Lugli 1953.

3. Gullini and Fasolo, *Il Santuario della Fortuna Primigenia a Palestrina* (Rome,
1953), pp. 450 ff. I cannot enter into discussion about the date of the upper part
of the sanctuary, but though I appreciate the general point of view of Fasolo and
Gullini, I am in this special case not convinced by their early dating of the upper
part of the sanctuary. I do in the main lines follow G. Lugli, *Rend. Lincei,* s. 9, IX
(1954), 51 ff., and *Arch. Cl.,* VI (1954), 305 ff. Fasolo and Gullini have expounded
their views in *Palladio,* n.s. IV (1954), 174 ff., and *Arch. Cl.,* VI (1954), 133 ff.
See also P. Mingazzini, *Arch. Cl.,* VI (1954), 295 ff. He interprets (and I am very
inclined to believe rightly) the round structure in front of one of the hemicycles
on the upper terrace as the *locus saeptus religiose* (Cicero *De divinatione* ii. 41. 85),
where the oracular *sortes* were found. I have always assumed, like Mingazzini,
that the basilica, caves, and hall were profane buildings connected with the temple (embedded in the cathedral), comparable to the basilica of the temple of
the lower town of Ardea (see E. Stefani, N.S., s. 8, VIII, 1954, 6 ff.) or the porticoes of the temple of Ceres which the younger Pliny restored, *Epist.* ix. 39.
"illam (the temple) *ad usum deae, has* (the porticoes) *ad hominum.*" H. Kähler
seems right, assuming that the round temple, which crowns the temenos, is the
shrine of Fortuna. See "Das Fortuna heiligtum von Palestrina Praeneste," in
Annales Universitatis Saraviensis. Philosophie—lettres VII, 3-4 (1958), 190–219:
the question of to which god the temple at the forum belonged is open.

4. In *Festschrift Bernhard Schweitzer, Neue Beiträge zur klassischen Altertumswissenschaft* (Stuttgart, 1954), pp. 297 ff. See also Schefold, *Pompejanische Malerei*
(Basle, 1952), with references; *Gnomon,* XXVII (1955), 41 f. and "Die Troiasage
in Pompeji," *Netherlands Yearbook for History of Art,* V (1954), 211 f.; *Die Wände
Pompejis* (Berlin, 1957).

author points out that Roman villas of the second and first centuries B.C. were the centers for that Hellenistic luxury and culture which we see in Pompeii at that time. Einar Gjerstad, in his studies of the Rostra on the Roman Comitium, and Erik Welin have both provided us with much material from the period between the Gallic invasion of 387 B.C., and the Sullan Age.[5] Luigi Polacco and Luisa Banti in her paper on the Italic triads[6] rightly attempt to repair the neglect of Roman activity in the artistic *koinē* of central Italy from the time of Etruscan supremacy to the final Roman unification of Italy about 100 B.C.

The great fortifications of central Italy—as described by Marion Blake and Giuseppe Lugli in their monumental works on Roman construction[7]—are now dated to the centuries after about 400 B.C. Here at least we have an important part of Italic architecture quite clearly belonging to the great centuries of the growth of Republican Rome (Fig. 10) and being part of its creative work after the Etruscan, Archaic period.

Guglielmo Gatti has led us in the same direction in identifying the Porticus Aemilia with the large concrete portico covered by coarse *opus incertum* that lies to the south of the Aventine and dating it to 174 B.C. (Figs. 11 and 12).[8] This has reopened discussion about the date at which concrete construction (*opus caementicium*) began in Rome. The concrete walls faced with *opus incertum* below the Porticus Octaviae obviously belong to the Porticus Metelli, which was erected in 147 B.C.[9] The evidence of the earliest domestic architecture of Ostia seems to support the view that as early as the third

5. For Gjerstad see chapter I, notes 2 and 21; Welin, "Studien zur Topographie des Forum Romanum," *Acta Rom. Suec.*, 8:0, VI (1953).

6. L. Polacco, *Tuscanicae dispositiones* (Padua, 1952), pp. 94, 97, and 139; Banti, "Il culto del cosidetto tempio dell'Apollo a Veio e il problema delle Triadi etrusco-italiche," *St. Etr.*, XVII (1943), 187 f.

7. Blake, *Ancient Roman Construction in Italy from the Prehistoric Period to Augustus* (Washington, 1947). Lugli, *La tecnica edilizia romana* (Rome, 1957)—quoted below as *Tecnica edilizia*. Cf. E. Sjöqvist, *A.J.A.* LXIII (1959), 104 ff.; N. Lamboglia, *R.S. Lig.*, XXIV (1958), 158 ff.; Gerkan, *S.S.A.*, CCXII (1958), 178–97; T. A. Richmond, *Y.R.S.*, XLIX (1959), 181–83.

8. Gatti, *Bull. Comm.*, LXII (1934), 123 ff. Lugli, *Tecnica edilizia*, pp. 450 ff.

9. Palladio, n.s. IV (1954), 143 ff. Lugli, *Tecnica edilizia*, p. 451.

FIG. 11. Porticus Aemilia, Rome. Probably 174 B.C. Concrete walls covered by *opus incertum*. About 50 B.C. this type of construction was replaced by *opus reticulatum* (Fig. 12).
Photo A. B. 1953.

century B.C. the Romans had already begun to abandon ashlar masonry, rubble, and mud brick and to develop the technique of building with concrete that was destined for so great a future.[10] As an illustration of this development we may take a house in Ardea[11] that was originally built of rubble and later, in the beginning of the first century B.C., was rebuilt with concrete faced with *opus incertum*. Noteworthy also are the results of the American excavations in Cosa. In this Roman colony, founded in 273 B.C., we see not concrete, faced

10. I have given my reasons for believing so in a review of Miss Blake's "Ancient Roman Construction in Italy," in *Art B.*, XXXIII (1951), 136, and in "Three Roman Contributions to World Architecture," *Festskrift tillägnad J. Arvid Hedvall* (Göteborg, 1948), pp. 62 f. Cf. Fasolo and Gullini, *op. cit.*, p. 325. See Lugli, *Tecnica edilizia*, pp. 363 ff., and "L'opus caementicium in Vitruvio," *Cl. Med.*, XVII (1956), 99–108.
11. Excavated and published by A. Andrén in the *Acta Rom. Suec.*, XVIII (=*Opus Rom.*, I, 1954, I ff.; Fig. 12); XXI (=*Opus Rom.*, III, 1959), I ff.

with *incertum*, but rubble.[12] This obviously reflects a transitional stage before fully developed concrete construction was introduced. We must also remember that the Greeks knew this material (cf. Strabo v. 4, 6). It is evident in any case that the Romans by the second century B.C. had developed the *opus caementicium* into an all-important material for both the monumental and the utilitarian architecture of the western world.

It would, indeed, seem to be essential, with our present knowledge of Roman architecture, to collect and to interpret the literary sources regarding building activity in central Italy between the Archaic and Sullan ages, adding the facts which the ancient authors have preserved to the archaeological revision of dates. Such an examination would no doubt establish that the centuries before Sulla were a most productive age for Roman architecture, an architecture characterized by a rather free Hellenistic style in contrast to the classicistic taste of the last century B.C., as we know from Etruscan reliefs and south Italian vase paintings. In so doing we must, however, avoid exaggeration and remember that the founding of the Sullan and later veteran colonies really represented a revolution for the towns of the Roman Campagna, as we also know at first hand from Pompeii. The veterans had seen the Hellenistic towns. Money was available from the wars. It is not at all surprising that towns such as Tibur (Tivoli) and Praeneste (Palestrina), where the new farmers settled down, were entirely rebuilt in this connection. It is also worth while to remember that in 78 B.C., the house of Lepidus in Rome was considered the finest of its age, but that thirty-five years later it had not even kept the hundredth place (Pliny xxxvi. 109). Many of our present datings are probably too recent, but we must realize that building activity on a luxurious scale increased swiftly in the first century B.C.[13]

FIG. 12. *Opus reticulatum*. The Aqueduct of Minturnae. Typical example of a Roman wall of best quality before the brick-covered architecture: cement covered by tufa-reticulate blocks and strengthened by square-hewn tufa blocks in the corners. In the substruction alternating layers of tufa blocks and more reliable (and expensive) limestone blocks.
Photo C. E. Östenberg 1957.

12. F. E. Brown, "Cosa I," *M.A.A.R.*, xx (1951), and E. Sjöqvist's review *A.J.P.*, LXXIV (1953), 441.
13. Lugli has rightly emphasized the importance of late Republican architecture in "Architettura italica," *Mem. Linc.*, s. 8, II (1950), 189 ff. Strabo (v. 3, 8) especially refers to the architecture of the generations before Augustus.

I want to emphasize again that it is entirely wrong to interpret what the Romans say about Etruscan influence in Rome as necessarily referring to something archaic, to something belonging only to the great age of the Etruscans (if not to their unknown homeland wherever it was). Much of what in their own times the Romans knew to be Etruscan was late Etruscan, or possibly Hellenistic with an Etruscan stamp. There was in the fourth and following centuries continuous Etruscan influence and no doubt exchange between Rome on the one hand and on the other its Etruscan *magistri elegantiarum* and their rich culture, which they—like the inhabitants of Capua and Pompeii—continued to develop under the favorable conditions of the Roman peace. The late Etruscans, however, seemed effeminate to their warlike Roman masters; in spite of their veneration for Etruscan culture the Romans added *obesus Etruscus* to their set of stock contemptuous phrases about their neighbors—among other such terms being *Graeculus, parcus Umber,* and *Lanuvinus ater atque dentatus.*[14] On the other hand the statue of the Arringatore in the archaeological museum of Florence seems to show Roman influence in Etruria. With its toga and Roman style it may be compared with the *togati* and lictors at the court of Antiochus IV.

To pass from general considerations to a discussion of details, we may reconsider regular town planning in Italy together with the established facts about the walls. Theories about fully developed prehistoric or Etruscan prototypes for regular towns and camps have been put forward repeatedly. The towns and camps with a regular plan—as we see them in late Republican or Imperial times—have been considered pre- or protohistoric petrifactions or fossils. Now that we have learned that the "regular" terramare were modern archaeological reconstructions inspired by exactly those preconceptions which they were said to prove, that their regular

14. See Catullus 39; Diodorus v. 40; Dion. H. lx. 16.8; Livy x. 16; Vergil *Aeneid* xi. 732–40; and others. Chapter 1, note 33. P. Romanelli discusses the same problems in Umbria in "Arte e cultura romana nell'Umbria" (*L'Umbria nella storia, nella litteratura, nell'arte*).

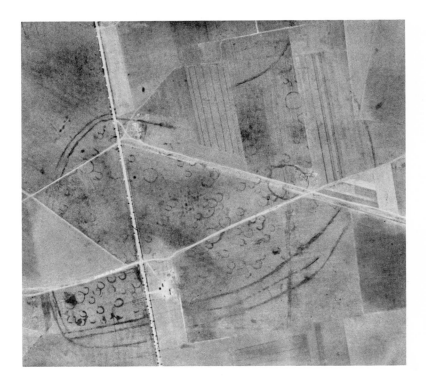

FIG. 13. Neolithic village, near the modern farm of Passo di Corvo, a few miles northeast of Foggia in Puglie. "Crop-marks" in the corn show buried ditches; excavated 1949.
Vertical photograph by John Bradford, May 1945.

planning never actually existed,[15] we must admit that so far there is not a scrap of evidence to prove the use of regular planning in the later Bronze Age and Iron Age villages of central and northern Italy. This holds true even for the loosely grouped oval huts of the Bronze Age settlements of Lipari, Promontorio del Milazzese, and Isola di Salina, excavated by Luigi Bernabò Brea, and for the neolithic settlements of Passo di Corvo (near Foggia) and Lucera, in spite of round or irregular oval enclosures and ditches[16] (Fig. 13). That primi-

15.   G. Säflund, "Le terremare delle provincie di Modena, Reggio Emilia, Parma, Piacenza," *Acta Rom. Suec.*, VII (1939); C. F. C. Hawkes, *The Prehistoric Foundations of Europe* (London, 1940), pp. 338 f.; J. E. Forssander, "Europäische Bronzezeit," *Kungl. Humanistiska vetenskapssamfundet i Lund. Årsberättelse* (1938–39), pp. 78 f. Fundamental remains: G. Patroni, *Athenaeum*, n.s. VIII (1930), 425 ff.

16.   L. Bernabò Brea and Madeleine Cavalier, *Civiltà preistoriche delle isole eolie e del territorio di Milazzo* (Rome, 1956), pp. 8 ff. and pp. 52–55. J. Ward Perkins, "Early Roman Towns in Italy," *Town Planning Review*, XXVI (1955–56), 127–154, and in the *Acta Congressus Madvigiani*, IV, 110 f. L. S. P. Bradford, *Ancient Landscapes* (London, 1957).

tive culture has in certain cases produced settlements with a definite form is well known, but the point is that no prehistoric material yet from Italy permits us to assume that the obscure legends about Roma Quadrata[17] or ancient Rome with a circular plan,[18] that have been cited in this connection, prove anything of the kind for central Italy during the period under discussion. The Romans themselves were troubled by the contrast between these tales and the crowded, irregular old Rome which they knew, with its *"forma urbis occupatae magis quam divisae similis"* (Livy v. 55). Livy's explanation was that it resulted from the hasty rebuilding of the town after the Gallic catastrophe.

If we turn from legends and from the information which they gave about old Italic villages to what we really know about the earliest communities, all our sources show that Rome was a most disorderly town. As far as we can see today, the same is true about the old Etruscan towns. Very likely their "city planning" resembled old, charming, and disorderly Tuscan towns of today—such as Monte Pulciano, Cetona, Sarteano, not to speak of famous and grand centers like Perugia.[19] In this respect ancient Athens and all other Greek towns before the development of regular city planning resembled the Italic towns. Both in Greece and in Italy (in spite of early attempts at planning in the center of the town) one feels that there is much truth in Corbusier's joke about the donkey being the first town planner. Philostratus (*Apoll.* ii. 23) not less amusingly contrasts the old crowded towns that had disorderly streets—like Athens—with those later ones, where centuries of urbanistic experience inspired regular

17. See Chapter 1, note 5; Plut. *Romulus* 9; Dion. H. i. 88.
18. Plut. *Romulus* 11. For primitive circular villages, see e.g., A. Kriesis, "The Enclosure Walls of El Kab," *A.J.A.*, LIII (1949), 261 f. or "The Neolithic Enclosure at Spiennes, Belgium," *Antiquity*, XXIX (Sept. 1955), 159.
19. What F. Castagnoli tries to establish about old regular towns in *Ippodamo di Mileto e l'urbanistica a pianta ortogonale* (Rome, 1956) pp. 15 and 67, to my mind only proves that we have no material showing real regular Etruscan town planning before the fifth century. I may also refer to Ward Perkins' communication "The Early Development of the Roman Town Planning," *Acta Congressus Madvigiani*, IV (Copenhagen, 1958) and his article "Early Roman Towns in Italy," quoted note 16.

plans. In the famous description of Hellenistic Athens it is considered as quite natural that the town, since it was so old, was irregular and untidy. Pausanias expresses it no less clearly when he speaks of the Agora of Elis (vi. 24). It was, he asserts, laid out, not regularly as the Ionians planned their cities, but without any strict pattern and with its porticoes and streets lying irregularly around the marketplace in the old-fashioned way (like the Agora of Athens, we are now tempted to add). The profound—and most natural—difference between the old irregular crowded quarters and rational town planning, which was inspired by Greek geometric reasoning and, of course, also by the inconveniences of the old towns, was evident to ancient observers no less than to modern students of ancient town life.[20]

In opposition to Giovanni Becatti's brilliant exposition,[21] I maintain that the western and southern parts of Ostia (Fig. 14), that is, those parts outside of the old castrum and outside of the regular quarters on public ground between the Decumanus and the Tiber to the east of the castrum, show us narrow crooked streets and irregular blocks, just such as our literary sources intimate about Rome. In the third and second centuries B.C., casual private enterprise could still compete with regular planning even on level ground.

---

20. Fundamental is Castagnoli's *Ippodamo di Mileto e l'urbanistica a pianta ortogonale*. For the Greek towns see A. von Gerkan, *Griechische Städteanlagen* (1924). P. Lavedan, *Histoire de l'urbanisme* (Paris, 1926); R. E. Wycherley, *How the Greeks Built Cities* (London, 1949), R. Martin, *Recherches sur l'agora grecque* (Paris, 1951), and his excellent exposition *L'urbanisme dans la Grèce antique* (Paris, 1956). For Athens, Dikaiarchos, *F.H.G.*, II, p. 254; Aristotle, *Politica* vii. 10, 4 (1330 b.). For Thebes (in spite of three catastrophes and reorganizations), Martin, *op. cit.*, pp. 79 ff. For Argos, Plut. *Pyrrhus* 32–33. See also my study "Zur Topographie des dorischen Argos," *Strena philologica Upsaliensis, Festskrift tillägnad prof. P. Persson*, 1922, pp. 264 f., and "Travaux de l'école française," *B.C.H.*, LXXVII (1953), 243, and LXXVIII (1954), 158 ff.; for Selinus, Martin, *op. cit.*, pp. 90 f.; and for Agrigentum, *ibid.*, pp. 91 f. with literature. For Rome I add to Livy: Tacitus *Annals* XV. 38; Strabo V. 3, 7; Diodorus XIV. 116; and Cicero *De lege agraria* ii, 35(96). P. Grimal, *Les villes romaines* (Paris: Que sais je? 1954), over and over again gets entangled in a conflict, on one hand clearly stating that the old metropoleis were irregular and, on the other, assuming regular town planning from oldest time in Italy.

21. *Scavi di Ostia*, I (Rome, 1953), p. 166. For this publication see also J. Le Gall's review, *R.A.*, s. 6, XLIX (1957), 60–76.

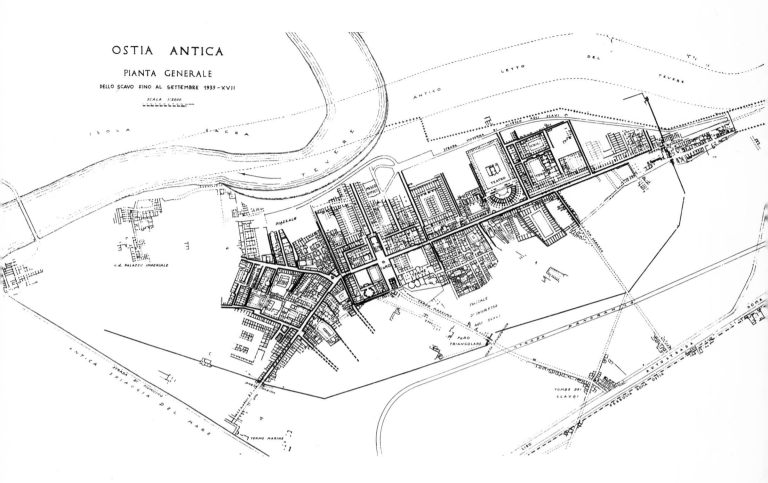

The oldest part of Pompeii around the forum shows tentative beginnings of regular planning, traceable in a system of two main streets crossing each other in the center of the town (Fig. 15). This small old town was encircled by a typical rampart street.[22] But unprejudiced study of the quar-

FIG. 14. Plan of Ostia. The regular, rectangular central part of the town with the main streets (cardo and decumanus) crossing each other at right angles on the forum (of the Imperial Age) is the old castrum of the fourth century, which was the origin of the present habitation.

22. A. von Gerkan, *Der Stadtplan von Pompeji* (Berlin, 1940). The rampart street: Vico dei Soprastanti—Strada degli Augustali—Vico del Lupanare—Strada dei Teatri. See also Castagnoli, *op. cit.*, pp. 26, 32, and 49. In this connection it would be of the greatest value if we could fix the dates of the "cardo-decumanus" plans of Paestum (Fig. 20) and Selinus; the opinions vary between sixth century and Roman age. For Paestum and Selinus, see now von Gerkan, "Zur Stadtlage von Paestum," *Studi in onore di Aristide Calderini e Roberto Paribeni III* (Milano: Varese, 1956), pp. 216–21, and Lugli, *Tecnica edilizia*, pp. 293–95 and 288. For the earlier discussion about Selinus see T. J. Dunbabin, *The Western Greeks* (Oxford, 1948), pp. 304 ff.; Wycherley, *A.J.A.*, LV (1951), 233; Boëthius, *Acta Athen. Suec.*, II (=*Opus Athen.* I, 1953), 174, note 4, and 177, note

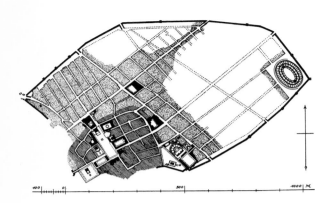

FIG. 15. Plan of Pompeii.
After von Gerkan, "Der Stadtplan von Pompeji," *Gesammelte Aufsätse* (1959), pp. 144–66.

ters inside the rampart street of old Pompeii suggests, as a matter of fact, that regular town planning in the proper sense of the word did not characterize the towns of Campania in Oscan and Etruscan times (that is, before the enlargements which resulted from the Samnite invasions in the fifth century B.C.).

In the same way an empirical study of the actual remains of old Italic towns seems to dispose entirely of the geometric shapes assumed by ancient and modern scholars. Everywhere such natural defenses as steep hillsides, valleys, and rivers determined their contours. "*Murus erant montes*," as Propertius said (iv. 4, 13). Where natural defenses—what Cicero calls "*nativa praesidia*"—were insufficient, they were supplemented by earthen embankments (*aggeres*), walls and moats, wooden palisades, or mud brick.[23] This was the shape of the old Italic towns before the great city walls of the fourth and following centuries. Livy as well as Vergil and the sculptors and painters of late Republican and succeeding ages were anachronistic and are completely misleading in that they almost always assumed the existence of towers and walls when their sources talked about old fortified towns. The real natural defenses of the primitive age are still to be seen in those Etruscan towns destroyed in the early wars with Rome—in a great town like Veii or in small anonymous oppida like Monte Fortino or S. Giovenale southwest of Viterbo or in Latin towns like Ardea, Satricum, or Antium, which were left in their old form with *aggeres* but without walls when the Roman frontier moved

13. I am, after renewed studies, inclined to date the planning of Selinus to after Hermocrates' concentration of the town at the acropolis, 406 B.C., and that of Paestum to the age after the Lucanian invasion, about 400 B.C. I am much indebted to Mr. John Bradford for permission to publish his plan of Paestum and for exchange of ideas about the date of the planning of that town. On Metapontum: Castagnoli, *Rend. Linc.*, s. 8, XIV (1959), 49–55.
23. Cicero *De republica* ii. 6 (11); Dion. H. ix. 68 (about Rome), Palisades: Appian *Bellum civile* i, 51 (Aeculanum). Mud brick: Vitr. ii. 8, 9 (Arezzo) and the remaining walls of Gela. P. Griffo, *Gela preistorica ed ellenica* (Gela, 1951), cf. P. Mingazzini, "Velia," *Atti M. Grecia*, n.s. 1 (1954), 28. Very likely the Greek wall in Paestum (first period of the walls) had a mud brick upper structure as suggested by von Gerkan in his article "Zur Stadtanlage von Paestum," quoted in note 22.

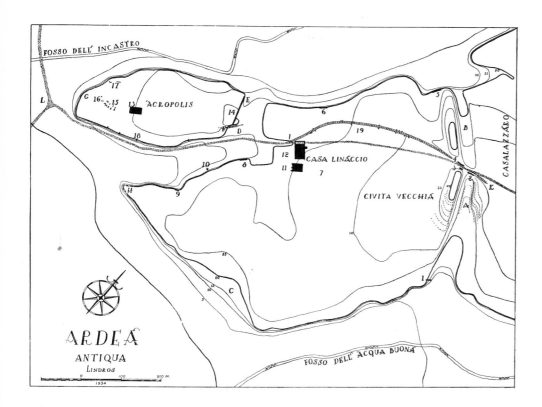

FIG. 16. Plan of Ardea. A.B.—the ditch (*fossa*).4—The gate in the agger of the main road from the Latin towns on the Alban Hills. 11, 12—Temple and basilica. 14—Terrace wall of the acropolis. 13—The main temple of Ardea.

By J. Lindros for the Italian-Swedish excavations, 1929–35.

southward[24] (Figs. 16–18). Modern historians have sometimes been mistaken in discarding what ancient authors say about old fortifications. In spite of their anachronistic fancies the information in our sources may be virtually right, though referring to primitive and natural defenses.

What we read about pomeria and about furrows ploughed around the planned towns by their founders[25] may, of course, be connected with such ancient towns, but neither this nor

24. Plan of Ardea: Boëthius, "Ardeatina," *Apophoreta Gotoburgensia V. Lundström oblata*, 1932, p. 349; *Boll. St. M.* v, 1–2 (1934), 1–6; Pl. 1; B. Tilly, *Vergil's Latium* (Oxford, 1947), p. 32. Antium: Lugli, *Tecnica edilizia*, pp. 270–71. The agger of Ardea may—if not older—belong to the Roman colonia of the fifth century B.C., but the only historical context for the agger of Antium would have been, it seems to me, the Volscan defense against the Romans before 338 B.C.

25. Varro *L.L.* v. 143. For the rite in the Roman colonies, see the well-known relief from Aquileia (*Storia di Venezia* I. Venezia, 1957, p. 195) and coins like those of Beirut. See R. Mouterde and J. Lauffray, "Beyrouth, ville romaine," *Publications de la direction des antiquités de Liban. Villes libanaises*, 1 (Beirut, 1952).

what we know about the pomerium of Rome[26] proves anything about the fixed geometric boundaries of the legends, quoted above, or of the Roman castra. As a venerable, inherited rite the ploughing was used all over the Roman Empire for Roman colonies. It was probably considered to be connected with and give authority to the regular castrum types, but the old legends about the pomeria, if they are thoroughly examined, tend to contradict any idea of a pre-established shape for towns. When the Romans constructed the mighty fortifications with cyclopean, polygonal,[27] or ashlar terrace walls of the fourth and following centuries B.C., the towns of central Italy acquired the definite, final boundary lines that revealed firm state control but made the most of any existing natural possibilities of defense. We have to keep in mind that in their earliest period these great fortifications in central Italy were still for the most part terrace walls that strengthened the natural defense lines of old hill towns or colonies founded on hills commanding the roads, such as Alba Fucens of 303 B.C., or Cosa of 273 B.C.[28] (Fig. 19). It was when the Romans fortified their dominion by colonies on flat land of the so-called castrum type—like the rectangular towns of Ostia (in its first period), Aosta (Fig. 21), or Torino—that they had to build city walls in the common meaning of that term, though even then they sometimes adhered to their old tradition and provided them with an agger on the inside and a ditch (*fossa*) without. This rectangular, convenient, and logical fortress pattern was used only where the state had to control the town because of its importance as a fortification.

Returning to consideration of regular planning of towns inside their fortification lines, I repeat that speculations about

FIG. 17. The agger of Ardea. A ditch and a rampart of the same kind, though provided with a mighty wall of tufa ashlar in front, were connected with the so-called Servian wall of 377 B.C. between the Porta Collina and the Porta Esquilina in Rome.
Photo B. Wahlgren 1956.

26.   Platner Ashby s.v. Tacitus *Ann.* xii. 24; Livy i. 44; Servius *Ad Aen.* v. 755. A. Momigliano, *J.R.S.*, XXXIII (1943), 121, and the article about the Luperci by A. Kirsopp Michels cited in chapter 1, note 6.

27.   Lugli, *Tecnica edilizia*, pp. 41–42 and 55 ff.; and "Conclusioni sulla cronologia dell'opera poligonale in Italia," *B. Ant. Besch.*, XXIX (1954), 141–44; Vitr. i. 5, 8.

28.   Cosa: see note 12. Alba Fucens: F. De Visscher, F. de Ruyt, S. J. De Laet, J. Mertens, *Les fouilles d'Alba Fucens de 1951 à 1953* (Bruxelles, 1955); *Rend. Linc.*, s. 8, XII (1957), 39 ff.; 163 ff. XIII (1958), 97 ff.; *Archaeology*, XII (1958), 124.

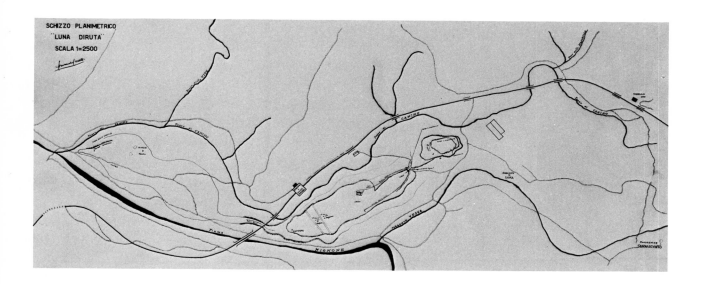

the planning of entire towns being a supposed Etruscan legacy have no basis whatever in archaeology. Anthony Kriesis calls the irregular old towns *"metropoleis,"* rightly contrasting them with newly founded colonies or re-established towns like Smyrna in the early fourth century, when there were opportunities for planning streets in straight lines, for *"rymotomia,"* as Strabo styled it, without interference from crowded blocks of houses already in existence on the site.[29] Nevertheless, as I have suggested, it seems as if there was, even in the disorderly old towns of central Italy, a tradition of axiality and symmetry in public and monumental buildings and places. In my opinion this was to a large extent the result of the Oriental legacy transmitted to the Etruscans in their early Orientalizing period or brought by them to Italy, together with the basic ideas of the Tuscan temples and atria which reveal the same spirit. It was evidently connected with the Etruscan rules for templa and for the orientation of sacred buildings and places of worship, and it must have been an important and inspiring element when the Italians in the sixth and following centuries B.C. began to develop regular town planning.

FIG. 18. An old Etruscan hilltown and mining center (Monte Fortino near Civitavecchia). The name is unknown, but the configuration of the site between the railroad to the north and the rivers Mignone and Vesca to the south is most typical, with an acropolis to the right (east), the town defended by steep hillsides with strengthening additional walls and by two rock-cut ditches to the left (west). On the heights to the left (west) of the town are chamber tombs and old iron mines.

Plan by Fernando Cordelli, most courteously put at the author's disposal.

29. Strabo xiv. 1, 37. Kriesis, "Versuch einer soziologischen Typologie des Stadtplanes," in the Upsala publication *Figura*, 1 (1951), 120 f. and "Ancient Greek Town Building," *Acta Congressus Madvigiani*, IV (Copenhagen, 1958), 27–86.

It is, of course, important in this connection to ask what we know about axial planning in Greece.[30] It seems to have been applied in Smyrna already in the seventh century B.C., but in Greek planning in classical times axial symmetry was by no means a prominent motive. The regular planning of the Ionians and, after the sixth century, of the mainland Greek towns did, of course, create monumental places with a certain symmetry (as for instance in Miletus), yet these monumental areas did not dominate and constitute a central axis but only rational and functional towns. The planners of, for instance, fourth-century Halicarnassus and Pergamon did in a charming way accommodate the towns to what the nature of the place suggested. They monumentalized the landscape in agreement with its natural lines, relief, and character (*construire le paysage*). In a town like Priene, its "functionalism" forced regular planning upon the site in spite of its natural configuration, the "*locorum difficultates*" (to speak with so-called Hyginus Gromaticus 178, 181, 194), but still without axial symmetry. But in Hellenistic times, at least from the third century onward, appears the Hellenistic "desire to provide each significant architectural unit, like the temple, with its own architectural environment, its own setting or surrounding."[31]

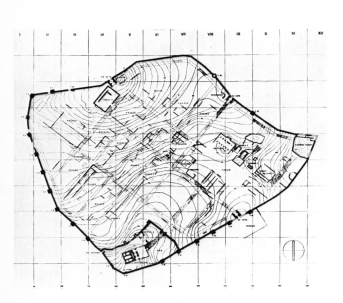

FIG. 19. Cosa (Ansedonia). A Roman colony of 273 B.C. Plan of the American excavation.

30. For the Etruscan and Roman traditions, see chapter 1, note 17. Among contributions about Roman axiality I may especially point out H. Jucker, *Vom Verhältniss der Römer zum bildenden Kunst* (Frankfurt am Main, 1950), p. 4 and *passim*; R. Scranton, *Art B.*, XXXI (1949), 247 ff. It is important to remember that axial planning can be traced in Greek towns, though much less than in Italy, long before the axial and symmetric designs of Hellenistic age. K. Hanell, *Acta Rom. Suec.*, II (=*Corolla Arch.* 1932), 228 ff., draws attention to tendencies to symmetric planning in the Mycenaean and classical Greek periods. See also Dorothea Gray, "Houses in the Odyssey," *C.Q.*, n.s. V (1955), 1 ff. For Smyrna, see J. M. Cook and E. Akurgal, *I.L.N.*, 28 (1953), 328–29.

31. A survey by Phyllis Williams Lehmann, *J.A.S.A.H.*, XIII, 15 f. See also among later contributions A. W. Byvanck in the *B. Ant. Besch.*, XXIV–V (1949–54), 36 f., and H. Kähler's description of Palestrina in *Die Kunst und das schöne Heim* 1955, p. 85. Martin has in his *L'urbanisme dans la Grèce antique* (cited in note 20) especially well emphasized the not axial Greek monumental architecture, coining the French definitions quoted above.

In this later Greek architectural planning we meet with an increasing predilection for axiality and symmetry, which no doubt had for its remote background the symmetric planning of monumental architecture of Egypt and of the old Oriental world, antecedents which, in my opinion, were the same as those of archaic Etruscan architecture. This gave rise to great architectural complexes like the sanctuary of Asclepius on Kos or the North Market of Miletus, both of which stood in strong contrast to the charming free disposition and independence of the majestic architectural units of Olympia for example, or the Acropolis of Athens.[32] This Hellenistic axial architecture certainly had importance for the late Republican architecture, but to explain its commanding position in the Rome of the last centuries B.C. and in the Imperial Age as due only to Hellenistic influence would, according to my opinion, be to simplify the matter and to forget the Italic traditions which the Greek architecture met in Rome. Axial symmetry was deep rooted in Italian architecture, and we can clearly trace it there long before the victories of the monumental axial planning in Hellenistic architecture.

In trying to trace pre-Hellenistic Etruscan architectural tendencies in Italy of importance for the late Republican and Imperial architecture, I must repeat that oldest Pompeii (Fig. 15), whether that small ancient hill town was originally Etrus-

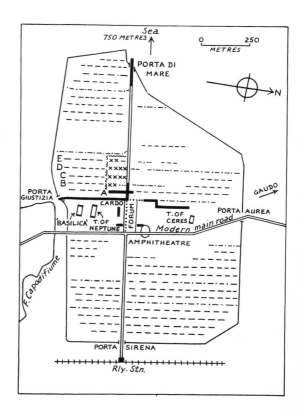

FIG. 20. Paestum.
Map drawn after an air photo by John Bradford.

32. Here belongs evidently the most important Palazzo delle Colonne in the Cyrenaica, G. Pesce, "Il Palazzo delle Colonne in Tolemaide di Cirenaica," *Monografie di archeologia libica*, II (Rome, 1950). Cf. the reviews by Becatti and C. Anti in *R.F.I.C.*, LXXIX (n.s. XXIX, 1951), 281 f., and LXXXI (n.s. XXXI), 178 ff. Mnesicles' Propylaea on the Acropolis of Athens are a most interesting but isolated forerunner to axial and symmetric monumental planning. J. A. Bundgaard's *Mnesicles* (Copenhagen, 1957) seems to me anyhow to be right in maintaining that no real basic axial design for the Propylaea can be traced. The symmetry of the building is due to the general influence of Hippodamean ideas, regular town planning, and the tradition from the older Propylaea, which Mnesicles' building replaced (pp. 72–73). As Bundgaard rightly says, Greek monumental buildings were built symmetrically along their longitudinal axis, but when grouping several buildings symmetry was not a natural principle with the Greeks (before the later Hellenistic age).

can or, as I believe, Oscan,[33] shows the beginnings of planning. As for old traditions which may have influenced the later regular Etruscan and Italic towns, there may also be something of importance in what Servius says (*Ad Aen.* i. 422) about the three gates, the three main streets, and the three temples that were requisite for every real town, in spite of the fact that his testimony cannot be reconciled with plans based on intersecting main roads and that it may be of a late date. His testimony may, perhaps, point to early attempts, but, of course, it does not prove that truly regular planning of entire towns was a legacy either from the prehistoric age or from old Etruscan culture in Italy, and it conflicts with what excavations have shown us up to now.

As I shall discuss in some detail below, it seems to me equally unjustified to assume that early regular town planning in Italy can be proved by the regular layout of some later towns which show intersecting main streets or by any known prehistory of the two types of Roman castra—that seen in fourth-century Ostia and that described by Polybius (vi. 27 ff.). The regular pattern of Selinus and Paestum was probably due to Italic influence in the fourth century (see note 22).

Archaeology has given us no evidence for the typical rectangular camps before the so-called "Castrum" in Ostia of the later part of the fourth century B.C. Historically, it seems most likely that this kind of military architecture acquired its fixed shape in connection with the organization of the Roman legions and heavy-armed infantry (hoplite) in the fifth century B.C.[34] Frontinus (*Strat.* iv. 1. 14) may have been right in assuming that the Romans got the idea for the blocks

33.   The whole problem is most unclear. The terracottas from the temple of Apollo at the Forum of Pompeii can be due to artistic influence, but Etruscan inscriptions may be claimed as proving that the Etruscans came to Pompeii earlier than in the last decades of the sixth century B.C. (as assumed by me in *Symbolae philologicae O. A. Danielsson dicatae*, 1932, pp. 1 ff.). On the other hand I cannot believe that the Doric temple on the Foro Triangolare was built in an Etruscan town and still assign the Etruscan Age to about 500–474 B.C.

34.   For these problems cf. M. P. Nilsson, "The Introduction of Hoplite Tactics in Rome," *J.R.S.*, XIX (1929), 1 ff.; Hanell, "Das altrömische eponyme Amt," *Acta Rom. Suec.*, 8:0, II (1946), 152, 195 f.; and Castagnoli, *op. cit.*, pp. 85–97 and 98–102.

and streets of their regularly laid-out encampments from the Greeks and in assuming that the camps of the old patrician cavalry consisted of scattered huts.[35] Polybius emphasized the similarity between the castra and the regular planning of the streets and blocks of the towns of his age (vi. 31. 10).

Linked with these negative considerations is, finally, the whole question of the *disciplina Etrusca* and the literary sources therefor. As clearly pointed out by Carl Olof Thulin, by Karl Lehmann, and by De Sanctis and his students, the Etruscan *limitatio* was originally a method of dividing new lands into fields. In built-up areas we know it only from late Republican colonies. Hyginus explicitly stated that this kind of regular plan was used only in later towns built on plains, as in the model Roman town planning of the two castrum types.[36] This system was probably derived from rather late colonies on flat land, where town builders had a free hand to apply new, rational ideas born of the reaction against the old crowded cities. Evidently, the Romans gave this regular town planning authority by referring it to old Etruscan rules which in reality had concerned only the templa and centers of the old towns and to old rites.

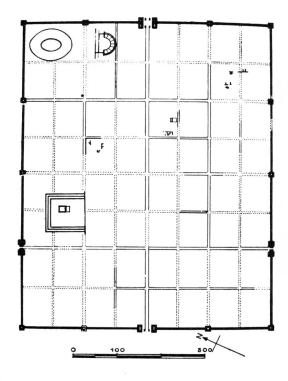

FIG. 21. Aosta.
After F. Castagnoli, *Ippodamo di Mileto e l'urbanistica a pianta ortogonale* (1956).

35.   According to Frontinus the Romans learned the art of planning the castra in the war against Pyrrhus. As Castagnoli remarks (*op. cit.*, pp. 101–2), this could be true about the camps of the type described by Polybius, but not about the planning with intersecting main streets, which we know from the fourth century in Ostia and probably also from Selinus and Paestum. What Frontinus says about the older irregular camps makes it more likely in any case that he is right combining the regular castrum with current Greek ideas but wrong in his dating of the Roman adaptations of them.

36.   The classical work is Thulin's *Die etruskische Disziplin*, especially vol. III. *Acta universitatis gotoburgensis*, XV (1909), 31 ff. For further discussion see Karl Lehmann, "Städtebau," in *R.E.* In this connection recent research on *centuriatio* of fields is also of great importance though the *centuriatio* of fields is largely distinct from the regular planning of towns. See Hyginus *Agrimens. Lachmann* I. 178, 11; Frontinus *Agrimens.* 27; Servius *Ad Aen.* I. 422; and further modern discussion and especially P. Fraccaro's studies collected in the third volume of his *Opuscula* (Pavia, 1957); Castagnoli, "Tracce di centuriazione nei territori di Nocera, Pompei, Nola, Alife, Aquino, Spello," *Rend. Linc.*, s. 8, XI (1956), 373 ff.; "I più antichi esempi conservati di divisioni agrarie romane," *Bull. Comm.*, LXXV (1953–55, =*Bull. del museo della civiltà romana*, XVIII), 1 ff.; "La centuriazione di Cosa," *M.A.A.R.*, XXIV (1956), 149 ff.; Bradford, "Fieldwork on Aerial Discoveries in Attica and Rhodes," *Antiquaries Journal*, XXXVI (1956), 57 ff., 175 ff.

If we now ask when regular town planning first appeared in Italic life, the background seems fairly clear. After scattered prehistoric villages there followed crowded hill towns with ditches and ramparts on their unprotected sides and, probably, rules about symmetry and orientation for public places and possibly some vague tendencies to lay out main streets intersecting each other in the center of the town as in old Pompeii.

Air photographs and pioneer work by John Bradford and others have created a new basis for research about Greek and Roman city planning by replacing hypothetical reconstructions with real evidence. Castagnoli, in his fundamental study about Hippodamus of Miletus and regular town planning, is one of the first scholars to give a general survey of the revolutionary results of recent topographical research about ancient towns.[37]

The regular quarters added to the north and east side of the old town of Pompeii (Fig. 15) are the earliest undisputed instance of regular town planning in an Italic town. It seems evident that Pompeii was enlarged in connection with the great Samnite immigration into Campania during the fifth century B.C. This immigration also completely changed the life of Capua, Naples, Cumae, Pompeii, Marcina, and other towns and created the Campanian people known to us from Roman history.[38] The first setting out of the regular quarters

37.   For Castagnoli see notes 19 and 20. For an interesting article with excellent illustrations see, "Roman Town Planning," by Paul MacKendrick, *Archaeology*, IX (summer 1956), 128–33. For aerial photographs see Bradford, *Ancient Landscapes* (London, 1957) and the catalogue of the *Mostra della fotografia aerea per la ricerca archeologica promossa dalla soprintendenza alle antichità della Lombardia e dalla fondazione Lerici* (Milan, 1957), bibliography, p. 61. Among the publications of the Fondazione C. M. Lerici-Politecnico di Milano especially noteworthy are: C. M. Lerici, *Fotografie aeree e prospezioni archeologiche* (Milan, 1956), *Rilievi aerofotografici e ricerca archeologica* (Milan, 1957), and *Campagna di prospezioni archeologiche nella necropoli etrusca di Monte Abbatone* (Milan, 1957). Published also in the *Quaderni di geofisica applicata*, 1956 and 1957. Cf. *Palladio*, VI (1958), 7, note 3.

38.   I am in full agreement with Gerkan, "Der Stadtplan von Pompeji" and "Zur Stadtlage von Paestum" (see note 22). Lugli, *Tecnica edilizia*, pp. 295–99, gives a full account of Amedeo Maiuri's fundamental research. He suggests (p. 295, note 3) that Maiuri's dates for the first periods of the city wall of Pompeii

of Pompeii belongs to the same century, which the Greeks considered as their classical age of regular town planning, perfected after earlier attempts. The results of this development of town planning in Greece itself are known to us thanks to David M. Robinson's excavation of Olynthus (destroyed 338 B.C.).39

The Greeks connected the new regular planning with Hippodamus of Miletus. He obviously was a leading architect who developed the urbanistic ideas in his Ionian homeland and brought them to Greece and Magna Graecia. Especially famous were his plans for the Piraeus and for Thurii. The coincidence between the suddenly increased urbanistic activity of the Hippodamean age in Greece and the same phenomenon in Italic towns does not, of course, necessarily prove that

(I *circa* 520–450, II *circa* 420–300 B.C.) should perhaps be lowered. According to my idea, expounded in my article "Gli Etruschi in Pompei" (see note 33) it seems likely that the Samnite immigration in the fifth century B.C. affected Pompeii in the same way as it did Capua, where the Etruscans, worn out by long wars, received the immigrants into the town (Livy iv. 37) and later (438 B.C.) were overthrown by the newcomers. In that case the enlarged city plan and the walls belonging to it would have been connected with an immigration which gradually reached the Campanian towns in the fifth century, and perhaps also in Pompeii (as in Capua), led to the dominion of the immigrants from about 438 B.C. and onward. The enlarged city may well belong to some early phase of this revolution in the life of Campania. Strabo (v. 4, 7) described a similar development in Naples, where the Greeks somehow succeeded in establishing a *modus vivendi* with the immigrants but only at the price of being forced to "treat their worst enemies (=the immigrants) as their best friends." The regular quarters of Pompeii, according to my opinion, show how the old Oscan, Greek, or Etruscan towns of Campania managed to receive the stream of immigrants. Castagnoli (*op. cit.*, p. 49) suggests the same development in Capua, but assumes for Pompeii, instead of the well-known Samnite invasion, an immigration of Greeks after the victory over the Etruscans in 474 B.C., which would give the same date (fifth century) as I suggest, but which is quite hypothetical (*op. cit.*, pp. 31–32). More attention should be paid to Maiuri's opinion (cf. Lugli, *op. cit.*) that the technique of the oldest period of the wall must be of pre-Samnite age. This would not in any case exclude a dating to the fifth century and a collaboration between the Oscans and the Samnites during the period of beginning immigration. For the Samnites in Cumae, Pompeii, and Marcina see Strabo v. 4, 4; v. 4, 8 and v. 4, 13.

39. Cf. D. M. Robinson's *Excavations at Olynthus*, especially vol. XII, and the reviews listed in *Studies Presented to D. M. Robinson*, I (1951), XLIII. I have expounded my views upon the material in *A.J.P.*, LXIX (1948), 396 ff. See further the literature quoted in notes 19 and 20, especially Castagnoli, *op. cit.*, pp. 17 f.

the Italians simply imitated the Greeks in their regular planning. Vitruvius strongly emphasized the difference between Greek and Italic usage (*consuetudo graeca, consuetudo italica*) in the description of the Hellenized Italic towns which he gives in the fifth book of his *De architectura*. He substantiated it for example by a statement (v. 1. 1) about the oblong Italic fora (such as those of Pompeii and of Lucanian and Roman Paestum) in which he contrasted them to the square piazzas of the Greeks. Obviously, the special conditions or traditions of Italic city life were operating here, but if we consider how swiftly, not to say immediately, Greek artistic achievements reached Italy, it seems clear that there was a connection between regular town planning in Greece and in Italy. To put it more precisely, the Greek ideas inspired the Italic town planners and military architects, but local traditions of symmetry and axiality and the system of intersecting main streets apparent in early Pompeii make us expect a special local stamp, a "*tuscanicorum et graecorum operum communis ratiocinatio*" (Vitr. iv. 8, 5) which we find in almost all artistic activity under Greek influence in Italy. If we analyze the earliest regular towns in Greece and Italy, we must in any case admit that Castagnoli is right in emphasizing how obvious and dominating the Greek pattern was.

The regular quarters of Pompeii show two broad main roads, *plateae*, in modern usage, decumani—Via di Nola and Via dell'Abbondanza. They are crossed at right angles by narrower streets, usually called cardines. Thus, large rectangular blocks were created facing the decumani with their short sides which measured at a maximum some 33–35 meters. Obviously, this town plan was laid out at the same time as the walls, but it seems evident that it was modified as the town gradually filled the space inside the line of walls, which remained the same from the fifth century B.C. to 79 A.D. The town plan of enlarged Pompeii shows what Cicero meant when he contrasted well-planned Capua on the Campanian plain with crowded irregular Rome on its seven hills (*De lege agraria* ii. 96). After Hyginus Gromaticus, Castagnoli calls blocks facing the decumani with their short side *strigae* and blocks running parallel with the decumani *scamna*.[40]

The same kind of city planning occurs in Marzabotto, originally an Etruscan colony of the early fifth (or the end of the sixth) century on the plain of Misano. Parts of two broad decumani, running from east to west and intersected by cardines are preserved. The blocks (*strigae*) measure roughly 35 by 165 meters. To me it hardly seems possible to doubt that the original layout of Marzabotto was Etruscan and belonged to the fifth century, well before its destruction by the Gallic invasion toward 350 B.C. Because of the architectural technique and for historical reasons Lugli is inclined to believe that after their victory over the Celts, the Romans rebuilt the old Etruscan town as a needed fortress.[41] Thus, according to him, Marzabotto ought to be classed among the Roman colonies of the fourth or following centuries which display the same system of streets and blocks as the enlarged Pompeii, that is, colonies such as Norba, Alba Fucens (about 80 B.C.), and Cosa (273 B.C.). Here Capua also belongs, according to its plan now revealed to us by air photographs.[42]

40. Hyginus Gromaticus *De munitionibus castrorum*. See Castagnoli, *op. cit.*, p. 100 on *scamna*; p. 83 (Fig. 38) for Alba Fucens, p. 97 (Fig. 52) for Zara; on *strigae*, pp. 21 f., 73–80. The short sides of the *strigae* or *scamna* often measure 30–35 m. = one *actus*, cf. *ibid*. p. 30, notes 59 and 48. The narrow streets inside the blocks were styled *stenopoi* or *angiportus*, as Castagnoli convincingly shows *op. cit.*, pp. 32–34, criticizing among others P. W. Harsh's "Angiportum, platea and vicus," *C.P.*, XXXII (1937), 44 ff. The decumani and cardines were called *plateiai* (*plateae*) as, for instance, old *plateiai* names of streets in Naples confirm in a striking way, Castagnoli, *op. cit.*, p. 35. Colonia Julia Karthago and Zara are good specimens of towns planned *per scamna*, see Castagnoli, pp. 97–98.

41. For the dating of Marzabotto, see P. E. Arias, "Considerazioni sulla città etrusca di pian di Misano (Marzabotto)," *Deputazione di storia patria per le province di Romagna*: *Memorie*, n.s. III (1953). Lugli has exposed his ideas about Marzabotto in *Tecnica edilizia*, pp. 378–97 and 460, but I agree with Ward Perkins, *Acta Congressus Madvigiani*, IV (1958), 113 f. and Arias.

42. For Norba see Castagnoli, *op. cit.*, pp. 81–83 and *L'antica città di Norba*. *Documentazione aerofotogrammetrica* (Firenze, 1957) by G. Schmiedt and Castagnoli; see further Lugli, *Tecnica edilizia*, pp. 137–42 (fourth century). For Alba Fucens see note 28 and *Ant. Cl.*, XXVII (1958), 363 ff.; Castagnoli, *op. cit.*, p. 83; Lugli, *Tecnica edilizia*, pp. 105–11. For Cosa see Brown *M.A.A.R.*, XX (1951); Castagnoli, *op. cit.*, p. 83, and Lugli, *Tecnica edilizia*, pp. 111–15 (273 B.C.). The whole group is discussed by Castagnoli in his chapter "Città romane tipo ippodameo," *op. cit.*, pp. 81–85 and 106. For Capua, see *ibid.*, pp. 44–49.

If, then, we compare this special type of planning *per strigas* in Italy with a Greek town like Olynthus, it becomes obvious that the Italic town planners were not merely influenced in a general way by contemporary Greek endeavors to create a well-planned town, as I have maintained in the past, following F. Haverfield[43] and others. As Castagnoli states (see note 19), they followed the Greeks in almost every detail. Thus, we must not only give up the old theories about a peculiarly Italic ancestry derived from the imaginary terramare and the Etruscan rules for city planning, the so-called *disciplina Etrusca*, but as a result of Castagnoli's analysis of Pompeii and Marzabotto (whether, as I believe, Etruscan or Roman), we must admit that in these towns it is very difficult to discern any specifically Italic modifications at all, even though it seems, at least to me, that the Italic usage which Vitruvius strongly emphasized implied such local modifications.

In Olynthus we find exactly the same system as in Pompeii, with what I, using the current terminology for Italic towns, may call decumani (running north-south) intersected by cardines (running east-west). The blocks thus created measure 35.40 (or 35) meters on their short sides (roughly the same as in Pompeii) which face the decumani, and 86.34 meters on their long sides (cf. note 39). The agreement in principle with the enlarged Pompeii and with the Roman colonies exhibiting the same system is obvious. Together with Olynthus belong, among other Greek towns, Rhodes, Akragas (Agrigento), Naples, and also Herculaneum. Castagnoli[44] seems to me to have strong reasons for maintaining that this is the kind of planning which gave to Hippodamus his fame as the town planner par excellence. It is obvious that it was a

43. *Ancient Town-planning* (Oxford, 1913), Boëthius: "Die hellenisierte italische Stadt der römischen Republik," *Acta Athen. Suec.*, II (=*Opus Athen.*, I, 1953). See further Castagnoli's introduction, *op. cit.*, pp. 7–11 and Kriesis' review of Martin, *L'urbanisme dans la Grèce antique* (quoted in note 20), *Gnomon*, XXIX (1957), 359–63.

44. Castagnoli, *op. cit.*, pp. 61–65. Rhodes: 408 B.C., Castagnoli, *op. cit.*, pp. 18–20. Akragas: probably earlier half of the fifth century, Castagnoli, *op. cit.*, pp. 22–25. Naples: probably late fifth century, Castagnoli, *op. cit.*, pp. 35–38. Herculaneum: Castagnoli, *op. cit.*, p. 34.

remarkable invention, which precisely in his time started to spread all over the Greek and Italic world. Typical for all the towns from the fifth and following centuries just referred to —Greek as well as Italic—is that the site determined the outline. The natural strength of the positions decided their boundaries. The enlarged Pompeii, Norba, Cosa, Alba Fucens, and Marzabotto show this feature especially well in strong contrast to towns on level surfaces which, like Aosta or Allifae (Alife),[45] had the strict rectangular shape of the Roman castra (see below).

Polybius (vi. 42) specially pointed out that the Greeks in contrast to the Romans selected naturally strong sites for their camps so as to avoid the toil of digging a ditch and because they believed that no artificial defenses were comparable to those afforded by the nature of the ground. The Greek camps were consequently located in the same manner as the old Greek and Italic towns just discussed. On the contrary the Roman camp of the second century B.C., described by Polybius (vi. 27–42), affords us a clear instance of Greek planning combined with Roman systematization. Here we actually meet Italic features such as I have looked for in vain in the enlarged Pompeii and the other towns with similar Greek planning.

As Castagnoli[46] very rightly points out, we now understand exactly what Polybius (vi. 31) meant when he affirmed that the streets and other constructions inside a Roman camp were planned like a town. In the camp which he described, there are two parallel decumani, the Via Principalis and the Via Quintana, crossed at right angles by cardines, that is to say, a regularity of precisely the same kind as in Olynthus, Pompeii, etc. But—and this is the point—this internal planning is here combined with typical results of Roman discipline and military traditions, which, as Polybius said, differed diametrically from Greek practice. The Roman camps had a

---

45. Castagnoli, *op. cit.*, p. 93. Blake, *op. cit.*, p. 231.
46. Castagnoli, *op. cit.*, pp. 98–102. For Polybius' description of the Roman castrum, see F. W. Walbank, *A Historical Commentary on Polybius*, I (Oxford, 1957), 709–23; P. Fraccaro, *Opuscula*, II (Pavia, 1957), 307–13. See also Livy xxxi. 24, 8.

strictly rectangular shape, a defensive rampart of earth with a ditch in front, gates in symmetrical, fixed positions, and a street inside. The rampart street was useful in several ways, especially in night assaults, since it secured the tents from the danger of being set on fire and kept the soldiers out of range of the enemy's missiles. The Romans, combining their own organization with the Greek regular planning, created a characteristic type of encampment, which was one and the same for all camps and familiar to every soldier, whether he joined the work of speedy construction or wished to find his tent. Another advantage was its ubiquitous adaptability. In spite of its Roman character, we conveniently call this type of encampment "Hippodamean," because of its obvious relations to Greek ideas of town planning in the fifth century B.C. Roman camps excavated in Spain (Numantia) at Carnuntum, and elsewhere, show clearly the same pattern which Polybius described.[47]

The military merits which I, following Polybius, have pointed out for the "Hippodamean castrum" also characterize certain towns which obviously had a background in another type of encampment with a still more accentuated impress of Italic tradition and Roman discipline. The most distinctive feature of this type is that two main streets—conveniently to be styled decumanus and cardo—cross each other at right angles and recall the tentative disposition of the same kind in oldest Pompeii. They start from four opposite gates, the Portae Principales of the decumanus and the Portae Pretoriae of the cardo.

These towns, or in many cases rather permanent castra, which display this pattern of two main crossing streets in contrast to the parallel decumani of the "Hippodamean camp" are generally considered to be the "Roman castrum" *par préférence*. We may, indeed, keep that name, because it probably had an old Italic ancestry and because it evidently was in any case considered as distinctive of the Roman spirit and, therefore, was destined to acquire the greatest importance for the configuration of Roman colonies and towns all over the

47. Castagnoli, *op. cit.*, pp. 98–102.

Mediterranean world under the Empire. I agree with John Ward Perkins[48] in maintaining that the military duties of the colonies contributed greatly to propagating the Roman castrum by stressing such obvious features as a network of straight streets, the wide central streets, and, connected with them, the rampart streets. How excellently such a town would function if attacked is obvious. No doubt the "Roman castrum" was a typical Roman achievement. But even if, as I believe, the city plans of Paestum (Fig. 20) and Selinus were due to Italic influence in the fourth century, what Strabo tells us about Nicaea in Bithynia[49] proves that a rectangular layout with two main streets cut at right angles was not alien to the regular planning of Hellenistic towns. Nicaea was a quadrangular town with four gates. They could all be seen from a stone in the middle of a gymnasium which was in the center of the town. Like the rebuilt Smyrna with its streets as nearly straight as possible (see note 29), Nicaea was a foundation of Antigonus Monophthalmus and Lysimachus. Both the history of the place and the gymnasium seem to exclude the hypothesis that the layout was due to the early Hellenistic admiration for Rome which we know from the history of Antiochus IV. It is in any case highly significant that Strabo considered the plan of Nicaea as something remarkable, in spite of the fact that its type of plan in his day was typically Roman.

The oldest known "Roman castrum" in an incontrovertible and final shape is, as I have pointed out, the permanent "Castrum" of fourth-century Ostia with its cardo and decumanus, its strict regular shape, its walls with ramparts on the inner side, and its city gates of Italic type passing like corridors through the ramparts.

It is most interesting to compare the "Castrum" of Ostia

48. In his lecture in the *Acta Congressus Madvigiani*, iv. For the "Roman castrum" see further Castagnoli's elucidating exposition, *op. cit.*, pp. 85–98, and discussion of all the colonies with more or less known planning.
49. For Paestum and Selinus see note 22. For Nicaea in Bithynia, Strabo xii. 4, 7 and V. Tscherikower, *Die hellenistischen Städtegründungen von Alexander dem Grossen bis auf die Römerzeit* (Leipzig, 1927), p. 135. Alexandria itself had two very broad streets, which cut one another into two sections and at right angles— Strabo xvii. 1, 8.

with the military outposts of Cosa and Alba Fucens, both of which were, in contrast to Ostia, situated on hills. Consequently, they have irregular defensive circuits strengthened by walls. At the time of the foundation of Cosa (273) and later in Alba a regular grid of streets derived from the "Hippodamean camp" was superimposed on the rocky and uneven terrain with its irregular boundaries.

Elsewhere (Hyginus Gromaticus 194), "*locorum difficultates*" were usually considered an excuse for not applying a regular town plan, but in these cities we are under the sway of rigid Roman discipline and its two types of regular encampments.

As Ostia developed from a fortress to a busy, commercial harbor town in the third and second centuries, quarters were built outside the wall. On the western side of the "Castrum" they were left to develop at random in spite of the town's situation on level ground. Evidently, Ostia soon lost its importance as a fortress. The constructions east of the "Castrum" on the public land between the decumanus and the Tiber were regularly planned, but the Roman state had no reason to control and hamper the growth of the important harbor town in other respects. The strict planning was no doubt a characteristic of important military towns founded by the state. Towns of the same type as the "Castrum" of Ostia were Minturnae (probably about 295), Pyrgi (probably third century), Fundi (Fondi, probably third century), Surrentum (very likely early first century), Lucca (second century), Allifae, Sena Gallica, and many other less completely preserved late Republican Roman colonies.[50]

More influenced by the "Hippodamean castrum" seem to me to have been the Augustan colonies Augusta Taurinorum (Torino) and Augusta Praetoria (Aosta, Fig. 21). The late Republican or Augustan planning of many of these towns still lingers in the towns of today. But the legacy from the organization of the Republican armies to medieval and later

50.   In addition to Castagnoli, *op. cit.*, pp. 84–95, see for Fundi, Lugli, *Tecnica edilizia*, pp. 152–54; for Sena Gallica, M. Ortolani and N. Alfieri, "Sena Gallica," *Rend. Linc.*, s. 8, VIII (1953), 152 ff.

ages survived not only in old Italic towns with preserved traces of the Roman planning, for, as I have already said, the "Roman castrum" possessed the most characteristic features of Roman style that spread over the Empire in the early great days of the *"immensa pacis romanae maiestas,"* as is still shown by many towns in Britain and France, or by the Colonia Claudia Ara Augusta Agrippinensium (Cologne), Timgad (Fig. 22), Egyptian Antinoupolis, Beirut,[51] and elsewhere.

To the antiquarians, inspirited by the *etruscheria* of the late Republican and Augustan times, the supposed connections with Etruscan town building seemed to give the regular Roman town plan a high and venerable antiquity and authority. This impression was mistaken, because the old Etruscan towns were, as far as we know, as confused as old Rome. These antiquarians also began to describe old capitals (metropoleis) as having been founded in the same regular way as were the later towns. With the same anachronism as about the town walls they generalized from whatever germs of regularity may have existed in the old crowded cities of archaic Italy without realizing how insignificant these were in the final urbanistic development of historic times, and they forgot that this development was linked with new ideas about town planning and the pressing problems of defense and increasing population. An old name like *Roma quadrata,* which probably belonged to some obsolete monument or some restricted scheme of planning in ancient days, was taken as proving regular planning of the entire primitive town and as giving historical background and authority to the recent results of contemporary town planning.

As far as our present evidence goes, we can conclude that regular town planning and the castrum were by no means fixed and stereotyped forms. They belonged, like the great walls, to the fifth and still more to the fourth and following centuries. To draw a comparison with another creative field, it was not the *"veteres versus"* of *"Fauni vatesque"* (Cicero *Bru-*

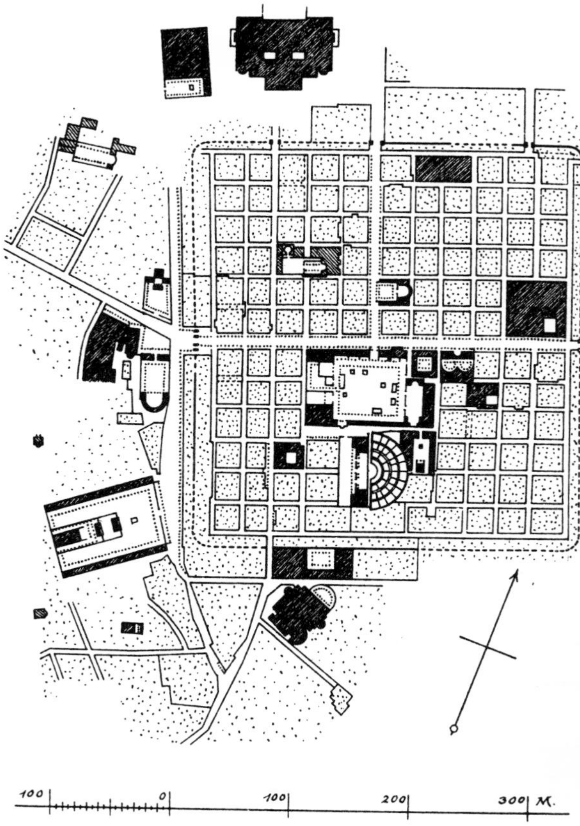

FIG. 22. Timgad. As in Ostia (Fig. 14) the roads and buildings outside the castrum do not follow its regular plan.

51. See Lauffray's useful survey, "L'urbanisme antique en Proche Orient," *Acta Congressus Madvigiani,* IV (Copenhagen, 1958), and his and Mouterde's "Beyrouth ville romaine," quoted in note 25.

tus 71) or the "*laudationes mortuorum*" (*ibid*. 62), but contemporary and Hellenistic ideas which were outstanding and new in Naevius' poetry.[52] In the same way, although old obscure traditions may have lingered in the new urbanistic organization, they actually counted for little in the final result. When they became systematized, it was a part of the same rational activity which the regular town planning itself represented both in Greece and Italy after 500 B.C. Like the whole cultural *koinē* of central Italy, the town plan was a result of common endeavors by Etruscans, Latins, Campanians, Samnites, and so on, but the final result—fortifications and castra as well as the strictly rectangular towns with regular plans—is a part of Roman history and victorious Roman organization. These developments will be understood when considered in connection with the growing population and increasing strength of Rome, with the walls, the great roads, and all the technical equipment of the overpopulated, vigorous towns (Strabo v. 3, 7).

We may also remember in this connection the high tenement houses of Rome and their social system (Vitr. ii. 8, 17), not forgetting, however, that the Roman army primarily was an army of peasants. We must be careful to credit the greatest centuries of Republican Roman history with what belongs to them instead of adorning the oldest days with the results of later activity, as some old Roman poets loved to do. We must understand the great walls and the systematized towns and camps not by falsely attributing their features to a prehistoric age, but by relating them to the history of which they were a part.

We now pass to the *tuscanicorum et graecorum operum communis ratiocinatio*, that is, to the results of the mixture of dominant Greek external forms and local traditions in Italy as they appear in various types of buildings.

52.   I refer again to De Sanctis' masterly exposition in *Storia dei Romani* and to Grimal's *Le siècle des Scipions*, quoted in notes 1 and 2. For the basic facts in the exposition of the Roman architecture of the Republic see D. L. Robertson, *A Handbook of Greek and Roman Architecture* (2nd ed.; Cambridge, 1943), and W. J. Anderson, R. P. Spiers, and T. Ashby, *The Architecture of Ancient Rome* (London, 1927); L. Crema, *L'architettura romana* (Turin, 1959).

This development becomes especially dramatic when influences from the Hellenistic towns gradually transformed public buildings in Rome and even more quickly penetrated private Roman life, bringing a new luxury into town houses and villas—Greek columns, wall paintings in modern Greek style, and other expressions of the Hellenistic culture of the proprietor. In the strife that started between old Etrusco-Italic Rome and the Hellenized town to come, we have to distinguish between the old local types and their gradual development under Greek-Etruscan and Hellenistic influences on the one hand and what the Romans felt on the other as imported Greek architecture, even when it became remodeled in Italy by the local traditions. We may start with the old types and the tendencies still surviving in Vitruvius' *De architectura*, recalling that he considered the form which they had acquired by the first century B.C. as inherited in its entirety from earliest antiquity.

In considering the so-called Tuscan atrium (Fig. 7), we must, in my opinion, start from what I have assumed to be the fundamental features: a court or hall with tablinum and side rooms at its inner side. Misled by Vitruvius' label *tuscanicum*, scholars have tended to regard as fundamental and primordial, not the Greek columns, architraves, and wall paintings, of course, but the entire architectural type as it was fashioned in the last centuries B.C., as we see it in Pompeii, and as Vitruvius described it. Here the problems are somewhat different from those of the regular town plan. The results that we see represent a late phase of the development, as do also the towns of the perfected castrum type, but in the case of the atria, we seem to be able to trace in Etruscan tombs of around 500 B.C., before all later innovations, the main and basic original features (Fig. 5) which define the type, even if in late Republican and in the Imperial ages they gave only the more or less obsolete outlines of an architecture which derived its most impressive features from the Hellenistic luxury of the last centuries B.C. Those basic features, as I have already pointed out, seem alien to Greek architecture and are probably of Oriental origin. As Amadeo Maiuri has shown,[53] the compluvium and impluvium belong to the later development of this type of house. This is also true of the fixed grouping around the *cavum aedium* of such rooms as the women's apartments (*gynaeconitis*) and the guest rooms. The shops to the right and left of the entrance (*vestibulum*) are obviously not in keeping with the original private character of the atrium house. They were a feature of its adaptation to the more lively commercial life of Italy in the third and following centuries B.C. and were an imitation of the rows of shops in the old business quarters. In other words, even apart from such unmistakably later adornments as Greek columns, paintings, and the peristyles, the *"cavum aedium tuscanicum,"* as Vitruvius described it, was the result of a long development belonging to the centuries before 100 B.C., with their rising commercial activity. The old atrium house of the Scipios in the Forum Romanum with its *"lanienae et tabernae"* (Livy xliv. 16, 10) shows us this kind of architecture coming into being.

What I have suggested as most probable about the atrium is evident in the case of the so-called Tuscan temple (Fig. 7). Here we do not need to depend only on an adjusted summary by Vitruvius. The descriptions of the temple of Jupiter on the Capitoline hill show us quite clearly old and genuine features such as a closed rear wall, an entrance (that is, a flight of steps) from the front side only, a low entablature, a high podium, and a large pronaos of 8+10 columns separated by wide intercolumniations. As a result of the exigencies of the cult, the Capitoline temple, like the newly excavated temple of the goddess Norta (Nortia) in Bolsena, had three cellas,[54]

---

53.   *N.S.*, 1930, pp. 381 f.; 1942, pp. 404 f.; 1944, pp. 130 f. Polacco, *op. cit.*, p. 117, note 118. A valuable study about the development of the atrium house under Hellenistic influence is A. Maiuri, "Gyneceo ed Hospitium," *Mem. Linc.*, s.8, v (1954), 449–67.

54.   Bloch, "Volsinies etrusque et romain," *Mel. Rome*, LXII (1950), 53 ff. For the Capitoline temple see Dion H., iii. 69, iv. 61, Polacco, *op. cit.*, pp. 80 ff., and A. Kirsopp Lake, "Archaeological Evidence for the 'Tuscan Temple'," *M.A.A. R.*, XII (1935), 89 ff. A survey of the various types of the "Tuscan temples" is given by A. De Franciscis in *Templum Dianae Tifatinae* (Caserta, 1956), pp. 28 ff. and by Castagnoli in "Peripteros sine postico," *Röm. Mitt.*, LXII (1955), 139–

but archaeological material proves that this was not essential for the type. Temples with three cellas and eight columns in front, others with one cella and with wings (alae) to the right and the left (Vitr. iv, 7), and yet others with one cella and a pronaos of the same width as the cella are probably as old as the three-cella type. We should bear in mind that these temples had a common frontal orientation, that the courts and altars before them naturally displayed a symmetrical organization, and that the Capitoline temple of 509 B.C. was decorated by the Etruscan sculptor Vulca from Veii (Pliny xxxv. 157). The abundant archaeological material from temples in Tuscany, Rome, and Latium shows us the archaic Greek style which Vulca and his Etruscan, Greek, and, very likely also, his Latin colleagues adopted with variations depending on their skill, personal taste, and the local traditions.

The history of terracotta decoration in Italy is typical. As Åke Åkerström has made clear[55] this kind of decoration was introduced into Italy about 550 B.C. The style was markedly Ionic, but was also much influenced by the art of the Greek mainland. But, whereas temples decorated with terracottas soon went out of fashion in Greek centers, this kind of decoration continued in use in Italy down to the Imperial Age. It acquired in the sixth century enriched and complicated shapes, for instance the huge acroteria of the temple at S. Omobono in Rome (Fig. 9), which remind us of both Villanovan huts and Phrygian rock façades, or the monumental figures on the ridge of the roof of the temple in Veii. The terracotta decorations did, nevertheless, follow the lead of Greek taste in their development through the classical to the Hellenistic style,[56] although gradually and with some retardation. In other words, an architectural form not of Greek origin but decorated in Greek style developed in Italy in a special way, following the Greek impulses century after century!

---

55. See "Untersuchungen über die figürlichen Terrakottafriese aus Etrurien und Latium," *Acta Rom. Suec.*, XVIII (=*Opuscula romana*, 1, 1954, 191 ff.).
56. See E. D. Van Buren's *Figurative Terracotta Revetments* (1921), and A. Andrén, "Architectural Terracottas from Etrusco-Italic Temples," (cf. chapter

The Hellenization went even further than the remodeling of architectural terracottas. Temple after temple, not only in the cities but also in the country, both in Rome and in Latium, was entirely rebuilt with Greek columns and architraves instead of the Tuscan columns and the low Tuscan entablatures. But again we find a fusion of Greek and Italic. A powerful conservatism dictated that the traditional plan of the old buildings should be retained. Despite their external Hellenization the Italic temples kept the traditional closed rear wall, the large pronaos, high podium, and stairs and entrance only at the front. As a rule the altars were built in front of the temples on the central axis. Here tradition and ritual considerations caused the Romans to resist change. Our witnesses concerning the Capitoline temple rebuilt after fires in 83 B.C., 69 A.D., and 80 A.D. provide eloquent evidence of this conservatism (see below).

The final result of this blend of Italic traditional design and the Greek orders of architecture is beautifully illustrated by the small temple in the Forum Boarium in Rome, the so-called temple of Fortuna Virilis (Fig. 23), and by the so-called temple of Hercules in Cori (Fig. 24). These also prove that such late Republican temples were the prototypes for the enlarged and monumental marble temples of the Imperial Age.

Vitruvius, in writing about *tuscanicae dispositiones* (iv. 7

FIG. 23. The so-called temple of Fortuna Virilis on the Forum Boarium in Rome. Greek columns, Italic podium, and prodomos. About 100 B.C. Photo Å. Olauson.

1, note 16); and his studies of the influences of classic style in Italy, in *Acta Rom. Suec.* 8:0, 1 (=*Dragma Martino P. Nilsson dedicatum*, 1939), 1 ff. and XIII (=*Opus Arch.*, v, 1948), 91 ff. For the interpretation of the statues on the ridge of the temple of Veii see M. Pallottino, *Arch. Cl.*, II (1950), pp. 122 ff., Pl. XXXVIII, and S. Ferri, *Arch. Cl.*, VI (1954), 118–21, Pl. XXVIII, who suggests that the figures were Apollo meeting Hermes, Aphrodite, with Ascanius (according to Pallottino Latona with the Apollo child) and Aeneas with Anchises. Pallottino's interpretation is evidently right.

For Phrygian rock façades of the Midas city (sixth century) and houses on doodle stones from Gordion (about 700) with gable roofs of which the timbers cross at the apex to form curving acroteria, see A. and G. Körte, "Gordion," *J.D.A.I.*, Ergänzungsheft 5 (Berlin, 1904) 221–23 and *A.J.A.*, LXI (1957), 323. In an important article, "Om figurdekoren i etrusko-italisk tempelarkitektur," *Arkeologiska forskningar och fynd, Studier utgivna med anl. av H.M. Konung Gustaf VI Adolfs sjuttioårsdag* (Stockholm, 1952), pp. 118–27, Andrén has shown how quaint and fantastic also the late Italic terracottas could be, see especially Figs. 2 and 3.

FIG. 24. The Doric temple in Cora (Cori). About 100 B.C. Photo Agne Hamrin.

—he never mentioned a "Tuscan temple"), by no means refers merely to the old architecture of the sixth or fifth century B.C., which could still be seen at many ancient sites (see Pliny xxxv. 157 f. and Vitruvius iii. 3, 5). Vitruvius was a classicist, but he wanted to modernize the old forms and make them useful in his own time. He wished to find the archetypal rules of the Greeks, by which he believed the work of the great classical architecture was directed, and to attempt thereby to regain the dignity of fifth-century architecture. And yet he was also a champion of Italic planning, of refined Tuscan columns, wide intercolumnar spaces with wooden architraves, oblong fora, and *cava aedium tuscanica*. But neither his atrium nor his Italic temple was purely an archaeological reconstruction. Our archaeological material shows us the living architecture that suggested his general rules, but it never agrees with them in detail. In other words, Vitruvius tried to impress upon his fellow architects what he considered to be the true and real Tuscan dispositions. Although Vitruvius must have known, for example, three cella temples which were wider than they were deep, like that of Volsinii (see note 54), he nevertheless prescribed a ratio of six parts in length to five parts in width (iv. 7. 1). When, among different types, he gives prominence as a model to the temple with three cellas, the reason obviously is that the Roman Capitolium (lavishly rebuilt after the disaster in 83 B.C.) possessed, in Vitruvius' own time, overwhelming authority as representative of the traditional Italic temple with Hellenistic exterior.[57] Very likely, too, Vitruvius really believed that the temple with three cellas was the Etruscan prototype, in spite of the fact that temples all round showed him, and show us, that such was not the case. Only where divine triads were worshiped did the temples have this shape. Very likely even in old Italy the three *"praesides imperii dei"* in Rome gave the type a special importance.

The history of the Capitoline temple recapitulates the whole development from archaic Etruscan architecture to Hellenization. As the centuries went on, walls and columns were, of course, re-covered with stucco and repainted (Livy xl. 51, 3). The old terracotta group of Jupiter in a quadriga on the apex of the pediment was replaced in 296 B.C. by another, very likely of bronze (Livy x. 23, 12). From indignant contemporary testimony about late Republican luxury, preserved by Pliny for the benefit of the moralists of his own age, we later learn of many items from private palaces, among them the marble floor (xxxvi. 185) and the golden ceiling (xxxiii. 57), which transformed the interior of the old Capitoline temple in much the same way as Renaissance and baroque decorations have changed the character of old Christian basilicas. But the old Etruscan structure with its low wooden entablature and Tuscan columns remained in the very center of Hellenized Roman life until the great fire of 83 B.C., when it had to be reconstructed—the oldest Roman traditions thus met with the modern Hellenizing tendencies. Dionysius of

---

57. See M. Cagiano de Azevedo, "I capitolia dell'impero romano," *Mem. Pont.*, s. 3, v (1940), 1 ff., and my remarks in "Vitruvio ed il tempio tuscanico," *St. Etr.*, XXIV (1955–56), 137 ff.

Halicarnassus (iv. 61) and Tacitus (*Hist.* iii. 72) in speaking of this rebuilding and in recording its short Vespasianic period after the fire in 69 A.D. (*ibid.* iv. 53) agree that the old foundations were kept; the plan was not to be changed, only height and luxurious architectural embellishments (such as Corinthian columns and marble) might be added: "*Isdem rursus vestigiis situm est*" (after the fire in 83 B.C.), "*Nolle deos mutari veterem formam*" (after the fire of 69 A.D.), and, to use Tacitus' masterly short references to rules also reported by Dionysius, "*altitudo aedibus adiecta: id solum religio adnuere et prioris templi magnificentiae defuisse credebatur.*"[58] These classic words explain the very essence of the new architecture that was in the making in the centuries before 100 B.C., with its gradual acceptance of Greek exterior decoration.

As we can still see on the Capitoline hill, the substructions and the high, archaic podium were kept. Greek columns and other luxuries could be permitted, as, for example, the gilded roof (Pliny xxxiii. 57), but the rebuilt Capitoline temple of the seventies B.C. was again provided with a low, broad wooden roof in Tuscan style in surprising contrast to contemporary temples, the so-called temples of Fortuna Virilis in Rome and of Hercules at Cori.[59] All the same Cicero (*Verr.* iv. 69) hailed the fire of 83 as sent by the gods, not to destroy the old temple but to revive it in more splendid and magnificent (i.e., Hellenized) form than ever before. When one thinks of how the traditions and memories of the old Etruscan temple of 509 B.C. were metamorphosed into the new Hellenic-Italic structure of Cicero's days, one is reminded of the enthusiasm which greeted the replacement of Constan-

58. In addition to Dion. H. iv. 59–61, I refer again to Ovid *Fasti* ii. 669, where we learn that even the altar of Terminus with a hole in the roof above was kept.
59. Vitruvius iii. 3, 5 and iv. 7, 4 f. That the roof of the temple of 69 B.C. was considered to be low is confirmed by Tacitus *Historiae* iv. 53 and Gellius ii. 10. For the wooden construction see the remarks on Tacitus' *Historiae* iii. 77 by E. Wistrand, *Eranos*, XL (1942) p. 167, and my remarks in *St. Etr.*, XXIV, quoted in note 57. Castagnoli has in *Arch. Cl.*, v (1953), 104–5, connected coins with a richly decorated gable and the rebuilt Capitoline temple. It seems to prove in a convincing way that the new temple was a sensation, but the type of gable on the coins is conventional and well known from the Italic red-figured vases.

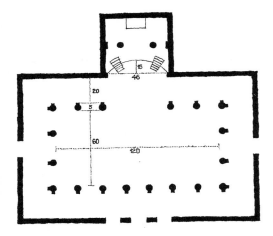

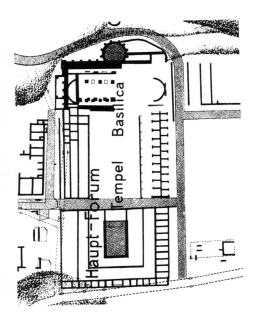

FIG. 25. The plan of Vitruvius' basilica in Fanum (Fano). Below: The forum of Augusta Raurica near Basel, which shows exactly the same disposition as Vitruvius described (v. 1, 7).
After E. Wistrand and F. Staehelin, *Die Schweiz in römischer Zeit* (3rd ed.; Basel, 1948).

tine's basilica by the St. Peter's which we know. The Hellenized Italic usage—*consuetudo Italica* in Vitruvius' words—does, indeed, rank among the conquering and destroying new styles in the history of architecture.

From the Capitoline temple and its preserved podium and plan we may once more return to the question of Roman symmetry and axiality. The Romans applied these aesthetic principles in all the architectural devices which they borrowed and made their own. Vitruvius was much concerned with *symmetriarum rationes* (see, e.g., vi. 3, 11) and with axiality. He proclaimed that the middle intercolumnar space of his modernized Greek temple was to be widened so that nothing might obstruct the approach to the statues of the gods ("*sine impeditionibus aditus erit*" iv. 3, 4). In his basilica in Fano (Fig. 25) he omitted the columns in front of the pronaos of the temple of Augustus. This temple was situated in the middle of the rear wall of the basilica and faced the temple of Jupiter and the center of the forum. The grouping of these buildings is a good example of axiality with a central axis running from the temple of Jupiter over the center of the forum and transversely straight across the basilica to the widened intercolumnar space in front of the Aedes Augusti (v. 1, 6–10). The Forum of Augusta Raurica near Basel offers an excellent parallel to Vitruvius' arrangement. The Forum of Trajan in Rome repeated it on a greatly enlarged scale (though without aedes and temple, Fig. 31) and the Forum of Alba Fucens also has the same disposition.

As Gullini and Fasolo point out in their great work on Praeneste (Palestrina, see note 3) these deep-rooted Italic traditions of axial symmetry acquired considerable strength in late Republican Rome. The splendid sanctuary of Fortuna in Praeneste, built on the slope below the old hilltop town (Castel S. Pietro),[60] reminds us of the Greek method of planning the town as a part of the whole landscape. An excellent paral-

60. The town, like Norba, was destroyed by Sulla (Strabo v. 311). The destruction is clearly proved by Strabo's description (*kakosis tes poleos*) and also by Appian (i. 94), who points out that the Roman soldiers got no booty in Norba, contrary to the case in Praeneste.

lel is offered by Vitruvius' description of the imaginary town of Dinocrates in the preface to his second book, and a still more effective one is his vivid picture (ii. 8, 11) of Halicarnassus in the Hellenized form given to the Carian sites by Mausolus and the rulers of his family. But on the slope of Praeneste great architects have brought the whole scheme with its rich supply of Greek architectural decoration under the control of Roman axial symmetry, grouping it around a central

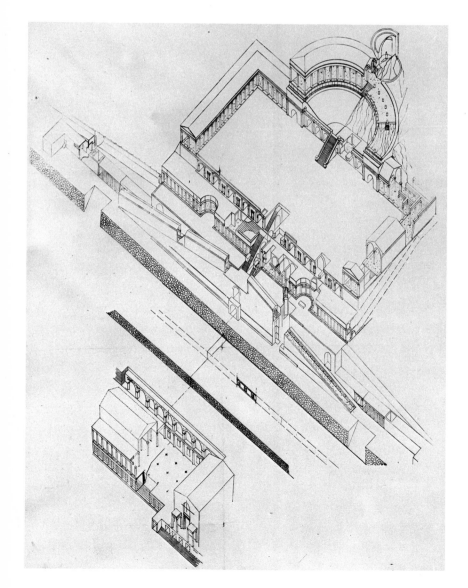

FIG. 26. The temple of Fortuna Primigenia in Praeneste (Palestrina).
After Fasolo and Gullini, *Il Santuario della Fortuna Primigenia* (1953).

FIG. 27. The Forum of Pompeii.
Photo Alinari.

axis that runs from the entrance below the forum and basilica to the round shrine above all the terraces and porticoes on the hillside. Of course, this is related to similar tendencies in Hellenistic architecture. Nevertheless, as a result of traditions derived from the Italic temples and the spirit of the Roman state, it has, as I see it, an obviously Roman stamp. Praeneste is also important because it shows us the degree of monumentality which the Romans had already attained in the late Republican Age and which became the model for the architecture of the Augustan Age. When we read Strabo (v. 3, 8) we must not forget that while praising the building activity of Pompey and Caesar and the family of Augustus, he also mentions "the later Romans" (that is, of the late Republican Age) before them.

The Roman style had from the day of Flamininus made a great impression in the Hellenistic world, as the temples of the goddess Roma and, for instance, the hymn to Rome by Melinno prove. I have already referred to the fact that Roman institutions were imitated by Antiochus IV in the Seleucid Empire. The importance of this new kind of Hellenism with a Roman character becomes especially clear with the spread of Roman building activity all over the Empire in the Augustan Age. The central axis created on the Agora of Athens by the Augustan Odeum is a most significant feature and is obviously Roman in spirit. We find it in the towns with the Roman castrum plan, in all the *capitolia*, in temples like that of Trajan at Pergamon with its strict porticoed court in front, and among the freely planned Hellenistic piazzas and royal peristyles. Roman axial symmetry is a part of Rome's influence in the first centuries of her dominion, in the same way as are other Roman features: the toga, the lictors, the fasces, the towns of castrum type, and the Imperial mausolea of Rome. The famous Tombe de la Chrétienne, that is, the tomb of King Juba II of Mauritania,[61] as well as Le Medracen in Numidia, obviously imitate the Mausoleum of Augustus and other Roman tombs of the same type with old-fashioned

61. For the temples of the goddess Roma in the Hellenistic world, see Nilsson, *Geschichte der griechischen Religion*, II (Munich, 1950), 167 ff. They have recently been treated in context with Roman propaganda and Greek admiration for Rome in the days of Flamininus by A. Alföldi, *op. cit.*, pp. 36 with notes 239 ff. See also Plut. *Titus* 16 and for Melinnos' hymn to Rome now C. M. Bowra, *J.R.S.*, XLVII (1957), 21 ff., especially p. 28. As for the Tombe de la Chrétienne, I insist upon that dating in spite of P. Romanelli's article in *Arch. Cl.*, IV (1952), 274 ff. Who after the dynasts of Numidia and Mauretania in the first centuries B.C. and A.D. would have built a Mausoleum like the Tombe de la Chrétienne? Its Roman style reminds one of the fact that Juba II styled his capital Iol Caesarea. See M. Christofle, *Le tombeau de la Chrétienne* (Paris, 1951). For the history of the tumuli in Italy see B. Götze, *Das Rundgrab in Falerii* (Stuttgart, 1939), pp. 8 ff. As always there may have been an exchange between Hellenistic, Egyptian, and Roman types. For royal Hellenistic tumuli cf. the tumulus of Antiochus I of Commagene (Nimrud Dagh), *Archaeology*, V (1952), 136 ff.; VI (1953), 246 f.; and *A.J.A.*, LIX (1955), 238. Roman technique of building (reticulate, concrete) also occurs in the Eastern provinces, see Ward Perkins, "The Aqueduct of Aspendos," *P.B.S.R.*, XXIII (1955), 122, and—for a villa of early Imperial age in Jericho—*B.A.S.O.R.*, CXX (1950), 11 ff.

Italic mounds on high circular substructures with Greek decoration. All this illustrates how important was the architectural legacy of Hellenized Republican Rome from the very beginning of the Imperial Age. Most illuminating are the words of Strabo about Nicopolis, outside Alexandria, and its modern Roman architecture, which even in a center such as the capital of the Ptolemies already surpassed the Hellenistic buildings (xvii. 1, 10, *ta de palaia ōligōrētai*).

The city of Beirut is particularly interesting with its modified castrum plan, its Marsyas on the Forum, and its coins showing the foundation of the colony by ritual plowing. The whole urbanistic system shown by its monuments and testified to by Josephus[62] gives a vivid impression of the Roman style that spread all over the Empire from late Republican and Augustan times and which persisted down to Nicomedia and Constantinople.

It is evident that in the centuries after 400 B.C. Roman architects not only rearranged the local architectural types according to a Hellenistic pattern, but also changed the borrowed Hellenistic architecture to suit the rules of old Italic architects. Vitruvius in the preface to his seventh book (paragraph 17) stresses the value of architectural work in Italy, saying that a temple built by C. Mucius would have ranked among the finest buildings of its age if it had been built with costly material (that is, with marble instead of stuccoed tufa or travertine with terracotta decorations). Here again we see the Hellenized Italic and Roman architecture, as far as new planning and adapted Greek decorations go, ready for marble and all the increased luxury of Augustan times. Cicero (*Ad Atticum* xiii, 35) regarded it as scandalous when Caesar, wishing to enlarge Rome, summoned a Greek architect. "*O rem indignam!*" This reminds us again that, after some two hundred years of Italic life, the entirely Hellenized Italic architecture was regarded as *consuetudo italica*—that is, as Italic or Roman in spite of its new embellishments. One may note in comparison that it was considered typically Roman to be

---

62. *De bello Judaico* i. 21, 11; vii. 3, 1; *Antiquitates Judaicae* xix. 7, 5; xx. 9, 4. Cf. note 51.

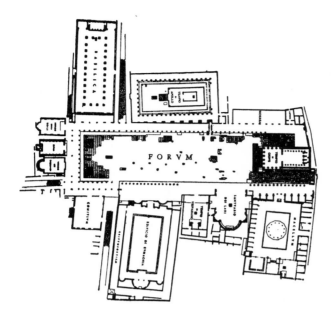

FIG. 28. Plan of the Forum of Pompeii with the basilica, the "khan" (Eumachia's peristyle building), and the macellum.

cleanshaven in the first century A.D. (Dio Chrysostom XXXVI, 17), and yet it was not altogether forgotten that the old Romans were bearded (*barbati*), like T. Quinctius Flamininus on the wonderful Hellenistic coin bearing his portrait. It was only the generation of Scipio Africanus, which, following the Hellenistic fashion of the time after Alexander the Great, created the clean-shaven Roman type.

Typical of the Hellenized architectural *consuetudo italica* is the Forum of Pompeii (second century B.C., Figs. 27 and 28). The old oblong shape and the axial disposition were kept (Vitr. v. 1 f.), but Greek porticoes were built instead of the old tabernae with upper floors and maeniana.[63] In the Forum Romanum and the Forum of Paestum (Fig. 29) they were combined with tabernae behind rows of Greek columns, usually in two stories. Vitruvius recommended them as something especially Italic,[64] but the type is altogether

63. Festus 135 M (Lindsay) A. Maiuri, *N.S.*, 1941, 371 f.

64. *Acta Athen. Suec.*, II (=*Opus Athen.*, I, 1953), 180, note 18. About the shops and the history of Basilica Aemilia see N. Sandberg, *Eranos*, XXXIV (1936), 82 ff.; and G. Fuchs, "Zur Baugeschichte der Basilica Aemilia in republikanischer Zeit" *RM*, LXIII (1956), 14–25. For the last excavations see Carettoni, *N.S.*, 1948, 111 ff. and Romanelli, *Gnomon*, XXVI (1954), 262.

FIG. 29. Porticoes with tabernae at the Forum of Paestum.
Photo A. B. 1955.

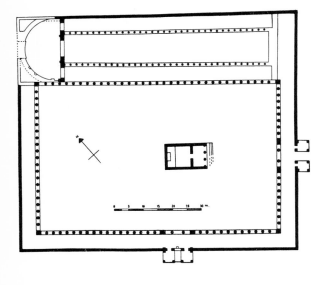

FIG. 30. Kaisareion in Cyrene.
J. Ward Perkins, *J.R.S.*, 1948, and *P.B.S.R.*, XXVI (1958), 137–94.

Greek, known from Greek *agorai* and (in a most elaborate shape) from the South Stoa of the fourth century B.C., at Corinth.[65]

As I see it, two mature traditions met when, in Caesar's time, Hellenistic piazzas surrounded by porticoes and having a temple on the longitudinal axis were used in Asia and Egypt as *Kaisareia*, that is, sanctuaries for emperor worship (Fig. 30). On the one hand it is evident that they stem from Hellenistic piazzas and Hellenistic hero worship. On the other hand they bear a striking resemblance to the Italic fora, exemplified by the Forum of Pompeii or the Imperial fora (Fig. 31), though with one very important difference, for it is typical of the Italic fora, even in their Hellenized shape, that the temple is always built against the rear wall, that is, at the upper end. In this I trace a legacy from the Etruscan temples with temenos and altar in front of the podium steps in contrast to Hellenistic porticoes where the temple was detached. It must have been most natural for the Romans to use the Hellenistic porticoes for the same purpose (in addition to what Hellenistic hero worship suggested), adapting them to the Roman tradi-

65.　O. T. Broneer, *The South Stoa and Its Roman Successors* (Princeton, 1954). Another monumental Greek portico with tabernae is the Hellenistic stoa of Sikyon, *Praktika*, 1952 (Athens, 1955), 388.

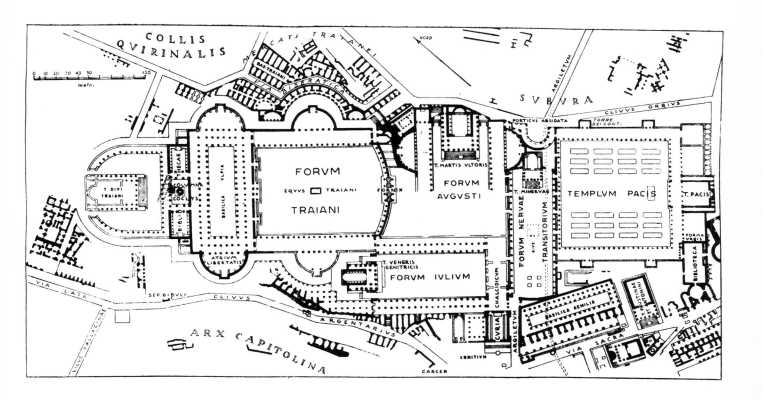

FIG. 31. The Imperial fora in Rome.

tion. Erik Sjöqvist has discussed this in a valuable article entitled "*Kaisareion*."[66] To what we know about *Kaisareia* of Alexandria, Antiochia, and Kyrene, he has been able to add the results of conversations with Professor A. J. B. Wace concerning the temple area dedicated to Ptolemy III and Berenice by the Greek garrison of Hermopolis Magna (Ashmunein), with its porticoes and axial symmetry—a splendid specimen of this kind of structure in its Hellenistic shape. It is of outstanding interest because of its early date (before 221 B.C.). It shows us exactly the prototype at which Campanians and Romans may have aimed when they started to Hellenize their axial fora.

A Hellenized piazza with strict axiality, a main temple with Greek columns and Italic plan, and Greek porticoes in front of rows of shops constituted the blend of Italic forum

66. *Acta Rom. Suec.*, XVIII (=*Opus Rom.*, I, 1954), 86.

and Greek piazza which the town planners in Italy created.[67] Sulla and Caesar tried to adapt the old, untidy Forum Romanum to its requirements, and the Imperial fora were all to follow its pattern. It had its social background in the Greek ideas about the *forensis dignitas*, the dignity of the public places, already expressed by Aristotle. The dealers of victuals were, for instance, banished from the tabernae at the Forum Romanum in the fourth century and only money changers and bankers were allowed to have their business there, just as jewelers succeeded the butchers on Ponte Vecchio in Florence in 1593. The fora were to be used for the transaction of public business, as Caesar expressed it when planning his forum in Rome, though here he was referring to the public squares of the Persians (Appian *B.C.* ii. 102). It is interesting to note that the development in Athens was not ahead of Rome. Only as late as in the early third century B.C., was an attempt made to remove the provision markets from the main Agora to its eastern end. The problem was solved in the second century B.C. by the "Middle Stoa" and the "commercial Agora" formed by that stoa and the South and East stoas.[68]

In the Forum Romanum the style of the statues of gods and men, as the coins show them and as literary testimony suggests, varied from archaic to classical Greek and Hellenistic baroque and Hellenistic realism. In the same way as Greek fashions remolded Roman history, Greek columns and other architectural items "conquered" the Italic temples, fora, atria, houses, portico-villas, and porticoes. Schefold is no doubt right in asserting that the second century B.C. was the decisive age for the creation of this enriched and Hellenized architecture in Italy.[69] At that period, one could already use Statius' words, *"innumeris spatia interstincta columnis"* ("openings

67.   To Roman structures of this kind we must, with R. A. Staccioli, add the cryptoporticoes of Aosta, Arles, and Bavai, *Rend. Linc.*, s. 8, IX (1954), 645 ff., and *Arch. Cl.*, VI (1954), 284 f.; Lugli, *Atti X Congresso di storia dell'architettura*, 1957, pp. 187–97. In Ferentino (*Arch. Cl.*, VI, 1954, 185 ff.), cryptoporticoes offered to the public a sheltered walk for summer days, as did the cryptoporticoes of the villas to their owners.

68.   For the Forensis dignitas see Varro, quoted by Nonius 532 M. and Aristotle's *Politics* vii. 11, 2 (1331 A–B). For the agora of Athens: *Hesperia*, XXII (1953), 35 ff.

69.   Schefold, *op. cit.*, note 4. For the portico-villas: K. M. Swoboda, *Römische und romanische Paläste* (2d ed.; Wien, 1924), pp. 29 ff.

punctuated by countless columns").[70] The mural paintings in the so-called Pompeian styles show the popularity of this kind of architecture in Rome and Italy about 100 B.C.

To this Hellenization belonged also the peristyles, which were added to the atria, as seen all over Pompeii. The Greek and the Roman domestic architecture was combined in the beautiful atrium-and-peristyle houses. But again Italic traditions asserted themselves. The Hellenistic peristyles were arranged in the Italic way with tablina and axial disposition, features that were alien to the Greek peristyles and which foreshadowed the characteristically rigid planning of the peristyle palaces of the Imperial Age.[71]

The basilicas can be linked with the Italic fora and peristyles (Figs. 28, 32). It seems that the idea of providing the nave, or rather the central court, with a high roof and upper lighting was Italic, perhaps Roman. Nevertheless, it would be dogmatic to ignore the fact that the basilicas had undeniable predecessors in Greek peristyles and hypostyle constructions. This seems to me especially clear when, like the Basilica Julia, the basilicas of Ardea, Alba Fucens, and Cosa, and Augusta Raurica, or the basilica in Fano which Vitruvius proudly described (v. 1, 6 ff., 9), they have a long side open toward the forum, thus enlarging the open space of the piazza and adding to it a shelter for the public, as in the Homeric lesche.

In order that the transactions of the officials should not interfere with business carried on in other parts of the buildings (Vitr. v. 1, 8), sometimes (but certainly not always) tribunes (*tribunalia*) were desirable. They were placed as tablina in the atria and introduced—as the tablina in the peristyle—axial symmetry.

---

70. *Silvae* III. 90. It may be worth while to point out that the portico along the south side of the decumanus in Ostia is Augustan. *Scavi di Ostia*, I, 118, note 4.
71. *Acta Rom. Suec.*, IV (=*Opus Arch.*, I, 1935), 182 ff. The Palazzo delle Colonne in Tolemaide di Cirenaica, referred to in note 32, has—in contrast to the Roman atrium and peristyle houses—a nonaxial entrance to the main peristyle, but otherwise it shows the tendency to create axial architecture in the Hellenistic world in its later stage. Typical is the villa near the Chiesa di S. Pietro in Alba Fucens, with its luxurious tablinum in the center of its southeastern side, *N.S.*, 1957, 164.

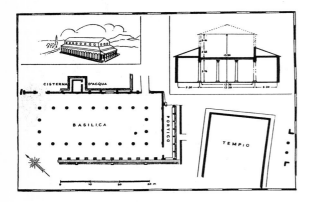

FIG. 32. The basilica of Ardea. Early first century B.C.
Plan and reconstruction by E. Wikén and J. Lindros from the Italian-Swedish excavations, 1929–35.

As Vitruvius shows in his description of the basilica, forum, and temple in Fano, and as we see, for instance, in the Forum of Augusta Raurica, the Italic axial symmetry could be combined with an open long side toward the forum. The basilica of Pompeii with its tablinum or aedes shows that basilicas, which had a short side (with a chalcidicum) toward the forum could also be reshaped in the same way. This axial systematization inevitably conflicted with the basic concept of a basilica's being a peristyle with colonnades on all four sides. It provides us with another interesting instance of how Greek architectural features were transformed under the sway of Roman traditions and requirements of Roman public life.[72]

So far our discussion has been concentrated upon Italic axiality and the Hellenization of the structural types with an old Italic tradition (the atrium, the Tuscan temple, and the forum). Before I end my remarks about mixed forms of Roman architecture with an Italic background a few words must be added about arches. They seem to have had an old Italic ancestry.[73] The monumental substructure below the Temple of Jupiter in Terracina (Fig. 33) and the amphitheater

FIG. 33. The terrace of the temple of Jupiter Anxur in Terracina. Arches without Greek decoration of the façade Note also the *opus incertum*.
Photo Alinari.

72. Welin, *op. cit.* (quoted note 5), pp. 111 ff. has rightly emphasized that the basilicas were, to start with, only roofed shelters connected with fora, to be compared with Greek leschai as described by Homer (*Odyssey* xviii. 329) and by Pausanias in his chapters about the lesche of the Cnidians in Delphi (x. 25, 1). Cf. also the colonnaded halls of the Argive Heraeum, P. Amandry, *Hesperia*, XXI (1952), 222. It seems evident that the basilicas only gradually replaced the old open air places for judicial and administrative purposes. See also Romanelli's review of Welin in *Gnomon*, XXVI (1954), 262. I have discussed these problems in *Netherlands Yearbook for the History of Art*, V (1954), 85 f. To me it seems clear that the basilica of Ardea (Fig. 32) shows the old type of these structures. It was a shelter for the pilgrims who came to the famous temples of the small town of Ardea (which about 100 B.C. seems to have been restricted only to the acropolis above the temple). The construction on the back side of the basilica is in my opinion not a tribunal but a water cistern. The Basilica Aemilia, like the Basilica Julia and the Basilica Ulpia, very likely never had a tribunal (cf. note 64), but for another view see Lugli, "Il 'pulvinar' nella basilica forense di Pompei," *Atti del VIII Congresso nazionale di storia dell'architettura*, 1953, pp. 261–70. For the forum of Augusta Raurica, see Fig. 25 and F. Staehelin, *Die Schweiz in römischer Zeit* (3d ed.; Basle, 1948), p. 600.

73. It seems evident that the clumsy imitation of an arch in the Tomba Campana in Veii, as well as the rock-cut arch of the Tomba della Capanna in Cerve-

FIG. 34. The amphitheater of Pompeii, with its unmasked arcaded façade. Photo B. Wahlgren 1956.

of Pompeii (Fig. 34), both dated to the first decades of the first century B.C., show that in late Republican Italy arches were a cherished monumental feature. The combination of arches and half columns with architrave, known from the Tabularium (78 B.C., Fig. 35), not to speak of such magnificent descendants in the Imperial Age as the Colosseum, was already being used in the second century B.C., as is shown by an Etruscan urn in the Worcester Museum and by sepulchral monuments from Delos and Syros. Archivolts carried directly by columns were in use about 60 B.C., as is seen in the paintings of the Villa dei Misteri[74] and in the early Imperial Age in the Casa della Fortuna in Pompeii (Fig. 36). The portico of Aemilius on the Tiber (Fig. 11), which was built in 174 B.C., shows another monumental feature, destined to enjoy a great future in Imperial and later ages, namely a façade that employs arches in two or more stories alternating so that the upper arches are placed over the piers of arches below.[75]

teri, foreshows this. That the rock-cut forms imitate built architecture seems quite evident in the tombs with sloping sides like the gates of Segni and Palestrina, *St. Etr.*, I (1927), Pl. 23; *Boll. St. M.*, II, I (1931–32), p. 17.

74. Maiuri, *Palladio*, I (1937), 121 ff. (Villa dei Misteri): G. M. A. Hanfmann, *Worcester Art Museum Annual*, V (1946), 15 ff.; *J.H.S.*, LXV (1947), 50. P. J. Riis, *Acta A.*, V (1934), 90, 93; *J.H.S.*, LXIV (1945), 50, note 34. Springer, *Kunstgesch. Altertum.*, 12th ed., p. 386.

75. G. Lugli, *Arch. Cl.*, I (1949), 157 ff.

A somewhat different aspect meets us when we examine Greek architectural types which were not gradually incorporated with the Roman traditions in the centuries before 100 B.C., but—in Rome with marked resistance[76]—were regarded as being foreign, not traditionally Italic (not *italicae consuetudinis*, as Vitruvius styled it). Such were the palestrae, the stone-built, permanent theaters and the baths as they first appeared in Rome.

We know that Pompey was inspired by the theater of Mitylene when he was planning his theater and its portico in Rome (Plut. *Pompeius* 42). Nevertheless, when he con-

76. See Plut. *Pyrrhus* 16 and also how indignant conservative Romans were because Scipio Africanus joined the gymnastics of the Greek palestrae (see chapter 1, note 35). Another typical instance is Livy's information *periocha* xlviii about the theater, which the censors started to build but which P. Cornelius Nasica stopped: "*tamquam inutile et nociturum publicis moribus.*" At that time a small Campanian town like Pompeii had had its stone-built theater for at least some fifty years.

FIG. 35. Tabularium at the Forum Romanum. 78 B.C.
Photo A. B. 1955.

structed a temple of Venus Victrix at the top of the central part of the cavea, he not only thereby disarmed conservative critics but probably also followed the idea of Roman comitia which had the Curia above the banks of stone or wooden steps of the cavea.[77] Also the low, broad stage and the monumental construction of the cavea (Vitr. v. 6) of Roman theaters remind us that these later loans were remodeled according to the exigencies of Italic life.

Most interesting in this connection is the development of the baths. For example, the Stabian loutra and the other baths of Pompeii or the first-century thermae of Augusta Raurica[78] show an irregular and evidently Hellenistic type. Here, the Roman axial systematization, shown by all the great thermae in Rome and by the second-century baths in Augusta Raurica, was due to some architect of the first century or about 100 A.D.—perhaps to Apollonius from Damascus and his plan for the baths of Trajan on the Esquiline hill (Cass. Dio lxix. 4, 1). Together with that goes also, for instance, the symmetrical peristyle of the Roman libraries, where the central axis runs from the dominating temple to the gateway. Libraries such as in the Templum Pacis in Rome or the library of Hadrian in Athens present a striking contrast to the free arrangement of the Pergamene library (Fig. 38).

The Hellenized Italic town described by Vitruvius in his fifth and sixth books was the result of two lines of development: the Hellenization of Italic features and the Italic remodeling of borrowed Hellenistic architecture. Over and over again Vitruvius emphasized the *consuetudo italica* in contrast to the *consuetudo graeca* (e.g., v. 1, 1; 7; 11, 1; vi. 7, 1). On comparing this Hellenized Italic town with a Hellenistic town of the East, one sees at once that new buildings are added and that items typical of the Eastern towns are lacking. The most important thing to note, however, is that the *consuetudo italica*

FIG. 36. Casa della Fortuna in Pompeii. The same construction with arches supported by columns is shown in the first half of the first century B.C. in the paintings of the Villa dei Misteri.
Photo Tatiana Warscher.

77.   For the comitia see E. Sjöqvist in *Studies Presented to David M. Robinson*, I, 400 ff., and L. Richardson, "Cosa and Rome: Comitium and Curia," *Archaeology*, X (spring 1957), 49 ff.

78.   F. Staehelin, *op. cit.*, pp. 475 f. R. Laur-Belart, *Uber die Colonia Raurica und den Ursprung von Basel* (Basle 1957), pp. 46 f.

of Vitruvius is not an old urbanistic scheme inherited from a remote, barbaric, or archaic Etruscan past, but that it is the thoroughly Hellenized Italic town of the centuries after about 400 B.C. Roman conservatism is revealed by the resistance of severe censors and—in the midst of all the Hellenistic luxury of the late Republican villas—by sighs like Cicero's "*revivescat M' Curius aut eorum aliquis, quorum in villa ac domo nihil splendidum nihil ornatum fuit praeter ipsos*" (*Paradoxa* v. 2. 38). The Roman traditions developed in old Etruscan Rome conflicted with the new ideas but at the same time made them productive in a new direction.

Another important feature, and one which Vitruvius largely neglected in his fifth and sixth books, is utilitarian architecture. The Romans boasted that they were unrivaled at building aqueducts, roads, and sewers (Strabo v. 3, 8). Dionysius of Halicarnassus (iii. 67, 5) maintained that nothing contributed more to the grandeur of Rome than those three demonstrations of Roman power. This is no doubt true—if we also include walls, castra, and so forth—but the Roman claim that all these were their inventions cannot be wholly accepted. Aristotle in his time had claimed that utilitarian architecture had and ought to have a beauty of its own created by suitability for its purpose—an idea which Roman authors from Cicero onward developed in a most interesting way.[79] As for the aqueducts, the idea of course was Greek, but the great contribution of the Romans was that by raising the channel of the aqueducts they brought the water to the town on a high level, as in the Aqua Marcia, which was built as early as 144–140 B.C. In the field of utilitarian architecture the late Republican warehouses with a high barrel-vaulted

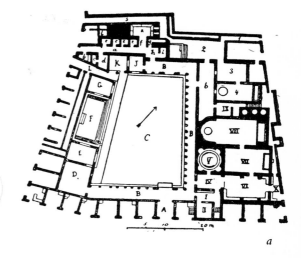

a

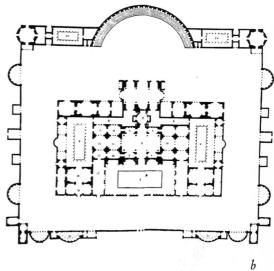

b

FIG. 37. Baths (loutra, thermae).
a) The Stabian baths at Pompeii (first period, second century B.C.). Compare with (*b*).
b) The systematized Roman thermae of the Imperial Age. Thermae of Diocletian.

79. Aristotle *Politics* vii. 11 (1331 A–B); *De partibus animalium* i. 5 (645 A). Cicero *De oratore* iii. 46 (180) shows in a most interesting way that the ideas about the special beauty of strictly utilitarian architecture, the *necessaria* to speak with Frontinus *De aquis* i. 16, belonged to late Republican times. I have discussed their importance in the Imperial Age in "Roman Architecture from Its Classicistic to Its Late Imperial Phase," *Acta universitatis gotoburgensis*, XLVII (1941), 27 f., and "Den romerska storstadens hyreshusarkitektur," *ibid.*, L (1944), 47 f. and (in English) 67 f.

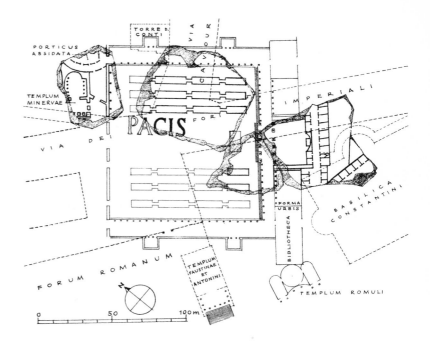

FIG. 38. The Forum Pacis in Rome ("Flavian forum"). Flavian Age. Reconstructed plan by A. Colini based on remains and fragments of the Forma Urbis.

FIG. 39. Remains of the aqueduct built by Q. Marcius Rex 144–140 B.C. (Aqua Marcia). Photo A. B. 1935.

nave in front of the tabernae[80] (Fig. 40) were probably inspired by Hellenistic models derived from the covered streets of the Orient. Here again we should remember that, beginning in the second century B.C., the armies brought impressions of Hellenistic towns back with them to Italy. This is especially important when we consider the towns at home that were reorganized for the veterans. But the Roman *opus caementicium*, or concrete, made it possible to develop the borrowed ideas in a new monumental way as early as about 100 B.C. The Trajanic market in Rome (Fig. 41) and the equally imposing structure of the same kind from Hadrian's time in Ostia[81] show the grandiose forms that this architectural idea acquired in Rome.

The Oriental bazaars of today can make this kind of architecture alive, and they suggest both a common origin and a common development of the type. When we see the Ma-

80. Such warehouses from the early first century B.C. are preserved in Ferentinum and Tibur (Tivoli). For Ferentino, see *Arch. Cl.*, VI (1954) 185 ff., A. Bartoli, "L'acropoli di Ferentino," *Boll. d'Arte*, IV (1949), 293 ff.; and for Tivoli, Boëthius-N. Carlgren, *Acta A.*, III (1932), 181 ff., and C. Carducci's considerations in his useful "Tibur" in *Italia romana. Municipi e colonie*, I. 3 (Istituto di studi romani, 1940), p. 61. For the Oriental prehistory, M. Rostovtzeff's short remark in *Dura Europos and Its Art* (Oxford, 1938), p. 47, and R. M. Riefstahl, "Mercati e fondachi coperti nell'Oriente islamico," *Roma*, X (1932), 159 ff.
81. *Scavi di Ostia*, I, 138.

FIG. 40. The Mercato of Ferentinum (Ferentino). Early first century B.C. Photo Ditta Santoro Blanca.

gazzini Republicani at the Porta Romana in Ostia and the Roman horrea of Imperial Age, we should also bear in mind the porticoed Hellenistic khan (caravanserai) and commercial marketplaces like the one of Dura-Europos. That architectural type also was imported into Italy and amplified and systematized in the Roman way.[82]

Turning from monumental architecture, from the domus and the public utilitarian architecture of Republican Rome, to tenement houses and rows of tabernae such as those along the Strada degli Augustali and the main streets north of the forum of Pompeii, we find more independence on the part of the Romans. This is due in part to that great revolutionary element in ancient architecture—concrete. As I have indicated in speaking of the Porticus Aemilia (see above), the use of concrete seems to have been perfected in Rome in the second century B.C. in connection with the needs of late Republican Rome. A rapidly increasing population made it necessary to find a cheap material suitable for high houses (*auxilium altitudinis*, Vitr. ii. 8, 17). Concrete was, indeed, of importance for almost all the monumental architecture already discussed, but it became decisive for many-storied tenement architecture that was clearly attested in Rome as early as in the

82. For the market place of Dura-Europos see *Excavations at Dura-Europos*, IX, Fig. 11. "Horrea republicana in Ostia," *Scavi di Ostia*, I, 112.

FIG. 41. The Mercato of Trajan at the Via Biberatica (see Figs. 68 and 74) outside the Forum of Trajan in Rome. Photo Alinari.

third century B.C., and which was considered typical of Rome in Cicero's time.[83] Vitruvius admits that concrete is useful for this kind of architecture, although he otherwise disapproves of it and doubts whether it could last more than eighty years (ii. 8, 8). As a matter of fact, below the *Caseggiato del portico delle mura del castrum* in Ostia we see a row of tabernae from as early as the third or the second century B.C., built with concrete covered by coarse *opus incertum*.[84] This primitive type of architecture was evidently the substratum for the architecture of Roman tenement houses, which we see all over the Ostia of Imperial times and on hundreds of fragments of the Forma Urbis (Fig. 42). The Forum baths of Pompeii (Fig.

83.   Livy xxi. 62; Diodorus xxxi. 18, 2; Cicero *De lege agraria* ii. 35 (96), *De officiis* iii. 16 (66); Plut. *Crassus* 2; Strabo v. 3, 7; Vitr. ii. 8, 17.
84.   *Scavi di Ostia* I, 98, note 4.

a

b

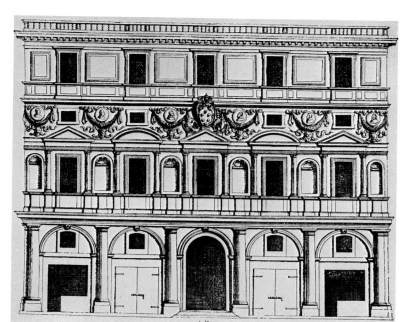

FIG. 42.

a) I. Gismondi's reconstruction of a
typical tenement house (insula) of the
Imperial Age. Cf. Fig. 73 ff.
b) Raphael's Palazzo del Aquila.
Lundberg, *Arkitekturens formspråk* (1954).

43), which in my opinion show a tenement house of the type
usually found in the capital, and the house with a portico toward the street at the Scalae Caci on the Palatine[85] show what
the Romans had achieved in this field as early as the beginning of the first century B.C. These represent the *egregiae habitationes* which were hailed by Vitruvius (ii. 8, 17) as solving

85. *Acta Rom. Suec.,* IV (=*Opus Arch.,* I, 1935), 167 ff.

the problem of housing in Rome (but they were by no means so frequent as his words may seem to imply).[86]

Having now considered Italic traditions, Hellenistic influence, and adaptations to local requirements, we may restate the fact that the *consuetudo italica* of Vitruvius, the Hellenized Italic town, came into being in the centuries before 100 B.C. The excavations at Cosa and, of course, pre-Sullan Pompeii give us the clearest idea of what was achieved before the culminating activity of the first century B.C. and the classicistic architecture of the age of Sulla, Caesar, and Augustus. It is absurd to overstress ancient tradition, assumed or real, in this revolutionary building activity or, on the other hand, to ignore that many of its principles were formulated by builders in the days of Appius Claudius Caecus and the Scipios. Once more I emphasize as a most desirable research project the re-examination of the testimonies about architecture in Rome from 400 to 100 B.C., as well as a re-examination of the style of the Republican monuments and our usual dating of them.

The great Hellenized program of the last centuries B.C. was a prelude to the extensive work summarized in Augustus' *Res Gestae* (19 ff.). It was the model for the architects who created Augustan Rome, introducing marble as material for the public buildings, enlarging all dimensions, and treating the Republican heritage in a classicistic spirit that we can trace back to Sullan days. Clearly, the Rome of the early Empire was by no means a direct copy of the Hellenistic towns. It was a new, enlarged, and more strictly classicistic edition of the Hellenized Republican architecture in its final form. In other words, even in the days of Sulla and Caesar the foundations of the urbanistic program of the Empire had been laid. In the second century A.D., Aelius Aristides de-

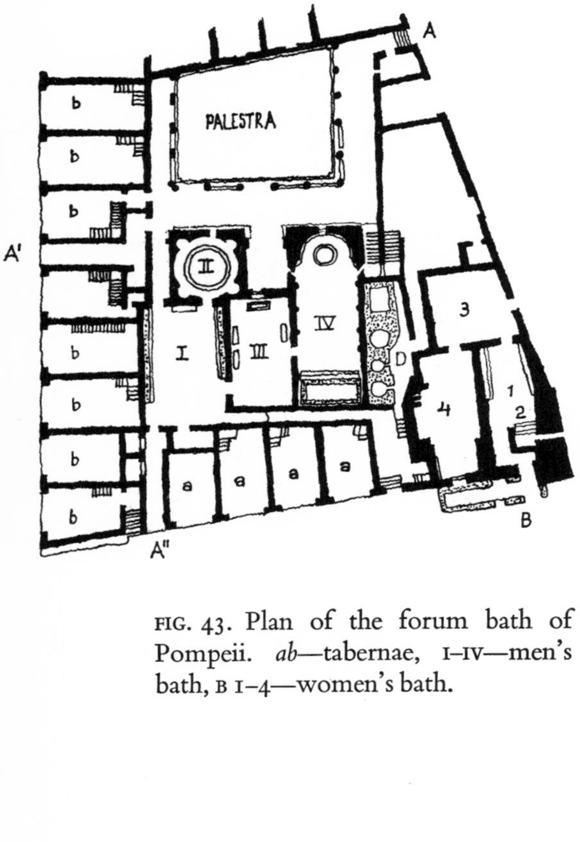

FIG. 43. Plan of the forum bath of Pompeii. *ab*—tabernae, I–IV—men's bath, B 1–4—women's bath.

86. It is for instance evident that adobe was much in use even in the Augustan Age: Vitr. ii. 8, 16; Suetonius *Augustus* 28 (=Dio Cassius lvi. 30) evidently aims at that, though in a rather illogical way contrasting the town of sunbaked bricks (*geine*) with his marble temples; Dio Cassius xxxix. 61; Zonaras x. 38 D. The natural comparison would have been the late Republican tufa temples and the monumental marble architecture of the Augustan Age.

scribed it in its fully developed form with gymnasia, baths, aqueducts, porticoes, and temples. Republican Rome had already created that system of material welfare which Aristides praised as public hygiene, which the Christians despised, and which Hadrian restrained in military life when he demolished separate dining rooms (triclinia), porticoes and subterranean porticoes for the summer time (cryptas), and garden paintings (topia), the type well known from triclinia and other rooms in Pompeii.[87]

In art, too, the importance of what was created in the centuries before 100 B.C. is sometimes overlooked. With its obvious affinity to Hellenistic—probably Egyptian—realism and its grim veracity akin to Cicero's descriptions of his contemporaries in his letters, the veristic Roman portrait of the first century B.C. is often considered to be the very beginning of Roman art. I do not wish to discuss here the nationality of

FIG. 44. Late Republican and Augustan coins, illustrating the various styles of the statues on Forum Romanum, temple courts, etc., in Republican and Augustan Rome.
a) Brutus—evidently based on a fourth-century "portrait" like the "Brutus" in the Palazzo dei Conservatori on the Capitolium.
b) Titus Tatius—romantic Hellenistic fancy portrait.
c) T. Quinctius Flamininus—contemporary Hellenistic portrait.
d) M. Claudius Marcellus—portrait in the veristic style of the first century B.C.
e) Augustus (classicistic).

87. *Scriptores Historiae Augustae. Hadrian* 10. 4.

FIG. 45. Schematic relief of a fortified
town on the column of Marcus Aurelius, Rome.
Photo Alinari.

the artists who interpreted the Romans in that way. Doubtless, the leading masters, at least, were Greeks or Etruscans. The Etruscan Hellenized portraits of the third and second centuries B.C. should always be kept in mind when we consider Republican Roman portraits. Even when in the second century B.C. direct contact with the Hellenistic world became more and more decisive for Roman art, Etruscan Hellenized "baroque" and realism continued to have great importance in Rome. Here it is difficult to distinguish Roman from Etruscan. There was an artistic unity, but it cannot be denied that from archaic times to the centuries of classic and Hellenistic influence Rome played a considerable part in the artistic life of Italy.[88] For proof we need only turn to the old Capitoline temple and to the late Republican coins with their reproductions of portraits of the fourth to the first centuries B.C. (Fig. 44). As von Kaschnitz pointed out many years ago,[89] we should also take into account here the so-called "Brutus" in the Capitoline Museum. When, in his description of the funerals in Rome (vi. 53), Polybius said that the Romans made their ancestral masks as lifelike as possible, this means—as I

88. As O. Vessberg has already maintained in "Studien zur Kunstgeschichte der römischen Republik," *Acta Rom. Suec.*, VIII (1941), 174, 254, and in other publications, G. Richter in *Three Critical Periods in Greek Sculpture* (Oxford, 1951), and J. M. C. Toynbee in "Some Notes on Artists in the Roman World" (*Collection Latomus*, VI, 1951) have proved the importance of Greek sculptors for both the realistic portrait of the last century B.C. and the Augustan classicism (cf. also Hanfmann, *Latomus*, XI, 1952). This seems obvious and has also been illustrated by Vessberg's study of Roman portrait art in Cyprus; *Acta Rom. Suec.*, XVIII (=*Opus Rom.*, I, 1954), 160 ff.: "The Roman portrait art was an art of the Roman Empire." I insist that we should not confuse the fascinating question about the introduction of modern Hellenistic art in late Republican Rome with testimony about the Greek artists in Imperial Rome. We should also remember both the importance of older art in Rome and of the Etruscan version of the Hellenistic styles when we consider their subsequent and continued victories in Rome and how they got changed in Roman life and adapted to Roman tradition (cf. Schefold, *op. cit.*, quoted note 4, pp. 297 ff., especially p. 300 f. and F. Brommer, "Zu den römischen Ahnenbildern" *R. M.*, LX/LXI [1953–54], 163). Appropriate remarks are made also by Polacco in his *Tuscanicae dispositiones*, Jucker (*op. cit.* in note 30) and Becatti, *Arte e gusto negli scrittori latini* (Florence, 1951), to which I owe very much.

89. *R.M.*, XLI (1926), 147 f.; *Mitteilungen des deutschen archäologischen Instituts*, III (1950), 158. "Brutus" may of course be Etruscan; in art and architecture cen-

see it—that some crude old traditions were perhaps retained, but, on the other hand and most important, that because of such old lore, or for some other reason, they adapted to their own use new possibilities offered by the realistic portraiture of Hellenistic art.[90]

Here we may add a word about the reliefs on the columns of Trajan and Marcus Aurelius (Fig. 45) and the panels of the triumphal arch of Septimius Severus on the Forum Romanum, in which, evidently, the traditions of triumphal painting were revived. The expressive "concentration on essentials at the expense of logical realism" in this great art has sometimes been explained as a more or less new achievement in an imperial age inspired by the wars in Germany and in the Orient.[91] No doubt the reports from the frontiers brought new life into this branch of art. But in principle this mode of telling a story was Etruscan and Hellenistic. This is proved by

tral Italy was, I repeat, a unity, even if local spirit no doubt many times reveals itself, especially in Rome. In any case "Brutus" belongs to the Hellenized Italic background of the Roman art of the last century B.C. To me it seems evident that the "veristic" late Republican portraiture had three sources: the ruthlessly realistic conception of the Romans which we meet with in Cicero's letters and in Sallust, the Roman-Etruscan version of Hellenistic baroque, classicism, and realism, and—finally—direct influences from Hellenistic realism including the portraiture of Ptolemaic Egypt. For another opinion about "Brutus" and the influence from older art in Italy and from Egypt see Gisela Richter, *Ancient Italy* (Ann Arbor, 1955), pp. 32–33, 89 ff. and especially 103, note 65 and Andrén's review in *Gnomon*, XXIX (1957), 606.

The old idea that Roman art started only with the strong new Hellenistic influences (realism and so forth) about 100 B.C. has doubtless caused much of the perplexity at the dating and understanding of "Brutus." See now A. Cedrena, "Teste votive di Carsóli," *Arch. Cl.*, v (1953), 197 ff.

90. See my discussion in the *Atti del 1º Congresso internazionale di preistoria e protoistoria mediterranea* (Florence, 1950), p. 112, and especially B. Schweitzer, *Die Bildniskunst der römischen Republik* (Weimar, 1948), p. 21. As pointed out by W. Schwabacher the coin portraits of Tissaphernes (see *Charites. Festschrift für E. Langlotz*, 1957, pp. 27 ff.) are most important for the prehistory of the Hellenistic realism, which the Romans adopted about 100 B.C.

91. See Toynbee, *loc. cit.* (note 88), and my remarks, *J.R.S.*, XLIII (1953), 190. It seems surprising to me that P. H. von Blanckenhagen in his contribution to the symposium on "Narration in Ancient Art," *A.J.A.*, LXI (1957), 80 f. has altogether overlooked the Etruscan ash urns while otherwise rightly emphasizing the importance for Imperial reliefs of "old Roman traditions of representing actual events for public consumption."

reliefs on Etruscan ash urns and sarcophagi (Fig. 46), especially where Greek legends were used as symbolic expressions for ideas about life and death, as on the Roman sarcophagi from the second century A.D. onward.[92] The large vases of the third century from South Italy present their stories in the same fashion, with stress on the main facts of the tale to the neglect of proportions and perspective, and with placement of background details above the figures and objects in the foreground.[93] This manner of narration seems to have been more or less discarded from official monuments by classicistic taste,[94] but it evidently lived on in the triumphal paintings with their special propaganda aims and scope. Here again we meet with an achievement of the centuries before 100 B.C. that was destined for a great future in the hands of artists of Imperial (and medieval) times, a Hellenistic mode of telling stories, transubstantiated in that independent colony of Hellenistic culture, the Etrusco-Roman West. In this Romanized form it belongs to the artistic program of Imperial Roman art, like the late Republican coins with their Hellenized goddess Roma, their symbolic representations, and their old Roman legends—as has lately been discussed by Andrew Alföldi (see note 1).

These observations go together with what I have ventured to suggest in spite of insufficient research about the Italic architecture of the fourth and following centuries: that it was under the spell of Hellenistic architecture and also, in its free use of various styles, revealed anticlassic tendencies characteristic of Italy.[95] Here, awaiting further exploration,

FIG. 46. Ash urn from Volterra. The siege of Thebes with Capaneus falling from the wall.
Courtesy of the Cabinetto fotografico della Soprintendenza alle antichità di Etruria.

92. As very well pointed out with reference to F. Cumont's *Recherches sur le symbolisme funéraire des Romains* (Paris, 1942) by A. Piganiol. See "Recherches sur les jeux romains," *Publications de la Faculté des Lettres de Strasbourg*, XIII (1923), 8, and "Les Etrusques peuples d'Orient," *Cahiers d'histoire mondiale*, I (1953), 350.
93. Good interpretations by C. Robert, *Archäologische Hermeneutik* (Berlin, 1919), p. 160 (Medea vase from Canossa) and C. Anti, "Il vaso di Dario e i persiani di Frinico," *Arch. Cl.*, IV (1952), 23 ff., V (1953), 171 and 229.
94. We do, however, see remains of it even on the mythological panels of Ara Pacis; see Toynbee, "The Ara Pacis Reconsidered and Historical Art in Roman Italy," *Proc. Brit. Acad.*, XXXIX (1953), 79 f.; for instance, the temple and landscape on the slab with Aeneas in Lanuvium; the cattle on the Terra Mater slab.
95. Here I refer again to Polacco, *op. cit.*, Pl. 2 and ff. with text.

b

FIG. 47.
a) The altar of the Agora of Athens.
Reconstruction. *Hesperia,* 21 (1952).
b) Ara Pacis.
Photo Alinari.

a

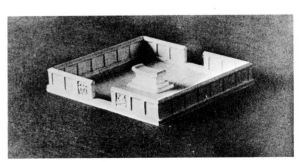

is a fascinating subject that would utilize the evidence of literature and more especially that of the Etruscan ash urns and sarcophagi. As early as Sulla's time classicistic taste seems to have reacted against the freedom of Hellenistic and Italic architecture. Thus far, this reaction belongs to our present theme, even if its decisive victory in Rome came only in the Augustan Age. In the Hellenistic world the movement was already in full swing in the second century B.C.,[96] adding the classicistic style to the other artistic tendencies simultaneously alive in the late Hellenistic Age: its baroque, its realism, and its Praxitelean sweetness. It is interesting that the Roman artists about 100 B.C. chose either the realistic or the baroque style of Hellenistic art for portraits. This shows how strong the earlier Hellenistic styles still were in Italy. The coins of this period, with their sudden conversion to classicism in Augustus' time (Fig. 44), are most helpful in illuminating both the earlier tendencies and the victory of classicism,[97] the end of the development which I have tried to follow through the centuries following 400 B.C.

The recent American excavations on the Athenian Agora have shown us how the Ara Pacis of Augustus testifies to the victory of classicism not only by the splendid classicistic style of its reliefs but also by the shape of the whole monument.[98] We must remember that it was erected in the heyday of the Augustan Empire. One might have expected that this central monument to the triumphs and the victorious peace of the new ruler of the world would be designed in the grandiose style of Hellenistic royal monuments such as the altar of Pergamon. Instead, the central but rather modest fifth-century altar of the twelve gods on the Agora of Athens was chosen as a model (Fig. 47).

96. See A. Boëthius, "L'ex voto dei fanciulli pythaisti nel Museo Barracco," *Studier tillägnade Henrik Cornell,* 1949, p. 24. Vagn Poulsen, *Meddelelser fra Ny Carlsberg Glyptotek,* 1948, pp. 31 f.

97. Vessberg, *op. cit.,* note 88, Pl. 11, pp. 114 (early classicism), 167, 198.

98. H. Thompson, *Hesperia,* XXI (1952), 47 f. See Toynbee, *op. cit.,* p. 91; T. Kraus, *Die Ranken der Ara Pacis* (Berlin, 1953), with D. E. Strong's remarks in *J.R.S.,* XLIV (1954), 141 f., and L. Byvanck-Quarles van Ufford, *B. Ant. Besch.,* XXX (1955), 39 ff.

FIG. 48. Wall painting from the so-called House of Livia on the Palatine. The fantastic new style criticized by Vitruvius.
Photo Alinari.

It is to this classicistic age that Vitruvius belongs. He stands between the results of the old development and the architecture of Imperial Rome. The classicistic architects of the later Hellenistic Age were his venerated teachers. With characteristic fervor he criticized the later, more wildly imaginative phase of the second Pompeian style (vii. 5, 3 ff.), and it is in this critique that we see Vitruvius as an active classicist struggling against what he considered the bad style and misleading rules of much Hellenistic architecture and art (Fig. 48). What he fought against was certainly not less influential than his classicism. Paintings such as those of the so-called Casa di Livia on the Palatine, the grandiose Hellenistic baroque style of the paintings in the Villa at Boscoreale, and sculptures such as the Belvedere torso (whether copy or original)[99] show

99.   See Gisela Richter, *op. cit.* (see note 88), p. 48, and my remarks in *Anthemon* (*Studies Dedicated to C. Anti*, 1955), pp. 13 f. Probably, Miss Richter is right in assuming that the Athenian sculptor, Apollonios, son of Nestor, who has signed

tendencies that are obviously in opposition to classicistic art. As for Vitruvius, he was, I repeat, *not* an antiquarian studying old styles for their own sake. The goal of his work was not to fight against all that was new and modern in his time but to combine the dignity of classic architecture, as he believed himself to have rediscovered it, with the needs of his own time and with Italic tradition.[100]

I have tried to show that his criticism of technique is quite sound, even if he is narrow-minded in seeing only its shortcomings and ignores the possibilities for improvement and development that were destined for great victories in the architecture both of Rome and of later western Europe.[101] On the other hand we should not forget that mud brick (Figs. 49 and 50), ashlar masonry, and *structura graecorum*, which he defends, also had a great future in Sicily, in Africa,

---

the torso—Philoktetes in Andrén's opinion—has made a copy, inspired by an original from the beginning of the second century B.C. But even if this is the case, it testifies to the vital power of the great Hellenistic style—as do the second Pompeian style and the paintings of the left and right walls of the "Hall of Aphrodite" in the Boscoreale villa. See Phyllis Lehmann, *Roman Wall Paintings from Bosco Reale in the Metropolitan Museum* (Cambridge, Mass., 1953), pp. 139 f. (especially Menedemus-Cinyras, Fig. 27) and K. Schefold's critique, *Gnomon*, XXVII (1955), 43.

100. Here I may still refer to my "Vitruvius and the Roman Architecture of His Age," *Acta Rom. Suec.*, 8:0, 1 (= *Dragma Martino Nilsson Dedicatum* 1939), 114 ff., although much ought to be added because of later research by Wistrand, F. Pellati, Polacco, C. J. Moe (*Numeri di Vitruvio*, Milan, 1945), and others.

101. *Eranos*, XXXIX (1941), 152 f. Everyone who has seen how the winters spoil the late Republican brickwork at Aquileia as soon as it is excavated will understand Vitruvius' critique ii. 8, 19. His words about testing of the material on roofs confirm that the Roman brick industry of Imperial Age started from roof tiles, which, of course, were of high quality. A great Roman achievement was to create a vast industry for small shaped bricks especially made to cover the surface of concrete walls.

Quite different was the Greek fabrication, now known from the kiln of Serra Orlando (*A.J.A.*, LXI, 1957, 158), from the theater of Taormina (Lugli, "L'architettura in Sicilia nell'età ellenistica e romana," *Atti del VII Congresso nazionale di storia dell'architettura*, 1950. Rome, 1955, pp. 1 ff.), and from Velia (Mingazzini, *op. cit.*, in note 23, pp. 26 ff.). The Greeks baked large-size bricks (average—Serra Orlando: 33 × 46 × 8; Taormina: from 35 × 51 × 9.5–15 × 24.5 × 4), whether intended for solid brickwork or in Roman practice for covering concrete walls. The bricks from Velia give a most interesting background to the practice of dating bricks, which the Romans in the Imperial Age developed for

and in the East.[102] He was, above all, a champion of a renewed classic style which was appropriate to the needs of his own age and which was also in harmony with the rules that had matured in Italy and Rome during the centuries before him. This explains how a teacher who was in many ways so reactionary could acquire such authority through the ages as is shown by excerpts from his work in Pliny, by the summary of Marcus Cetius Faventius, by the famous words of Sidonius Apollinaris about Vitruvius as the architect par excellence,[103] by his reputation in medieval times and later. He belongs to one of the most important transitional periods in the history of art, the decades of Augustus' reign, when classicism, perfecting its Roman form, became the style of the Empire and thereby also the leading conception of ancient art and architecture when the Renaissance abandoned the medieval traditions and the legacy from the late Roman Empire and rediscovered classic naturalism.

---

their great brick industry (Chap. IV, note 27). When Diodoros (xiv. 116; see Livy v. 55) speaks about *keramides politikai* that were distributed to the builders after the Gallic catastrophe, he obviously aims at old roof tiles with some kind of official marks. It is difficult to find Vitruvius' critique of the *opus caementicium* of his time (ii. 8, 2) better confirmed and illustrated than by what Gullini, *Arch Cl.*, VI (1954), 187–89, tells about the deterioration of the great terrace building of Ferentino. But see H. Bloch, *A.J.A.*, LXIII (1959), 235.

102.   For *structura graecorum*, see Wistrand, *Eranos*, XLI (1943), 137, and my remarks in "Den romerska storstadens hyresarkitektur," *Acta universitatis gotoburgensis*, L (1944), 31, note 44, and in the English summary on p. 64. For the continued life of the Greek constructions (without concrete) see, for example, J. Ward Perkins, *Proc. Brit. Acad.*, XXXVII (1951), 277; *J.R.S.*, XXXVIII (1948), 62 f., or the material from Ephesos (J. Keil, *Ephesos*, Wien, 1955) and other towns in Asia Minor.

103.   Sidonius Apollinaris *Epistulae* iv. 3, 5 and in general H. Koch, "Vom Nachleben des Vitruv," *Deutsche Beiträge zur Altertumswissenschaft*, I (Baden Baden, 1951). Cf. D. Detlefsen, *Philologus*, XXXI (1872), 385.

FIG. 49. Mud brick sarcophagi, fourth to third centuries B.C. Campo di Diana, Lipari.
Photo B. Wahlgren, May 1956.

FIG. 50. The city wall of Gela with its upper part built of mud brick. Probably all fourth century B.C. (Timoleon's age).
Photo H. M. the King of Sweden 1954.

CHAPTER III

THE GOLDEN HOUSE OF NERO

It may seem premature to discuss the Domus Aurea of Nero (Figs. 51–53), for much fundamental work remains to be done on it. First of all, a complete description of the remains of the main palace of the great villa below the terrace of the Thermae of Trajan must be prepared. Another essential requirement is a survey and map of the wide grounds surrounding the main palace—as outlined by C. C. Van Essen in his most valuable article "La Topographie de la Domus Aurea Neronis."[1] It will also be necessary to analyze the ruins in front (that is, to the south) of the great apse of the terrace of the Thermae of Trajan (in the Orto di Dorotea Rotolanti).[2] The slightly different orientation and the general impression of these remains seem to me to indicate a post-Neronian origin; however, this question will have to be carefully examined. The apsidal construction, known from old excavations on the

---

1. *Meded. Koninkl. Nederlandse Akademie van Wetenschappen, afd. Letterkunde,* n.s. XVII (1954), 371 ff. His exposition "La découverte du Laocoon," *ibid.,* XVIII (1955), 291 ff. makes it clear that when Pliny xxxvi. 37 speaks of the Laocoon group as having been found in "Titi domu" he uses the word "Domus" in Tacitus' sense and that he means only: in the Domus Aurea establishment—anywhere in that large district. Different view: G. Lugli, *Arch. Cl.,* x (1958), 197–200.
2. Lanciani, *Forma Urbis,* Pl. 30; Van Essen, *op. cit.,* 386 f.

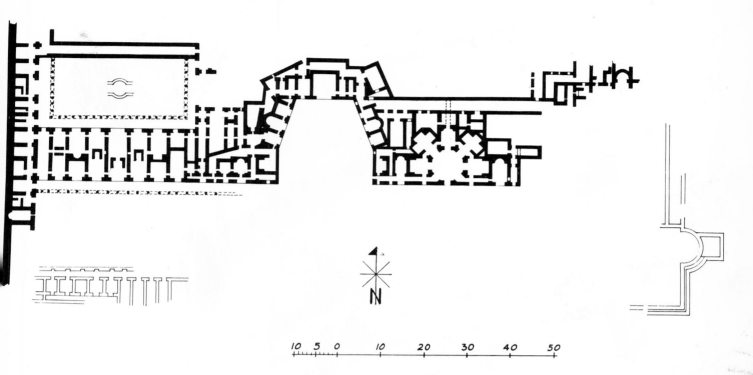

FIG. 51. The Domus Aurea. Further research is necessary to clarify the connection between the main building, the ruins in front of its western part, and the apse, etc., to the east. On the east side of the peristyle in the western wing a barrel-vaulted hall and a nymphaeum have now been excavated. Plan after Lugli and Lanciani revised by Vittorio Messina 1956.

eastern side of the court in front of the palace, must also be studied. In spite of such deficiencies in our knowledge, some suggestions will be offered here about the place of the Domus Aurea in the history of Roman architecture, and I shall discuss, in general, its role in Roman life and Roman history.

There is ample literary evidence to show that, in ancient times, many farmhouses stood in the countryside surrounding the cities of Italy. At the same time peasants also lived, as today, in hill towns and went out to their fields at dawn. In the fields the peasants had huts which were available for short sojourns in harvest times or for the shepherds (Fig. 3). There were, moreover, the greater farms and manor houses, the so-called Roman villas whose agricultural function was beautifully described by Cato, Varro, and Vitruvius. The descriptions of the farm of Manius Curius Dentatus give us a reliable glimpse of the simple life in the villas of the early third century B.C. In *De legibus* Cicero contrasted the luxury of the rebuilt house of his father with the homestead of his grandfather which—according to the old custom—was like that of Curius in the Sabine country. A small "farmer" like Horace makes us feel the deep-rooted tradition in this country life derived from the *priscae virtutes* and *mores* of legendary ploughmen, like Cincinnatus, "*ab aratro aut foco exeuntes.*"

a

FIG. 52. The Colosseum Valley.
a) Reconstruction in the Museo della Civiltà Romana, Rome. In front the Circus Maximus and the Palatine and to the right of the Colosseum the temple and portico of Claudius on the Caelian Hill. Studying the Domus Aurea we introduce: (1) N. of the Palatine the porticoes along the Via Sacra (Fig. 61). (2) Instead of the temple of Rome and Venus the Vestibulum. (3) Instead of the Colosseum the lake. (4) Behind that, instead of the Baths of Trajan the palace (Fig. 51).
b) The valley from the temple of Venus and Rome (left) to the Baths of Trajan (the terrace visible just behind the Colosseum to the right).
c) Plan of the valley (after Van Essen) with its Neronian palace and the great Trajanic reservoir (Sette Sale).

These old politicians, warriors, and farmers, such as Dentatus with his stove, his turnips, and his answer to the Samnites who tried to bribe him ("*Malo haec in fictilibus meis esse et aurum habentibus imperare*"), and the parsimonious old Roman honesty—recorded from the second century B.C. by authors like Cato, Ennius, and Polybius—all are in strong contrast to the characteristics of the generations of Varro, Cicero, Sallust, Propertius, and Horace.3

The villa of Scipio Africanus seemed simple to later generations,4 and as early as the second century B.C., Hellenistic luxury in private houses, as displayed in marble, Greek columns, peristyles, and mosaics, increased rapidly, although it was not to culminate until after the Sullan Age.

For the study of the Domus Aurea it is most important to remember that in the last centuries B.C. the villa had come to be a real center of Hellenistic luxury. The elder Pliny, especially, has recorded the indignant opinions expressed about it.5 We see it illustrated in towns like Pompeii and Herculan-

---

3. Cicero *De legibus* ii. 1 (3). Cato maior 16 (55). Pliny xxxvi. 111 f. Sallustius *Catilina* 12. Forni, *Athenaeum*, XXXI (1953), 173. Horace *Od.* ii. 15, 10 ff.
4.   Seneca *Epist.* 86. 4.
5.   Pliny eagerly uses these early and original reactions against the Hellenistic luxury for the moralistic reflections of his own age. See for example xix. 24; xxxiii. 57; xxxiv. 13 and 34 (*fictilia deorum simulacra in delubris usque ad devictam Asiam, unde luxuria*); xxxv. 6 and 157 f.; xxxvi. 4 ff., 48 f., 110. The harvest in the *Odes* of Horace is rich. I have noted as especially typical: ii. 3, 17; ii. 14, 21; ii. 15; iii. 1, 33 ff. and 45 (*cur invidendis postibus et novo sublime ritu moliar atrium?*); iii. 24 (*caementis licet occupes Tyrrhenum mare*); iii. 29, 10 (*molem propinquam nubibus arduis*). See also Prop. iii. 2, 8 ff.

b

c

eum and in the villas around the Bay of Naples with their paintings and their early importation, or imitation, of marble in various colors. The testimony of Cicero and Vitruvius, the remains of villas, and paintings like those of Boscoreale, as interpreted by Phyllis Lehmann, show colonnades, peristyles, apsidal halls for lectures and philosophical discourses, domes, and all the rich variety of Hellenistic luxury. The influence of the Hellenistic palaces is also evident in imaginative landscape architecture and various luxurious oddities.[6]

Although it is evident that the palaces of the Hellenistic world were the source of inspiration, a comparison between the House of the Faun in a provincial town like Pompeii and the royal palaces excavated on the acropolis of Pergamon, for

6.   Early apsidal constructions (*exhedrae, scholae*): Plut. *Pompejus* 42; *Brutus* 14 (in the peristyle of the theater of Pompeius); the great villa discussed in *Palladio*, v (1941), 145 f. Suet. *De gramm.* 17. Vitr. vi. 7, 3; in the baths v. 11, 2 (*"exhedrae —in quibus philosophi . . . disputare possint"*). Cicero *Ad fam.* vii. 23 (*"exhedria . . . in porticula Tusculani"*). For the Greek background: the Mouseion in Alexandria (Strabo xvii. 1, 8), F. Poulsen, E. Dyggve, and K. Rhomaios, *Das Heroon von Kalydon* (Copenhagen, 1934). For domed constructions: see K. Lehmann, "The Dome of Heaven," *Art B.*, XXVII (1945), 19 ff. To what Lehmann (p. 20, note 176) says about "wooden domes used in Etruria from archaic times on" we can add also a circular vestibulum (with flat roof) in a still anonymous tomb near "*il grande tumulo degli scudi*" in Caere (Cerveteri). In my view this is a feature belonging to the luxury of the Etruscan domus. That such a vestibulum should carry on traditions from Italic round huts and tombs seems most unlikely to me. See further: E. Baldwin Smith, *The Dome* (Princeton, N. J., 1950) and *Architectural Symbolism of Imperial Rome and the Middle Ages* (Princeton, N.J., 1956), especially p. 124, note 51 (about Varro's aviary).

example, suggests that the Romans surpassed their models—as Pompey decided to do when he built his theater (Plut. *Pompey* 42). When Horace (*Odes* ii. 18) speaks of the Regia Attali as a culmination of wealth, he no doubt has in mind the whole acropolis with piazzas, porticoes, library, temples, and monuments.

The Romans imitated and elaborated, but at the same time, as I have explained above, they remodeled in accordance with their own traditions or simply Hellenized their old types of houses. The predilection for symmetrical disposition (*symmetriarum rationes*—Vitr. vi. 3. 11), for axiality, and for the tripartite inner side of the atria remained, when atria were

FIG. 53. The Octagon of the Domus Aurea with stairs for running water from behind. The same arrangement in different sizes and from different ages is shown in Figure 58. The oblique (scratched) walls in front belong to the substructions of the Thermae of Trajan, in which the remains of the Domus are embedded.
Plan by Vittorio Messina 1956.

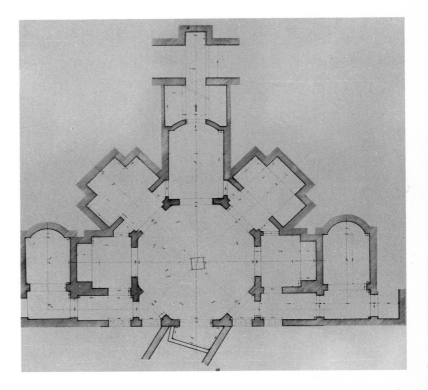

provided with Greek columns, paintings, and peristyles, and distinguished the Italic palaces from their Greek models. Peristyles, reshaped by Italic symmetry and axiality (Fig. 54)—as in the Villa dei Misteri outside Pompeii, for example, or the late Republican villa in Tibur that Hadrian rebuilt[7]—were in great favor in these luxurious villas. Pierre Grimal and lately Karl Schefold have brought this out very well. The large atrium and peristyle houses in the Republican strata of Ostia[8] help us to understand that by about 100 B.C. villas and domus in Rome were already the leading centers for the new luxuries. So far as we can see, the private houses in Ostia and the villas stand out in striking contrast to the late Republican temples of tufa and travertine and all the old-fashioned discipline of the state, as Pliny, too, observed in a noteworthy phrase: "*Tacuere tantas moles* [great columns of costly marble] *in privatam domum trahi praeter fictilia deorum fastigia*" (xxxvi. 6).

7.   See G. Lugli, "Studi topografici intorno alle antiche ville suburbane. VI. Villa Adriana," *Bull. Comm.*, LV (1927), 139 ff.; H. Kähler, *Hadrian und seine Villa bei Tivoli* (Berlin, 1950), p. 90.

8.   *Scavi di Ostia*, I, 101 f. Grimal, *Les jardins romains* (Paris, 1943), pp. 167 f., 234 ff. Schefold, "Pompejis Tuffzeit als Zeuge für die Begründung römischer Kunst," *Neue Beiträge zur klassischen Altertumswissenschaft. Festschrift Bernhard Schweitzer* (Stuttgart, 1954), 297 ff.; *R.M.*, LX / LXI (1953–54), 297 f.

FIG. 54. Peristyle in the Roman way provided with tablinum and side doors like the atria. Casa di Triptolemo. Pompeii.
Photo A. B. 1935.

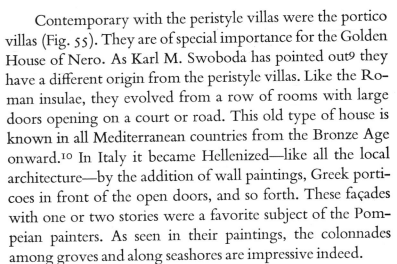

Contemporary with the peristyle villas were the portico villas (Fig. 55). They are of special importance for the Golden House of Nero. As Karl M. Swoboda has pointed out[9] they have a different origin from the peristyle villas. Like the Roman insulae, they evolved from a row of rooms with large doors opening on a court or road. This old type of house is known in all Mediterranean countries from the Bronze Age onward.[10] In Italy it became Hellenized—like all the local architecture—by the addition of wall paintings, Greek porticoes in front of the open doors, and so forth. These façades with one or two stories were a favorite subject of the Pompeian painters. As seen in their paintings, the colonnades among groves and along seashores are impressive indeed.

These colonnades along the seashore remind us of Horace's words about the terraces of the villas projecting into the sea (*Odes* ii. 18. 20; iii. 1. 33; iii. 24. 2). The portico façade could be used as a screen in front of a peristyle villa, but the original form of this kind of architecture was a long, narrow palace with a row of open chambers inside the colonnade that faced the sunny side, if built for winter and spring, or looked out over a view, the sea, or other attractions. A typical instance is the so-called Villa di Arianna southeast of Castellammare di Stabia.[11] A central hall with a painting of Ariadne is flanked by triclinia with small sunken gardens. To the right and the left extend rows of chambers and in front of these

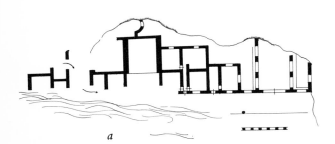

FIG. 55. A porticus villa with an open view toward coast and sea. So-called Villa di Arianna (Scavi A) at Stabiae (above Castellammare di Stabia). After Libero d'Orsi. The lower colonnaded terrace can be compared with the terrace along the sea front of the Damecutta villa on Capri shown below. Photo H. M. the King of Sweden.

b

9. *Römische und romanische Paläste* (2d ed.; Wien, 1924), pp. 29 ff. I agree with D. Mustilli when he, in his important paper "La villa pseudourbana Ercolanense," *Rend. Nap.*, XXXI (1956), 19–22, emphasizes, against Swoboda, that the peristyle and porticus villas were equally luxurious. He may be right in saying that the rich development of the porticus villas belonged to luxurious late Republican architecture and perhaps was somewhat later than the Hellenization of the atrium and peristyle houses, but overwhelming material from the Imperial Age is against the assumption that the palatial peristyle architecture went out of date.

10. Cf. the market or stoa at Hagia Triada, discussed by R. H. Hutchinson, *Town Planning Review*, XXI (1950), 215. To take this building as a prototype of the classical stoa, etc., is in my opinion erroneous. The type was ubiquitous. Swoboda's suggestion, *op. cit.*, p. 30, that the original type in Italy had a corridor in front of the rooms is unfounded and seems most unlikely.

11. The Scavi A, described by Libero d'Orsi, *Gli Scavi di Stabia* (Naples, 1954), 10 f., Pl. 31, and *Come ritrovai l'antica Stabia* (Naples, 1956),

runs a portico; below that is a terrace about one hundred yards long—an ambulatio such as the ancient writers on dietetics recommended. The whole building is oriented toward the Bay of Castellammare, Vesuvius, and the delightful beauty of those surroundings. The view reminds one at once of Cicero's words in a letter to M. Marius (*Ad fam* vii. 1, 1) about the view from his cubiculum toward the Bay of Stabiae. The villa at the Torre Damecutta on Capri was built in the same spirit, as were some of the houses on the south side of Pompeii.[12]

This Hellenized Italic villa architecture with its love for Greek art and Greek culture, with all the Greek legends and motifs of the so-called Pompeian wall paintings, with agricultural traditions, and love of nature has been well interpreted by Pierre Grimal, Karl Lehmann, and Phyllis Lehmann[13] —not to mention Horace's famous: "Amid your varied columns you are nursing trees, and you praise the mansion which looks out on distant fields. You may drive out Nature with a pitchfork, yet she will ever hurry back, and ere you know it, will burst through your foolish contempt in triumph."[14]

There has been a certain failure to appreciate how thoroughly all this was incorporated into Italic and Roman life and farm traditions by late Republican times. It is evident that we misinterpret the villas of the Imperial Age if we do not realize how much of their luxury and architecture had already been made Roman by the first century B.C. There was, of course, much that was new and foreign in the luxury of Imperial times, but the owners of late Republican villas

12. K. Lehmann and F. Noack, *Baugeschichtliche Untersuchungen am Stadtrand von Pompeji* (Berlin and Leipzig, 1936).

13. Grimal, *op. cit.*; K. Lehmann, *Thomas Jefferson, American Humanist* (New York, 1947), Jefferson's Monticello and the University of Virginia are indeed an American renewal of the Roman traditions. Phyllis Lehmann, *Roman Wall Paintings from Bosco Reale in the Metropolitan Museum of Art*, especially pp. 82 ff. For the cultural impact of the Pompeian paintings and their importance as expressions of living Hellenism in Italy I refer again to Schefold's works, quoted in note 8 and chapter II, note 4.

14. *Epist.* i. 10, 22–25 (Loeb edition).

FIG. 56. Roman villa. Landscape. Stucco from the Villa Farnesina in Rome. Museo delle Terme.

had already laid out the program. Did not Strabo refer to the Oriental and Hellenistic luxury of these palaces as "Persian" (v. 2, 5), and did not Horace "hate Persian elegance" (*Odes* i. 38)? It seems clear that the late Republican nobles rivaled, if they did not surpass, their Hellenistic teachers, their "seducers," to use Cato's term.[15] They belonged entirely to a luxurious cultured life, with Greek architectural forms—that is to the *consuetudo italica*, the Hellenized Italic life discussed in the previous chapter.

How far the fancies and refinements of these villas went even in Varro's time is shown by the description of his aviary (*R.R.*iii. 5, 8). He claims that he surpassed even the great improvements in the villa of Lucullus at Tusculum. The modern reader is reminded of the stuccoes from the Villa Farnesina (Fig. 56) and the elaborately arranged settings in the gardens of Campania (as seen in their ruins and wall paintings) when he reads about the channel and the bridges in Varro's

---

15.   A. Alföldi has made interesting comments on the important results of this union between Roman and Hellenistic in his article "Die Geburt der kaiserlichen Bildsymbolic," *Mus. Helv.*, IX (1952), 213, 235 and *passim*. Otherwise, he is one of the scholars who have been somewhat inclined to underestimate the Hellenism of the Republic, but in his brilliant paper "Die Geschichte des Throntabernakels," *La Nouvelle Clio*, 1950, pp. 537 f. he has pointed out that a new kind of Hellenistic architecture arose in the villas of the late Republican Roman aristocracy.

villa at Casino, about the groves, the fish basins, and the colonnades covered with a net of hemp and filled with all kinds of birds. A path gave access to a tholos, a round-domed building with columns, which was surrounded by a wood planted with large trees. There was netting between the columns so that, while there was a view of the wood, not a bird could escape into it.

"Inside under the dome of the rotunda the morning-star by day and the evening-star at night circle around near the lower part of the hemisphere, and move in such a manner as to show what the hour is. In the middle of the same hemisphere, running around the axis, is a compass of the eight winds, as in the horologium at Athens, which was built by the Cyrrestrian; and there a pointer, projecting from the axis, runs about the compass in such a way that it touches the wind which is blowing, so that you can tell on the inside which it is" (trans. in the Loeb Classical Library).

I suppose that the painting that resembles an orrery on a ceiling in one of the villas excavated by Libero d'Orsi outside Castellammare di Stabia (Fig. 57) has some connection with these astronomical caprices. Does it, perhaps, depict a pavilion with a spherical grid for celestial observations instead of a roof?[16] In any case, the magnificent thermal building called Tempio di Mercurio at Baiae shows what the Roman domes were like in early Imperial times and that they already could be covered with mosaics.[17]

All this—the love of nature, the old agricultural traditions, the Hellenized architecture, and the fanciful luxury and refinement—has to be kept in mind if we are to understand the villa that Nero laid out in the center of Rome. As Pliny indicates (xxxvi. 111), the villa was called Domus Aurea because the façade of the main palace was gilded (as was the

16. Libero d'Orsi's report quoted note 11, Pl. 9. See now Olga Elia, *Pitturae di Stabia* (Napoli, 1957), pp. 26–29, Pl. 1. For ancient clocks, which may have some connection with the painting, Fig. 57, cf. A. G. Drachmann, "The Plane Astrolabe and the Anaphoric Clocks," *Centaurus*, III (1954), 183 f.

17. A. Maiuri, "I campi flegrei," *Itinerario dei musei e monumenti d'Italia*, no. 32, p. 68.

a   b

FIG. 57.
a) Roof painting from a villa at Stabiae. Compare with (*b*).
Courtesy of Libero d'Orsi.
b) The famous Orrery by Benjamin Martin (of London) acquired by Harvard College in 1767.
Courtesy of the Harvard University Collection of Historical Scientific Instruments, Cambridge, Mass.

theater where Nero in 66 A.D. received the Parthian King
Tiridates—Dio Cassius lxii. 6). But both this costly decoration and the very word *aureus* had a symbolic meaning well
known from such expressions as *aurea aetas*, *aurea saecula*, and
aurei dies. Like the Augustan era and Rome, Nero's reign was
from its beginning hailed as golden: *aurea formoso descendunt
saecula filo*.[18] As is clearly shown by Tacitus (*Ann.* xv. 42) the
word *domus*, like the Italian word *villa*, means the entire establishment, including the palace, gardens, and fields. We
note in Martial (*De spect.* 2) that even the word *aula* could be
used in the same way, for after mentioning the lake of the
Domus Aurea, its "*invidiosa atria*" and its "*superbus ager*," he
ends by saying that the Claudian portico on the Caelian hill
was "*ultima pars aulae deficientis*." Although our sources (Tac.
Ann., Suet. *Nero* 31, and Martial, *De spect.*) are absolutely
clear, it seems necessary to emphasize that neither the earlier
villa—the *Domus Transitoria* by which Nero started to unite
the Palatine and the Esquiline in the first years of his reign
(Suet. *Nero*)—nor the Domus Aurea were big palaces which
occupied the whole valley. Instead, they were fanciful landscape gardens containing magnificent casinos in the center of
Rome, a "*rus in urbe*" (Martial xii. 57, 21), which included
buildings around an artificial lake, perhaps baths, and other
structures like the marvelous temple of Fortuna, built of
translucent marble (*phengites*, Pliny xxxvi. 163). We know

18. Seneca *Ludus de morte Claudii* iv. 1, 9. For the Augustan aurea aetas see Vergil *Aeneid* vi. 792 f. and Ovid *Ars am.* iii. 113. What Pliny said about the gilded
façade of the Domus Aurea, xxxiii. 54 and xxxvi. 111, is clearly against an (in itself improbable) assumption, which has been made, that only the vaulted dining
hall of Nero (Suetonius *Nero* 31) was gilded. Discussing the importance of gold
one may also remember that the chariot of the *triumphatores* was gilded (for instance Livy x. 7, 10; Horace *Epode* ix. 21; *Seneca rhetor Controvers.* x. 1, 8. R.
Pipping has shown in a most interesting article, *Arv*, vi [1950], 33 f., that the
idea of the golden car lived on in medieval times). Scholars who have traced special connection between the gilded façade of Nero and his pretended connections
with the Sun God, Helios, and his "*regia—clara micante auro*" (Ovid *Metam.* ii. 1)
seem to overlook how very common gilded façades, statues, etc., were. Gilding
had a general, symbolic meaning if not taken only as a decorative scheme. Gold
gave only a general impression of happiness, divine power, or divinization, and
it does not in itself permit any further conclusions.

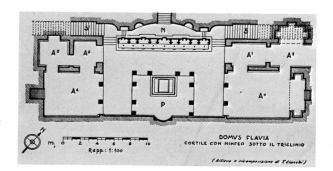

a

b

c

FIG. 58.

a) A sunken triclinium under the open sky in the Neronian palace on the Palatine. See especially the stairs for running water that cooled the air (N). Compare the same arrangement on a larger scale in the Octagon of the Domus Aurea, Fig. 53.

N.S., 1949.

The same palatial tradition is to be seen, for instance, in (*b*) and (*c*).

b) The Casa del Centenario in Pompeii.

c) The Norman palace La Zisa in Palermo (twelfth century A.D.).

omething of the luxury connected with the palace buildings of this villa from the Neronian remains beneath the palace of Domitian on the Palatine (Fig. 58). There was a sunken garden with a biclinium, resembling the sunken peristyle of the palace of Domitian (Fig. 59). In the upper parts of this Neronian palace, which seems to have belonged to the Domus Transitoria, we can still see most luxurious marble floors with varied colors and designs. In the sunken garden were miniature marble stairs, down which water poured, in front of the biclinium, and in the side rooms there were charming paintings inlaid with gems.

Even in Neronian times there appears all the exquisite luxury known from the domus in Ostia of the third and fourth centuries A.D.[19] We must avoid exaggerating the novelty, remembering Tacitus' explicit statement that Rome was accustomed to luxury before Nero and his Domus Aurea. Pliny considered the villa of Publius Clodius, which had cost 800,000 sesterces, as rivaling the pyramids. He also says categorically that Nero did not surpass the luxury of Scaurus' edile in 58 B.C.; xxxvi. 103, 111–13). This is further evidence in support of my previous statement about the luxury of late Republican villas.

After the fire in 64 A.D., Nero had a free hand in extending the plans indicated by the building of the Domus Transitoria (Figs. 51 and 52). He enlarged the grounds of his villa to include all of the valley around a lake where the Colosseum was built by Vespasian some sixteen years later. To the south, this fantastic country seat in the center of Rome reached as far as the temple of Claudius on the Caelian hill, which he almost destroyed in carrying out his new plans (Suet. *Vespasian* 9). In the east, it extended to the present via Merulana, where

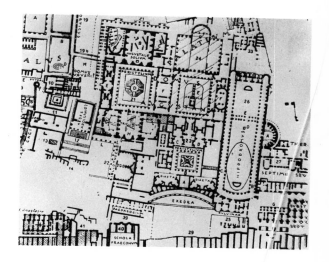

FIG. 59. Domus Augustiana. From left to right:

1) Reception wing with central peristyle and apsidal *cenatio praecipua* (H).
2) Peristyle with basin, island, bridge, and a cubiculum on the island.
3) Sunken peristyle (on a lower level to the south) with entrance toward the Circus Maximus (A) and three domed rooms at the upper (north) side.

To the right (east) of the two peristyles (2 and 3) and at the same lower level as peristyle 3 is the hippodrome garden of the palace, with its palatial, apsidal, so-called *palco* in the center of the eastern long side.

After F. Castagnoli, *Roma antica*. Part 1 of Castagnoli, Cecchelli, Giovannoni, Zocca, *Topografia e urbanistica di Roma* (Roma, 1957).

. *Scavi di Ostia*, I, 155 ff.; G. Becatti, "Case ostiensi del tardo impero," *B.d.A.*, XXXIII (1948), 102 ff., 197 ff., proves convincingly that the planning of these domus is alien to the Roman traditions and is probably the result of influence from Syria, but the refinements are mostly typical for the Hellenized Roman palaces of late Republican and early Imperial times. For the Neronian Palace on the Palatine see *N.S.*, 1949, 48 ff.; and for the luxury, Seneca, *Epist. ad Lucilium* 86, 100.6; Statius *Silvae* i. 3, 36–37; i. 5, 42–43.

the gardens of Maecenas began.[20] On the western side the villa extended to the Palatine and the Velia; on the north the landscape garden may have stretched as far as to the Forum of Augustus.

Van Essen[21] has surveyed the grounds of the Domus Aurea in an attempt to estimate its extent and fix its exact limits. His hypothesis that Nero tried to separate his villa from the town by extending it to suitable natural boundaries seems most convincing. Nero evidently attempted to re-establish between the Palatine, the Caelian, and the Esquiline hills a wide, shallow valley about two hundred acres in extent. As ancient parallels to this concept of a villa with natural boundaries, one might take Hadrian's much larger villa at Tibur, or the villa of Maximian, as I believe, in the delightful low area more or less enclosed by hills near Piazza Armerina. And the same ideal of an isolated and spacious abode was realized in the Imperial villa which Augustus and Tiberius created out of the whole island of Capri, adding to its old Greek village numerous palaces and resting places, such as the small cubiculum at Axel Munthe's San Michele.[22]

"All Rome is transformed to a villa! Romans, flee to Veii, if only the villa does not also spread itself to Veii!" complained a pasquinade in Nero's Rome (Suet. *Nero* 39) in a somewhat altered echo of Ovid's words about Vedius Pollio's domus (*Fasti* vi. 639 f.) and Sallust's words about late Republican "*domus atque villae in urbium modum exaedificatae*" (*Catilina* 12). With similar fantastic exaggeration Pliny twice as-

FIG. 60. Refinements of late Roman palatial architecture in Ostia.
a) Plan of Domus di Amore e Psiche.
b) View from room E through the main hall (B, leading to the Tablinum C) toward the unroofed garden area I and its beautifully decorated arcaded niches for running water.
Photo G. Svanström.

20. Castagnoli has proved that the great water reservoir called Sette Sale belonged to the Baths of Trajan, *Arch. Cl.*, VIII (1956), 53.
21. *Op. cit.*, note 1, pp. 376 ff., with the extent of the Domus Aurea, Van Essen (p. 384) compares the Vatican state (44 hectares = 109 acres). Van Essen's interpretation of Nero's famous words (Suet. *Nero*. 31) about the Domus ("*quasi hominem tandem habitare coepisse*") as aiming at the solitude of the evacuated Domus Aurea valley may seem narrow and romantic, but I agree that Nero's words, which Suetonius ridicules, probably have to be understood as connected with the Roman predilection for countryside life contrasted with the meaningless bustle and vanity fair of the towns, which Horace and other Roman poets detested.
22. As interpreted by A. Maiuri, *Capri, Mythus und Wirklichkeit*, pp. 181 ff.

serts (xxxiii. 54; xxxvi. 111) that the Domus Aurea indeed enclosed the whole town! Tacitus emphasized that the sensational thing about the Domus Aurea was not gold and jewels (*Ann.* xv. 42). He said the Romans were accustomed to such luxury from the late Republican and early Imperial ages.[23] According to Tacitus and Suetonius, the really amazing thing was that in the very center of Rome Nero's architects—Severus and Celer—had created a piece of landscape with groves, pastures, herds, wild animals, and artificial rural solitude—as the Romans loved to see it in both the Republican and the Imperial periods.

When we try to figure out what Severus and Celer produced in the years between 64 and 68 A.D., our main literary sources are descriptions already referred to (Tac. *Ann.*, Suet. *Nero*), and the poem that Martial wrote after Vespasian and Titus had opened the grounds of the Domus Aurea to the Roman people (*De spect.* 2). To these we should also add the topographic survey of the terrain and the famous remains of the ground floor in the main palace of the Domus Aurea which are preserved in the terrace below the Thermae of Trajan.[24]

Let us start, with Martial, from the Forum. The old narrow and crooked Via Sacra (Tac. *Ann.* xv. 38) was buried and so was all that part of old Rome, *Roma vetus*, which lay

---

23. This familiarity receives additional confirmation on the very spot from the luxurious rotunda and cryptoporticoes that were destroyed when Nero's Via Sacra and atrium were laid out. See M. Barosso, "Edificio romano sotto il tempio di Venere e Roma," *Atti del III convegno nazionale dell'architettura. Roma 1938* (1941), pp. 75 ff.

24. For older research see Platner Ashby s.v., Swoboda, *op. cit.*, p. 51; F. Weege, "Das goldene Haus des Nero," *J.D.A.I.*, XXVIII (1913), and Van Essen's survey cited above note 1. Especially important are G. Lugli's surveys of the monuments in *I monumenti antichi di Roma e suburbio*, 1, "La zona archeologica" (Rome, 1930), 200 f.; supplemento (Rome, 1940), pp. 96 f., *Roma antica, il centro monumentale* (Rome, 1946), pp. 348 f.; *Monumenti minori del Foro Romano* (Rome, 1947), 165 f. To the interpretation of the word Domus in the sense of the whole establishment is now to be added Van Essen's convincing article about the finding place of Laocoon outside the palace building of the Domus Aurea. I have made my first attempt to characterize the Domus Aurea in *Eranos Rudbergianus* (=*Eranos*, XLIV, 1946), 442 ff. See also below, note 37 and J. Ward Perkins, "Nero's Golden House," *Antiquity*, XXX (December, 1956), 209 ff.

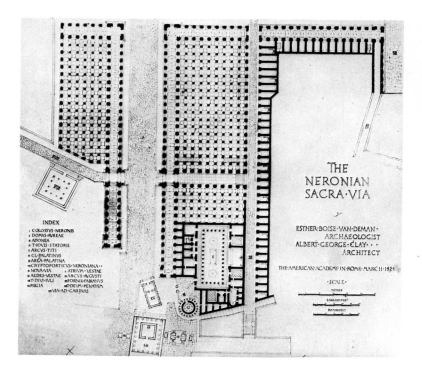

FIG. 61. The Neronian Via Sacra. Cf. Fig. 52.

Reconstruction of the street and the porticoes in agreement with actual remains by E. B. Van Deman.

to the right and left of the Via Sacra. On the new level a broad straight ceremonial street was laid out (Fig. 61) between great porticoes.[25] This model portico street of the *urbs nova* of Nero (cf. Suet. *Nero* 16) led to a terrace that served as the entrance hall of the Domus Aurea ("*invidiosa feri atria regis*" Martial). Giuseppe Lugli and Maria Barosso[26] have given us glimpses of the *urbs vetus* which was buried below the porticoes of the new Via Sacra and the entrance hall at its eastern end. Our sources make it clear that the colossus of Nero stood in this entrance hall, which is now replaced by Hadrian's Temple of Venus and Roma; the colossus was then moved to a pedestal facing the Colosseum that was removed only in our time. Martial (*De spect.*) and Dio Cassius (lxix. 4, 4) indicate clearly that the colossus stood in an atrium, probably a rectangular court surrounded by porticoes. Hadrian's temple and its surrounding colonnade seem to repeat

25.   Miss E. B. Van Deman has rediscovered the plan of the Neronian Via Sacra, *M.A.A.R.*, v (1925), 115 f. The atrium on her plan is conjectural. Later research has shown that her reconstruction of the porticoes along the Via Sacra and of building XVI is unfounded.

26.   See Lugli, *Monumenti minori del Foro Romano*, pp. 139 f. and, above, note 23.

the Neronian plan in a still more monumental style. The colossus was made by a Greek, Zenodoros, and was 119½ feet high.

It has been suggested that the colossus represented Nero as Helios. Of course, as recently pointed out by Eduard Fraenkel, already in Augustus' time Horace's early ode (i. 2) shows that "typical Hellenistic ideas about the incarnation of a god in the body of a ruler were, though not directly taken over, yet employed in a mitigated form" in Rome. But the assumption that the colossus in the Neronian atrium should have illustrated such a coalescence happens, as a matter of fact, to be completely unfounded. Lucan (*De bello civili* i. 45 f.), who has been quoted in this connection, shows clearly that Nero was not identified with Helios while alive. After his death he was free to choose between the scepter of Jupiter or the car of the sun, in short, "*quis deus esse velis*," and also the place where he wished to establish his dominion. Pliny tells us that the clay model of the colossus at any rate showed a striking likeness to Nero (xxxiv. 46). It was a great sensation, then, in Vespasian's time, the statue, with a new or remodeled face, was changed into the statue of Helios.[27]

The new Via Sacra was included in the Imperial palace. We do not know, however, whether both the straight Clivus

Fraenkel, *Horace* (Oxford, 1957), pp. 251 and 249 with note 1, where he recalls the "limitations to which Horace has subjected this idea." For the colossus Platner Ashby s.v. I have given my reasons rejecting the idea that the colossus should have shown Nero as Helios in *Eranos*, L (1952), 129 ff. and *Neue Beiträge zur klassischen Altertumswissenschaft. Festschrift B. Schweitzer*, 1954, pp. 358 ff. In the latter contribution I have corrected my previous suggestions about the pegmata which were stored in the porticoes of the Neronian atrium and of the temple of Hadrian (Martial; Dio Cassius lxix. 4, 4), returning to the old and previously correct view that they were the machinery of the amphitheater. For the practice of changing heads on the statues see also Suet. *Gaius* 22 and what the Anonymus published in Banduri, *Imperium Orientale*, 1, 92 tells about Constantine; his head was put on a colossal statue of Apollo in Constantinople. E. Welin, "Studien zur Topographie des Forum Romanum," *Acta Rom. Suec.*, 8:0, VI (1953), 179 f., comments in a convincing way upon the architectural meaning of the word atrium in late Republican and Imperial ages. How the different meaning of the word atrium (atrium of a domus and peristyle court) should be explained is, as A. von Gerkan points out (*Gymnasium*, LXII, 278), most uncertain.

Palatinus of Nero and the new Via Sacra which still runs under the Arch of Titus were open to the public. In any case it is quite obvious that to the great displeasure of the people, Nero, by his atrium and his Via Sacra, solved the same problem that Caligula settled by making the Temple of Castor and Pollux his vestibule. This problem was solved in a third way when Domitian created a stately entrance from the Imperial palaces to the Forum by means of a typical reception hall, which in Imperial times was probably called *atrium regium* and in the sixth century was converted into the church of Santa Maria Antiqua.[28]

Beyond all the marble architecture of the Forum and the Via Sacra, from Martial's *"invidiosa feri atria regis,"* one beheld the wide artificial landscape of the Domus Aurea. Where the Colosseum stands was a lake surrounded by villages—a view such as the painters loved to depict (Fig. 62). There was nothing new in this. Varro tells us that round pools were common in the Roman villas (*L.L.* v. 26), and as early as Horace's time large artificial fish ponds were part of their usual luxurious equipment (*Odes* ii. 15). But the lake was brought into the town and a view was created that resembled suburban Renaissance villas with their landscape gardening, groves, and pastures.

In other parts of the villa everything was gilded and decorated with gems and mother-of-pearl, said Suetonius. In the dining rooms there were ceilings of ivory plaques through which flowers could be scattered. Some of these ceilings were pierced with pipes for spraying perfumes, a piece of information that reminds us of the *"lacunaria diducta"* in Trimalchio's house (Petronius *Sat.* 60) and the *triclinia versatilia* in which Heliogabalus suffocated his guests beneath heaps of flowers (*Script. Hist. Aug. Antoninus Elagabalus* 21). When describing all this, Suetonius is speaking about the palace of the villa, the *Domus Aurea* in the modern sense of the word, which it is still

28. See in addition to my articles cited in note 27 my article "The Reception Halls of the Roman Emperors," *B.S.A.*, XLVI (1951), 25 ff. Septimius Severus intended to build a new vestibule of the Palatine in connection with the Septizonium; the Severus *vita* in the *Script. Hist. Aug.* 24, styles it = *atrium regium*.

possible to visit in the substructure of Trajan's baths on the slope of the Esquiline overlooking the Colosseum valley (Figs. 51 and 52). When in 104 A.D., Apollodorus from Damascus built the great Thermae of Trajan that were destined to be the models for all future Roman establishments of the same kind, he began in the usual Roman way by creating a new level on a huge terrace. The parts of the palace which did not interfere because of their position or height were left standing when the terrace was filled in. In other words the bottom floor of the palace remained intact inside the terrace. It has been visited by artists and others since the Renaissance and has been gradually excavated in modern times.

Trajan's façade is in the typical style of the Roman tenement houses.[29] Through the plain southern apse of the Trajanic terrace one reaches the façade of the Neronian palace. Its western (left) part is, as seen by Swoboda, Grimal,[30] and

29. This style is also known from the terrace buildings of a luxurious villa on the Pincio in Rome. K. Lehmann and J. Lindros, "Il palazzo degli Orti Sallustiani," *Acta Rom. Suec.*, IV (=*Opus Arch.*, I, 1935), 196 f.

30. Grimal, *op. cit.*, pp. 165 f. Swoboda, *op. cit.*, p. 51, Pl. I and especially II b. The sellaria along the façade must have been delightful in spring, on sunny winter days, and in autumn. Back to back are sellaria facing north and belonging to the peristyle behind the western part of the villa toward the Esquiline. They in their turn must have been a welcome refuge in hot summer days as was the cryptoporticus behind the splendid rooms along the façade of the east wing, which also protected the palace from the pressure and moisture from the Esquiline hill (as an "intercapedine"). This remark may once more emphasize how interesting a study of the function of all the rooms of the domus would be.

FIG. 62. Harbor or lake surrounded by architecture. Wall painting from Pompeii. Naples.
Photo Alinari, Rome.

FIG. 63. Porticus villas in Campanian paintings. Above: Painting from Stabiae, now in the Naples Museum. Below: Painting from the house of Lucretius Fronto in Pompeii.
Fototeca Unione, Rome.

others, a façade typical of a porticus villa with *sellaria* (rooms with doors wide open to the portico in front of them). Toward the center of the façade—if the apsidal construction on the eastern side of the court indicates the end of the palace—the portico was interrupted by a sun court of a type well known from Pompeian wall paintings (Fig. 63). It faces south and must have been delightful in winter and early spring. The east wing is different from the western. There, the most conspicuous room is octagonal in plan (Fig. 53). It has a circular dome with an opening in the center, like the oldest dome in Baiae, the luxurious pre-Neronian building between the convent of Santa Maria Nuova and the Basilica of Maxentius (see note 23), the Flavian Santa Maria della Rotunda in Albano, and, most notably, the Pantheon. At the rear of the room water cascaded down a steeply stepped artificial channel. The Roman villa of Minori (between Amalfi and Salerno) has a cascade of exactly the same type placed on the central axis of a barrel-vaulted hall in the center of a large rectangular court. The hall in Minori faces a high arch on the other side of the court through which there was an open view toward the sea—a disposition which makes one feel that the asymmetrical position of the Neronian octagon and its waterfall is rather surprising. The cascades of the Domus Aurea and Minori repeat, on a monumental scale, the *"iucundissimum murmur"* (Pliny *Epist.* v, 6. 22–23) of the fountains in charming peristyles and gardens of Pompeii and the stairs with cascades, which I have already mentioned, in the Neronian palace on the Palatine (Fig. 58). They are also to be compared with the luxuries of the domus of fourth-century Ostia.

In the *sellaria* along the façade and around the octagon, niches were made for the great collection of sculptures that Nero brought with him from Greece: *"Violentia Neronis in urbem convecta et in sellariis domus aureae disposita"* (Pliny xxxiv, 84). The walls of these fanciful rooms along the façade were encrusted with marble. In the scattered remains we recognize the same luxury which Nero's Palatine palace shows and which our sources describe. The vaulted ceilings had delicate stucco decorations with exquisite paintings in the classicistic style like the famous *volta dorata*. This is evidently the part of the palace in which the painter Famulus, attired in a toga and dignified even on the scaffolding, spent the few hours of his working days painting.[31]

The plans of the reception rooms along the façade determined the shape of the rooms and localities behind the main part of the palace. These localities were secondary, and neither in them nor in the long cryptoporticoes was there any marble facing. The walls and the vaulted ceilings were stuccoed and painted with brilliant, daring sketches in the style

31. Pliny xxxv, 120. As A. Maiuri's *Roman Painting* in the Skira series (Geneva, 1953) probably will be (and indeed merits to be) the most used book about Roman painting for the time being, I wish to point out that he has made a most curious mistake in translating Pliny's words about Famulus (Fabullus) and making him work in his toga "without a moment's respite." The right translation is to be found for instance in S. Ferri's *Plinio il vecchio. Storia delle arti antiche* (Rome, 1946), pp. 187–189.

which is now well known to us from the villas of Castellammare di Stabia (see note 11). The general disposition with its
delicate framework belongs to the so-called fourth Pompeian
style that mirrors, of course, the richness and luxury of palaces from the Neronian Age to the Flavian. Here there is no
refined classicism, no marble, no place for gems and mother-
of-pearl as there was in the now barren and despoiled *sellaria*
facing Nero's countryside. By a curious mistake these utilitarian parts of the palace and their paintings have often been
used to illustrate Neronian luxury. To a great extent they also
became models for grotesque paintings.

The buildings in front of the western wing present a
problem. The façade might have had a height of two or even
three stories and resembled the screens of the theaters, the
monumental outer walls of the *natationes* of the Thermae of
Caracalla and Diocletian and the Septizonium. Was this façade visible only from a rectangular courtyard of which the
buildings in question formed the outer wall? Or was the view
open so that one could contemplate the lake and all that
countryside which had been created over the remains of the
crowded quarters of the center of *Roma vetus*? Was all that
visible through the wide doors of the *sellaria* between the columns of the portico and across the sun court, just as in the
Villa di Arianna at Stabiae everything faced the Bay of Castellammare? Could the wanderer in the landscape, looking
toward the Domus, appreciate the fantastic vaults and niches,
the rich colors, and the sculptures included in the rooms behind the columns of the portico? It would have been a splendid contrast, a luxurious background to the countryside,
comparable with the temple of Fortuna Primigenia on the
hillside of Praeneste, and in fullest agreement with the traditions of the porticus villas, as we know them from the Pompeian paintings.[32] But though it may seem most likely that
the Neronian porticus villa resembled the Campanian architecture (Fig. 63) of the same kind, we must admit that only
excavations on the south side of the court can tell us if or to

---

32.   The Porticus villas (Fig. 63) illustrate exactly what the Neronian palace
might have been like if it had an open front side with flanking wings.

what degree the view from and toward the monumental façade of the palace was obstructed. Until it is excavated we cannot know whether it was open, entirely closed, or if there was a wide arch in front of the sun court serving as an open window toward the lake and the landscape, as in the villa in Minori.

In my opinion it is not possible to state with certainty the exact use of any of the many rooms of the palace, except the library.[33] A detailed study of all the various localities remains to be made. Suetonius explicitly mentioned two baths (*balineae*) and a notable circular dining hall (*praecipua cenatio rotunda*). Of the two baths, one was for salt and one for sulfurous water. This reminds us of the two thermae of the second period of the Villa of Hadrian and suggests that the two baths of Nero may have been situated outside the palace in the open air. Perhaps the baths of Titus, the *velocia munera thermae* that Martial praises, were built in the same place as the private baths of Nero.[34]

Suetonius' description of the *praecipua cenatio* is lamentably short: "*Praecipua cenationum rotunda, quae perpetuo diebus ac noctibus vice mundi circumageretur.*" That is all! An implied *cenatio* with the adjective *rotunda* is, of course, the subject of *circumageretur*. This has sometimes gone unnoticed because, in modern usage, the word *rotunda* often means a dome-covered round building. As our text actually stands, it seems evident that the *cenatio* was a merry-go-round, a revolving construction, probably lightly built of wood. "Perpetually day and night" may be one of the typical exaggerations in Suetonius' descriptions of the follies of the emperors. But one must admit that the words "*vice mundi*" make one wonder if Suetonius' wording is imprecise. He may have meant that the hall was provided with a rotating spherical ceiling.

Concerning this most sensational part of the Domus

33. Lugli, *I monumenti antichi di Roma e suburbio*, I, 211; Gregori, *Accademie e biblioteche d'Italia*, XI (1937), 21; C. Callmer, "Antike Bibliotheken," *Acta Rom. Suec.*, X (=*Opus Arch.*, III, 1944), 160 f.

34. Perhaps the dome illustrated and discussed by K. Lehmann in "The Dome of Heaven," p. 12, note 84, belonged to the Neronian balinea.

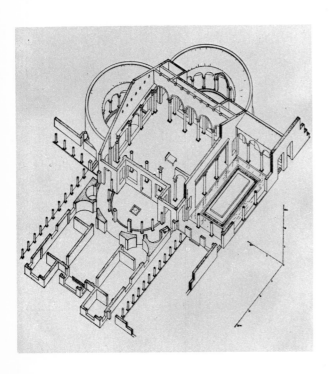

FIG. 64. A dining hall in Hadrian's villa near Tivoli.

After Heinz Kähler, *Hadrian und seine Villa bei Tivoli* (1950).

Aurea we may ask again whether it was perhaps a separate building set out in the wide grounds of the Domus Aurea like the fantastic *cenatio* at the western side of the stadium of the Villa of Hadrian (Fig. 64). Was it reminiscent of the cosmic tents of the kings of Persia or the tent of Alexander the Great with its fifty gilded posts supporting an imitation firmament of rich workmanship? Perhaps the dome of the Domus Aurea was something like these and like the dome-shaped audience tents of the Mongol khans. Was it in some way constructed inside a hall which belonged to the main building like the dining rooms in the northern part of Hadrian's Villa—formerly interpreted as Latin and Greek libraries? Or was it placed in the sun court of the façade like the tholos in the painting of a porticus villa in the house of Lucretius Fronto (Fig. 63) in Pompeii?[35]

Andrew Alföldi has put this tantalizing dome in a general relation to the banqueting halls of the Hellenistic kings and

35. For the cenationes of Hadrian cf. Heinz Kähler, *Hadrian und seine Villa bei Tivoli* (Berlin, 1950), pp. 31–44 and 122–28, Pls. I (D, E, and K)–V and VIII–X. Kähler is evidently right in comparing the cenatio at the stadium with the main apsidal hall of the Domus Augustiana (p. 123, Fig. 26). The description of Pertinax' death in the biography in the *Scriptores Historiae Augustae* (*Pertinax* 11) seems to prove that the hall in the Palatine palace was called *Sicilia et Iovis cenatio*. Philo, describing a villa of Caligula in *Legatio ad Gaium* (364), obviously refers to a hall of the same kind as the *"megas oikos."* In the latter cases the cenationes were inside the palaces like the apsidal halls of the palace of Piazza Armerina (see the plan in Gentile's guide *La villa imperiale di Piazza Armerina*, 3 and 46). Nero's *cenatio rotunda* can have been in one of the palace halls with special devices for rotation. One should also remember that the word *rotundus* can mean simply "circular." Was the *cenatio rotunda* perhaps only a rotating floor for instance in the octagon, Fig. 53? Or does Suetonius aim at a revolving heaven (ouranós, cf. Cassius Dio's description of Pantheon LIII.27) in the octagon (as has been suggested under the assumption that *plinthium sive lacunar* in Vitruvius' list of dials, ix. 8. 1, should be read *Panthium sive lacunas*)? Both suggestions seem to me to be too farfetched, considering the wording of Suetonius as it actually runs. I believe that the simile *vice mundi* and the whole context must imply globe shaped, vaulted (*sphairoeidēs*). Cicero expressed himself in a similar fashion when speaking of heaven. To avoid mistakes it may be pointed out that the building with a dome on the Neronian dupondius struck in Rome and Lugdunum between 64 and 66 A.D. represents the macellum as shown by the inscription *MAC AUG*. Cf. Marilyn Stokstad in *Spink and Son Numismatic Circular*, October–November 1954; C. Vermeule, *A.J.A.*, LIX (1955), 258 f.; and K. Walzinger, "Die Macellum-Dupondien des Nero," *Numismatik*, II (1933), 1 ff.

Dionysiac ideas about royal happiness. Other scholars, notably Hans Peter L'Orange, Karl Lehmann, and Earl Baldwin Smith have not only compared Nero's revolving dining hall with Oriental architecture but have tried to explain it by tracing more wide-ranging connections[36] with Oriental and especially Persian royal architecture and deification—what Strabo (xi. 13, 9) called *sebasmós theoprepḗs*. Lehmann, among other evidence, quotes Hesychius' gloss *ouranos* ("heaven"): "The Persians also" used the term "for the royal tents and courts whose round awnings they called heavens." Here, certainly, we have to remember light Oriental structures, which, no doubt, inspired Roman domed architecture, for instance the high buildings of Babylonia which still in Strabo's time (xvi. 1, 5) were built of beams and pillars of palmwood with ropes of twisted, plastered, and painted reeds round them, and doors coated with asphalt, all being vaulted on account of the lack of timber. These, too, may have their connection with the *cenatio rotunda*, while, in turn, the Roman concrete structures no doubt inspired Oriental architecture.

L'Orange has revived the whole discussion by inspiring studies. His suggestion that the whole Domus Aurea complex was a palace of Nero-Helios, a palace of the Sun, must, as far as I can see, be discarded as completely unverified.[37] Again, I emphasize its obvious connection with the Hellenized late Republican villas. But most inspiring was and is L'Orange's ingenious idea that the Neronian *cenatio rotunda* was closely related to the hall and fire temple of the Sassanid King Chos-

---

36. Alföldi's articles are cited in note 15. For the Persian tents and domes see Baldwin Smith's works and K. Lehmann's "The Dome of Heaven," cited in note 6. Lehmann gives an excellent account of starry domes and makes it clear that there was a direct tradition connecting Jupiter or Helios as kosmokrator with the same cosmic decoration in a symbolic Christian sense where Christ appears as kosmokrator, and he draws attention to the new life, meaning, and strength which the pagan motives drew from Christian ideas. But I think that we have to admit that we can not prove any real religious connection between all this and the revolving dining hall of Nero.

37. For L'Orange's suggestion that the Domus Aurea was a "Sonnenpalast" see *Serta Eitremiana* (= *Symbolae Osloenses*, Fasc. suppl. XI, 1942, 68 ff.) and *Studies on the Iconography of Cosmic Kingship in the Ancient World* (Oslo, 1953), pp. 28 f., *Apotheosis in Ancient Portraiture* (Oslo, 1947), pp. 60 f. For criticism see my

roes II, who was defeated in 624 A.D. by the Byzantine Emperor Herakleios. This remarkable structure has been discussed by Ernst Herzfeld, Fritz Saxl, Lars Erik Ringbom, Sven Eriksson, and others.[38] To me Eriksson's analysis of the material seems conclusive. The Byzantine sources (Nicephorus Patriarcha, Georgius Monachus, and Georgius Cedrenus, from the ninth to the eleventh century) tell us about an image of Chosroes in a hall, which Cedrenus described as being spherical. Nicephorus and Georgius Monachus speak only about a fire temple, whereas Cedrenus mentioned both a palace and a temple.

---

articles cited in the notes 24, 27, and 28, and Vermeule in *A.J.A.*, LIX (1955), 258 f. I have only lately noted that J. M. C. Toynbee in *Numismatic Chronicle*, s. 6, VII (1947), 133 ff. has, like me, maintained that the Domus Aurea should be understood mainly as a great Italian villa of early Imperial type. In "Wochentagsgötter, Mond und Tierkreis," *Studia graeca et latina gotoburgensia*, III (Stockholm, 1956), 85 ff., S. Eriksson has analyzed current misinterpretations of our literary sources.

38.   Herzfeld, "Der Thron des Khosro," *J.P.K.S.*, XLI (1920), 1 ff., 103 ff.; F. Saxl, "Frühes Christentum und spätes Heidentum in ihren künstlerischen Ausdrucksformen, 3: Darstellungen der Weltkönig-Idee," *Wiener Jahrb. f. Kunstgeschichte*, II (1923), 102 ff.; L.-I. Ringbom, "Graltempel und Paradies," *Kungl. Vitterhets, Historie och Antikvitetsakademiens handlingar*, LXXIII (Stockholm, 1951); and "Zur Ikonographie der Göttin Ardvi Sura Anahita," *Acta Åbo Humaniora*, XXIII, 2 (1957), 24–26. Eriksson, *op. cit.*, pp. 111–12, seems to me convincing in combining Ringbom's reconstruction of the Sassanid Takht-i-Taqdis in Gandjak or Shiz, with the literary evidence about Chosroes' palace and temple. For archaeological evidence regarding Takht-i-Suleiman see *Bulletin of the American Institute for Art and Archaeology*, 1937, 2. Ringbom's conclusion is that the Takht-i-Taqdis consisted of a round lake surrounded by a portico very much like the lake of the canopus at the villa of Hadrian, together with a barrel-vaulted throne hall and behind that a temple with a central cupola surmounting a pillar. According to Eriksson's very plausible explanation this pillar was the base of Chosroes' statue below the starry dome, in the temple, mentioned by the Byzantine authors. In other words, the ruins in Shiz seem to show exactly what the sources describe (and confuse): a palace combined with a fire-temple in which the statue stood. To my mind Eriksson in his pursuit of unfounded conclusions about cosmocratores, etc., sometimes overlooks the fact that architectural forms may have once had a symbolic importance but, all the same, have lived on even since they have lost their original meaning and strength.

Nobody who has studied ancient devices of rotation has any reason to ridicule the assumption that Nero's cenatio—like Chosroes' revolving turret—was pulled by oxen, horses, or mules. But Eriksson (*op. cit.*, pp. 118 f., note 2) may be right in suggesting that a hydraulic press, using water power such as that of the cascade in the Octagon, Fig. 53, made the cenatio rotate.

In addition, the Byzantine sources describe representations of the sun, the moon, and the stars, arrangements for artificial rain and thunder, and a statue of Chosroes on a high pillar in the temple. Western medieval sources (*Exaltatio sanctae crucis* and the *Martyrologium* of Ado from Vienna), though also mentioning sun, moon, stars, and thunder, evidently only speak of the palace and tell us about a costly throne (not image) of Chosroes in a revolving tower which was made to rotate by draft animals in the basement. Persians of the tenth and eleventh centuries, Firdausi and Tha'alibi, also describe the palace as a splendid hall with a throne and a marvelous planetarium. It seems probable that the data concerning the sun, moon, stars, and planetarium belong to either the temple or the palace. These buildings were evidently connected with each other and easily confused in the legends of Chosroes' palace.

I agree with K. Lehmann that Nero's dining hall "is beyond suspicion of being a literary fantasy." The medieval stories and Suetonius' words, as they stand, seem to support each other. But though considering Nero's rotating hall (or heavenly dome) in connection with the Oriental architecture, where it probably belongs, L'Orange's reasoning seems to me too restricted. Frederick P. Bargebuhr in an article, "The Alhambra Palace of the Eleventh Century,"[39] has published and discussed a poem about an Arabic palace, in which, among other marvels, we meet with a dome, "that rotates in

39. *Journal of the Warburg and Courtauld Institutes*, XIX (1956), 198 ff. and 228 ff. Bargebuhr speaks about Yūsuf's dome as "a dome made to appear to be rotating" and believes that the rotation of which Ibn Gabirol speaks in the poem quoted "was in effect produced by lights." Bargebuhr recalls that in the famous "Hall of the Caliphs" in Madinat az-Zahrā a huge cistern was filled with quicksilver. When it was put in motion, the whole place appeared to be rotating. One would be tempted to adduce the phengitis temple of Fortuna of the Domus Aurea (Pliny xxxvi. 163), but I cannot see any cogent reason to doubt that both the cenatio of Nero and Yūsuf's dome were really rotating. To me Yūsuf's dome is a third example of this fanciful, probably Oriental architecture as developed in the Hellenistic world and inherited by the Romans perhaps as early as their late Republican, "Persian" palaces, but in any case by Nero's architects. The notices about Chosroes' planetarium (Firdausi, Tha'alibi), and the stars, sun, moon, rain, and thunder in his palace (Byzantine sources), as well as the information

its circumference." Above all, when we meet this fantastic architecture in the Sassanid Empire, in Rome and the Roman villas, from late Republican times and onward, or in Arabic Spain, we must remember that its grandeur was a late result of a joint development of common features in East and West—even if the hall of Chosroes had its own Oriental traditions of king worship and they, as I am most inclined to believe, were the remote background of all these kinds of architecture.

Chosroes' dome, as we know it from the medieval descriptions, was deeply influenced by the development of Parthian and Persian culture and architecture under Hellenistic and Roman influence. From this formal point of view we could even turn the argument upside down and say that the dome of the Domus Aurea might well be regarded as the ancestor of Chosroes' hall, which had a most obvious Hellenistic and Roman heritage, admirably analyzed by Karl Lehmann, in spite of the fact that both may have had a distant common Oriental ancestry in ancient Persian days.[40]

The testimony about the Republican and early Imperial palaces, Nero's buildings, and the refinements of this Roman palatial architecture which appear in the late domus of Ostia (Fig. 60) with their otherwise un-Roman planning and character (see note 19), help us to visualize the great development of Hellenistic traditions under the constant influence of the legacy of Rome on the one hand and the influence of the architecture of the Parthian and Sassanid world on the other. Thanks to the excavations in Ostia we can now get a clear notion of how far this development had advanced before the foundation of Constantinople. Syria and Constantinople

---

about the oxen which pulled the revolving turret in the *Exaltatio sanctae crucis* and the *Martyrologium* of Ado from Vienne, show us varied aspects of this kind of building—of which Nero's cenatio is an early example and the Arabic rotating hall in Spain a late offspring. All this material, taken together, seems to me to bar any temptation to believe that Ado's description of Chosroes' revolving turret could be only a legend, perhaps inspired by the tales about Nero's cenatio, but we must remember that the explicit description of the revolving hall of Chosroes is only to be found in medieval sources from western Europe.

40. "The Dome of Heaven," pp. 24–25,

FIG. 65. Mosaic, Mosque of the Ommiads, Damascus. Eighth century A.D.

were the great centers from which internal development and amalgamation spread. Comparing the eighth-century mosaics of the Mosque of the Ommiads in Damascus (Fig. 65) with, for instance, the mosaics from the palace of Piazza Armerina (Fig. 66) we cannot help feeling that the great tradition from Hellenistic, Imperial Roman, and Parthian palaces was still alive in the Arab world. Moreover, when we compare Roman and Turkish baths (Fig. 67), it becomes evident that the same tradition lived on through the Ottoman Age. A similar thought occurs to us when we see in the Norman palaces of Sicily, for instance in La Zisa in Palermo (Fig. 58), mosaics and running water like those of Nero's sunken triclinium on the Palatine or of the domus of Ostia, when we read in Boccaccio, Fazello, or Gregorovius' *Wanderjahre*[41] about La Cuba, Palermo, or when we hear Leonardo Alberti describe the fishpond Albehira in the fanciful landscape architecture of La Zisa with an island and a bridge that recall the same features in one of the peristyles of Domitian's palace on the Palatine (Fig. 59).

It seems obvious that much of this was a Roman and Byzantine legacy to the Arab world. In Sicily it met with the

41. *Wanderjahre in Italien*. The chapter about Palermo, pp. 328–31 in the Agrippina-verlag edition (Cologne, 1953), in spite of false attribution gives a glorious picture of the Cuba and Zisa palaces. See also Bargebuhr, *op. cit.*, for the same kind of luxury in Arabic Spain.

Roman heritage in another form, propagated from France. To that great tradition belong both the dome of the Domus Aurea and Chosroes' revolving hall with their probable Persian and Oriental background and their evident and decisive share in both the results and the cultural interchange of some of the most creative periods in history: the Hellenistic, Roman, and Parthian ages. Very often no doubt it lost the original meaning, which it may have had among the Persians, in Hellenistic and later palatial architecture and remained only as a profane architectural form and a decoration; trappings which, "like all terrestrial garments, wax old" to quote Carlyle's *Sartor Resartus*.

In other words it seems to me more than likely that L'Orange, Lehmann, and others were intuitively right in connecting the aviary of Varro and the Neronian dome with the Persian influence, which Strabo (v. 2, 5) noted in the late Republican villas and which Appian detected in Caesar's forum (*B.C.* ii. 102), though the *cenatio praecipua* no doubt had precedents on Italic soil in late Republican times and became adjusted to Italic traditions in the Roman villas and domus. But when L'Orange (with rather mixed and uncertain evidence from the Oriental side) pictures Nero as an Oriental cosmocrator below a starry dome, Suetonius and all the Roman sources which he adduces fail to support his conclusion. It is not only that Suetonius makes no mention of stars. On every point Eriksson seems to me to be right in his criticism. L'Orange's hypothesis ceases to convince at the point where he leaves formal architectural relations and claims that he can also interpret Oriental symbolic meaning. I do not think that we can say any more than has already been said by Alföldi about the Neronian dome, its supposed stars and movements like those of the universe.[42]

Of course, court philosophers and flatterers may have attempted symbolic Oriental interpretations. Everybody who has read the poets of the first century A.D. remembers those

42. *Op. cit.*, note 15. Eriksson, *op. cit.*, does not always seem to pay enough attention to the early instances of short-lived Oriental and Hellenistic flattery and hero worship in the first centuries of the Empire.

new elements of Oriental apotheosis and Oriental flattery which Martial stigmatized in Trajan's Age of the Roman Renaissance (x. 72) and to which Juvenal alluded when he said that the whole of the Tiber is polluted by the Orontes (iii. 63 f.). So far, I do not consider it impossible that in certain quarters the dome may have been associated with Oriental ideas, destined for a great future in the late Empire, when the rulers were deified and enmeshed in a system of elaborate court ceremony. But we cannot prove it, and we should not overemphasize such whims and doubtful antecedents. Over and over again after such exaggerations the cult of the emperors returned to its basic stable shape. We saw that start in Augustan days. Horace "ventured toward a compromise with certain religious conceptions of the Hellenistic East" in an early ode (i. 2, *Iam satis terris*). But after that follows *Quem virum aut heroa* (i. 12), where, as Fraenkel says (Horace, p. 297), all that is said about the ruler is kept within the bounds of strictest Roman propriety without the faintest hint at a deification.

Only with Diocletian and Constantine did *adoratio*—akin to the Persian *proskynesis* and to other impressive Oriental ceremonies that were renewed in the Neo-Persian empire—attain stable importance as an expression of the supremacy of the state in Italy. We can, of course, never know all that court poets prated about—and Martial, Juvenal, Seneca, and Tacitus (*Ann.* xiii. 3) ridiculed—but we are certainly mistaken if we take altogether hypothetical interpretations of the Domus Aurea more seriously than Martial and the others took the flatteries. For that reason we must not minimize the fact that

FIG. 66. Mosaic from the palace of Piazza Armerina. Sala della pesca.

FIG. 67. The bath of the sultans in the Terschana Seraglio, 1710. Drawing by a Swedish officer in the service of King Charles XII, illustrating the Roman-Byzantine technical and artistic tradition.
Courtesy of the Nationalmuseum, Stockholm.

the vaulted *cenatio* and the whole luxuriously renewed Roman villa in the center of Rome had its forerunners in late Republican villa architecture of mixed Roman, Hellenistic, and Oriental ancestry.

But it is more important and real than all these tantalizing considerations to turn to the more or less contemporary sources and to listen without prejudice to what they allege. First, I once more recall that Strabo spoke about late Republican or Augustan villas as Persian and that the idea of the *cenatio rotunda* perhaps reached Nero from them—even if it originally was Oriental. But in spite of all this we must keep in mind that not a single word indicates that contemporary praise or criticism was concerned with Oriental origin or religious ideas expressed by the Domus Aurea, either as a whole or in part. Nothing proves that it was understood as a palace of the sun. It was seen from quite a different point of view. A villa was brought into the town (Tac. *Ann.* xv. 42). It was built by spoliation of the citizens (*ibid.* 52) and was hated, for it had deprived poor people of their homes. It was an expression of reckless egoism and a source of envy (Martial *De spect.* 2). It was a prison for Famulus' art (Pliny xxxv. 120) and for the collection of stolen Greek works of art (Pliny xxxiv. 84). The gold and the gems were less objectionable; the Romans were accustomed to luxury before Nero (Tac. *Ann.* xv. 42). Nero's own verdict was that now he could at last begin to live as a human being (Suet. *Nero* 31).

The Domus Aurea was not finished in the period between 64 and 68 A.D. Otho spent 50,000,000 sesterces to complete it (Plut. *Otho* 7). Nevertheless, Vitellius and his wife criticized the Domus Aurea as being badly built, poor, lowly, and lacking in elegance (Dio Cassius lxv. 4), somewhat snobbish comments which may seem less unreasonable, however, if we remember Pliny's statement that the late Republican *insania* of Scaurus surpassed the luxury of the palaces of Nero and Caligula (xxxvi. 113). In strong contrast to Vitellius' demands and to Nero's imperial egotism stands the spirit that finally ended the fairy tale of the Domus Aurea, namely, the democratic sense of responsibility of Vespasian, Titus, and Trajan and their realistic policies. Their model was rather Augustus' simple house on the Palatine (cf. Suet. *Augustus* 72), his carefulness not to expropriate private houses for public use (*ibid.* 56), and his destruction of the vast and luxurious domus of Vedius Pollio in Rome:

Disce tamen, veniens aetas, ubi Livia nunc est porticus, immensae tecta fuisse domus; urbis opus domus una fuit, spatiumque tenebat, quo brevius muris oppida multa tenent. Haec aequata solo est, nullo sub crimine regni, sed quia luxuria visa nocere sua. ("But learn, thou age to come, that where Livia's colonnade now stands, there once stood a palace huge. The single house was like the fabric of a city; *it occupied a space larger than that occupied by the walls of many a town. It was levelled with the ground, not on a charge of treason, but because its luxury was deemed harmful.* Caesar brooked to overthrow so vast a structure, and to destroy so much wealth, to which he was himself the heir. That is the way to exercise the censorship; that is the way to set an example, when the judge does himself what he warns others to do."—*Fasti* vi. 639 ff., Frazer's translation).

The Roman pasquinade, already cited from Suetonius' *Nero* (39), and Martial's poem about the Domus Aurea and its demolition (*De spect.* 2) seem to echo these words of Ovid, except that in Martial's poem from the Flavian Age the point of view of public welfare is given more emphasis. The colossus, also ridiculed by Juvenal in his eighth satire (line 230), was changed to Helios. Thereby the envied vestibule of the tyrant and the Via Sacra were thrown open to the public as a temple of Helios. The Arch of Titus probably belongs to the years when the Domus Aurea was made public, and it may thus be regarded as a symbol of the change. The porticoes of the temple of Claudius on the Caelian hill, which Nero had usurped (Suet. *Vespasian* 9), again offered their shadow to the Roman people.

On the slopes of the Esquiline, from which the poor people had been driven, the public Baths of Titus were now built. But by far the greatest monument of the democratic policy of Vespasian and Titus was, of course, the Amphitheater, which was built where Nero's lake had been. In connection with this the Ludus Magnus (not mentioned by Martial) was constructed, and some machinery of the Amphitheater was stored in the colonnades of the former vestibule.[43] The tyrant's delight became the delight of the people. To the words of Martial we may add that the Flavian temple of Peace with its public library was constructed on or close to the northern outskirts of the villa and that the art treasures of the Domus Aurea came to be exhibited there (Pliny xxxiv. 84). The revolution completed itself when, after a fire, the Baths of Trajan were built above the Neronian palace on the Esquiline and when Hadrian built the temple of Venus and Roma above the vestibulum. That erased the last remaining parts of the Domus Aurea. Instead of the Imperial villa in the center of the town we see the largest pleasure grounds created by any megalopolis for the masses.

There is, though, a certain charm in conjuring up, behind the great social architecture still visible, a phantom vision of Nero's creation. It is a dazzling late chapter in the history of the Roman villas of late Republican and early Imperial times as well as of the Oriental and Hellenistic *paradeisoi* and palaces. And the palace on the Esquiline above the lake and the artificial countryside, although in existence only some forty years, was in many ways remarkable in the history of Roman architecture. It was one of the first great buildings of brick-faced concrete. In its planning and its vaults, the octagon and the row of *sellaria* show already the "baroque" style that later characterized parts of Domitian's palace, the villa of Hadrian at Tibur, and Imperial palaces in general.

43.　See note 27.

CHAPTER IV

THE DOMESTIC ARCHITECTURE OF THE IMPERIAL AGE AND ITS IMPORTANCE FOR MEDIEVAL TOWN BUILDING

Und keine Zeit und keine Macht zerstückelt
Geprägte Form, die lebend sich entwickelt.
—GOETHE

The *urbs nova* heralded by Tacitus (*Ann.* xv. 43)—the utilitarian brick-faced concrete architecture (Fig. 68) of second-century Imperial Rome—created a new starting point for the urbanistic development of the Western world. Older elements (which we see in Pompeii and Herculaneum in the forms they assumed before 79 A.D.) had real importance for the future only in their second-century form and systematization.

Before discussing questions concerning the survival in medieval town life of this truly revolutionary creation in the field of utilitarian architecture, I wish to premise a general remark about the different lines of inheritance from Roman antiquity to medieval times and the Renaissance. There is, of course, the danger that I may present these in too schematic a way, or that I may be thought unaware of complex cross-currents between the main lines of development. Nevertheless, it seems necessary to try to outline this evolution.

FIG. 68. "Via Biberatica" outside the Forum of Trajan in Rome. Cf. Figs. 41 and 74.
Photo J. Lindros 1934.

The legacy which everyone recognizes is generally studied in the splendid classicistic monumental architecture of the first two centuries of the Empire. As social facts and as solutions to the recurrent demands of town life, its various architectural types will reappear in our discussion, but it is unnecessary for our present argument to describe its well-known external features. In their Roman form, however, and as expressions of Roman civilization and social ideals, these features gradually disappeared as the pagan empire became "a society with no prestige values, whether inheritance, gifts, or occupation" (to use Berenson's words about modern times), and thus was unable to renew or protect its architectural system. As early as 551–52 A.D. cattle passed through the Imperial fora (Procopius viii. 21, 10 ff.) and in 536–37 the temple of Janus in the Argiletum street was a neglected antiquity (Procopius v. 25, 23 ff.). It would indeed be of great value if the time when the various features of the great Roman urban system ceased to be used could be fixed not only for temples and fora but also for thermae, *horrea*, theaters, and circuses. It would be valuable too if it were shown how the pagan system of material welfare had to yield to the Christian urbanism of the fourth and fifth centuries A.D., with its new sacred civic centers, and how both pagan and Christian institutions were affected by the downfall of the Western Roman Empire. A decisive fact was that Rome, especially after the victory of Islam, lost its Mediterranean trade.[1] As a result, Ostia fell into ruins and the towns of Italy lost whatever bourgeoisie had re-established itself after the social revolution of the third century, and with it the creative force in the civic urban system.

The great classicistic architecture of the Roman state was visible as a tantalizing ideal in the late Empire and in the ages of Charlemagne and Frederick II of Hohenstaufen, but was truly rediscovered only by the Renaissance. As shown by—among others—Christian Elling and by Herbert Koch,[2] the renewal of what the artists and architects of the Renaissance believed to be classical actually involved to a considerable extent their own fresh artistic creations, however much these may have been inspired by—not to say bound up with—what the ancient remains suggested. It was a typical instance of what Wolfgang Schadewaldt, in speaking of the Homeric renaissance of the Greek saga, calls *gebundenes Erfinden*.[3] This most fascinating activity forms the best-known and most discussed chapter in the history of the legacy of Roman town architecture.

In part, this classicistic tradition had already been destroyed by the very different taste displayed in the architecture of the late Roman Empire. All of us now admit that the period of the Basilica of Maxentius, the Basilica of Treves, the Curia of Diocletian, and the Aurelian Wall was one of the greatest creative periods in Roman architecture. It is characterized by reduced classic decoration. What Frontinus

1.   Recent illuminating studies by E. Sjöqvist, "Studi archeologici e topografici intorno alla Piazza del Collegio Romano," *Acta Rom. Suec.*, XII (= *Opus Arch.*, IV, 1946), 77 f., and "De romerska akvedukternas öden under senantiken," *Arkeologiska forskningar och fynd. Studier utgivna m. anl. av H. M. Konung Gustaf VI Adolfs sjuttioårsdag*, 1952, pp. 139 ff. Frances J. Niederer, *The Roman Diaconiae. A Study of the Use of Ancient Buildings by the Christian Church Prior to 806 A.D.*
2.   Christian Elling, "Villa Pia in Vaticano," in *Studier fra Sprog- og oldtidsforskning*, CCIII (Copenhagen, 1947); H. Koch, *Vom Nachleben des Vitruv* (Baden Baden, 1951).
3.   *Von Homers Welt und Werk* (Stuttgart, 1951), p. 195. A recent useful contribution is Ragnhild Billig, "Die Kirchenpläne 'al modo antico' von Sebastiano Serlio," *Acta Rom. Suec.*, XVIII (= *Opus Rom.*, I, 1954), 21 f.

FIG. 69. The basilica of Maxentius and Constantine at the Via Sacra in Rome. The façades were stuccoed and flanking columns and marble decorated the entrances, but buttresses, windows, and the plan and height, demanded by the scope of the building, are what really characterize the style—not the traditional Greek ornaments.
Photo A. B. 1956.

called *necessaria*, the necessary features in planning and structure, are its dominating monumental values. Its background is the stern, functional style of the façades of Roman utilitarian architecture (thermae, insulae, etc.), and the notion that the practical requirements of actual necessity produce as a result charm of style (*suavitas quaedam et lepos* in Cicero's words).4 This unclassical monumental architecture was typical of the time of Aurelian, Diocletian, and Constantine, and it was taken over by the Christians in their fundamentally changed urban system—a system which, based on a new creed and filled with a new spirit, replaced the grandiose pagan town architecture and its cultural standards. All over the Empire the same development can be observed. What the Chris-

4. Frontinus i. 16. Cicero *De Oratore* iii. 46 (180). See chapter II, note 79. F. W. Deichmann, *Frühchristliche Kirchen in Rom* (Basel, 1948).

tian architects produced in Rome and in Jerusalem when Constantine called upon them to create a monumental Christian architecture[5] was the Roman contribution to the Christian architecture to come. The late Roman façade style and its direct offspring, early Christian architecture (i.e., that of the third to sixth centuries A.D.), became by organic development the inheritance of early medieval times and as a matter of fact dominated that period. This is the second route from Imperial Rome through medieval times.

To this legacy belonged also the instructions for town architecture in the code of Justinian, which remained valid in medieval times,[6] and also the architectural tradition derived from the Roman portico villas which, as has been shown by Karl M. Swoboda, was still alive in medieval palaces.[7] Here we must also remember the palatial luxury of the third and fourth centuries A.D. (as it has been revealed to us by Calza's

FIG. 70. The basilica of Trier (so-called Protestant church). The building had a richly decorated entrance, balconies along the long sides, and was stuccoed, but the windows and the buttresses, connected by arcades as the piers of the aqueducts, no doubt determined the main, unclassic impression.
Courtesy of the Landesmuseum Trier.

5. Most important Eusebius *Vita Constantini* ii. 46, 1–3. Cf. E. Wistrand, "Konstantins Kirche am heiligen Grab in Jerusalem," *Acta Universitatis Gotoburgensis*, LVIII (1952:1), 13 and 17 f., and J. Ward Perkins, *J.R.S.*, XLIV (1954), 148, and *P.B.S.R.*, XXII (1954), 69 ff.; and K. J. Conant, "The Original Buildings at the Holy Sepulchre in Jerusalem," *Speculum*, XXI (1956), 1 ff.
6. W. Braunfels, *Mittelalterliche Stadtbaukunst in der Toskana* (Berlin, 1953), p. 88.
7. *Römische und romanische Paläste*, pp. 77 ff., 133 ff., and 185 ff.

latest excavations in Ostia) and the survival of that kind of architecture on the Adriatic coast and probably in Venice.[8] Through this tradition many classicistic features were passed on to medieval times—as Franz von Juraschek, among others, has recently suggested. The Ionic columns of the narthex of Santi Giovanni e Paolo in Rome are an interesting feature which belong to the reconstruction of the cardinal of Sutri during the papacy of Pope Eugenius III (1145–53). As Karl Lehmann remarks in his article "The Dome of Heaven," it is always difficult to say whether such classical features are a result of direct unbroken tradition or a symptom of proto-Renaissance.[9]

In connection with the unbroken legacy from the late Roman Empire to medieval life, we should also mention the predilection for peristyles and porticoes, and we should remember that peristyles were not always parts of palaces. It is more important, no doubt, for their development in medieval times that they were at least as typically part of utilitarian architecture: of warehouses, of barracks like the Caserma dei Vigili in Ostia, of marketplaces like the Piccolo Mercato, the Horrea di Hortensius in Ostia, and Eumachia's building in the Forum at Pompeii, and of Hellenistic hotels like the caravansary of Kassope in Epeiros with its court measuring 14.2 by 11.7 meters, flanked by porticoes.[10] Like the Byzantine and Oriental caravansaries, the western medieval peristyles continued to be integral parts of the architecture of the time because they were useful fragments of the old urban system in spite of the decay of its original spirit. They lived on in spite of the impoverishing catastrophes of the sixth century, in spite of the Norman invasion and the Saracens, and in spite of Byzantine and other influences that obscured the original

8.   See Chapter III, note 19. For Venice, see G. Fiocco, "La casa veneziana antica," *Rend. Linc.*, s. 8, IV (1949), 38 ff.

9.   F. Von Juraschek, "Weiterleben antiker Baunormen an Bauten des 8 Jahrhunderts," *Z. Schw. Alt.*, XI (1950), 129 f. For SS. Giovanni e Paolo see A. Prandi, *Il complesso monumentale della basilica celimontana dei SS. Giovanni e Paolo* (Città del Vaticano, 1953), p. 154. Lehmann, "The Dome of Heaven," *Art. B.*, XXVII (1945), 13.

10.   *J.H.S.*, LXXIII (1953), 120.

FIG. 71. The Circus building at S. Agnese in Rome, showing the monumental effect of buttresses in late Roman architecture.
Old photo before the present systematization of the surroundings.

pattern. This classical heritage which persisted in medieval monumental architecture must be contrasted with the well-known Renaissance revivals already mentioned.

From this more or less monumental architecture, which continued in use mainly because of the influence of the Church, let us turn to the third type of tradition from Imperial Rome: the entirely utilitarian architecture (Figs. 42, 68, 72–78), like the Roman tenement houses of the second century A.D.—the insulae with their rows of shops (tabernae) along the streets.[11] At this point we may inquire whether there also survived into medieval times a humble and persistent, though gradually degenerating, tradition from this remarkable creation of town life in the Imperial Age. Apart from the general interest of research into medieval survivals of ancient Roman tradition, this study would be of special interest because, as Pierre

11.   That the word insula means tenement house is in my opinion self-evident, as I have stated in "La 'insula romana' secondo Leon Homo," *Colloqui del sodalizio*, II (Rome, 1956). A. de Marchi's most valuable article, "Ricerche intorno alle insulae o case a pigione di Roma antica," *Mem. R. Istituto Lombardo*, XVIII (1891), 241 ff., gives all the evidence. See also F. G. Mayer, "Römische Bevölkerungsgeschichte und Inschriftenstatistik," *Historia*, II (1953), 331 ff.; and, for the tabernae, Giancarla Girri, "La taberna nel quadro urbanistico e sociale di Ostia," *Istituto di archeologia, Università di Milano*, I (Roma, 1956), and T. Kleberg, *Hotels, restaurants et cabarets dans l'antiquité romaine* (Uppsala, 1957), especially pp. 39–73.

FIG. 72. The new matter-of-fact architecture, displayed by the military style
of the Aurelian walls during the first
periods (275 A.D. and early fourth century). Porta Asinaria before the latest
reconstruction. To be compared, for
instance, with the contemporary classicism of the triumphal Arch of Constantine.
Photo Alinari.

Lavedan says,[12] housing is not only one of the most neglected chapters in the history of medieval architecture but also one of the most important, for it reveals much of the life and spirit of the anonymous common people that we often fail to see. This is, as we shall later point out, exactly the area in which Roman traditions may have remained alive.

As we see in Ostia and on the Forma Urbis (Figs. 77 and 78), houses of the domus type (that is, the atrium and peristyle houses) were in an aristocratic minority when compared with tenement houses of Imperial Rome, the *"immensus numerus insularum,"* to quote Suetonius (*Nero* 38). The excavations in Ostia, the fragments of the marble plan of Rome from about 200 A.D., called "Forma Urbis," and above all the *Libellus de regionibus urbis Romae*, prove by actual count that tenement houses were predominant in Imperial Rome.[13] The centuries that followed the great creative period of the late Empire and the grandeur of the early Christian Age depended passively on such earlier developments as the apartment houses.

The basis for any discussion of the persistence of this heritage from the Roman tenement houses is, of course, the study of Ostia and Imperial Rome itself. The history of the tenement houses is quite different from that of the domus, which had developed around the atria or peristyles with a closed façade. The insulae have a quite different origin, the row of tabernae. It seems to me completely useless to discuss how these rows of shops came into being, and whether isolated tabernae or a row of them came first. Let us limit our inquiry to the earliest forms actually known and begin with the row of independent rooms, each with a wide door toward a court or street—the tabernae as they appear in our descrip-

12.   "Représentation des villes dans l'art du Moyen Age" in Grabar's *Bibliothèque de documentation* (Paris, 1954), p. 51.

13.   For the "Libellus de regionibus urbis Romae" (fourth century A.D.) I use A. Nordh's edition in *Acta Rom. Suec.*, 8:o, III (Lund, 1949), but see also *Codice topografico della Città di Roma*, edited by R. Valentini and G. Zucchetti, I (Roma, 1940), 63–258. "Forma urbis," *ibid.*, pp. 49–62, and H. Jordan, *Forma urbis Romae regionum XIV* (Berlin, 1874), cited below Forma Urbis (Jordan).

tions of the oldest Forum Romanum and also the Forum of about 200 B.C. in Plautus, and in Ostia from the third century B.C. onward.[14] The function of the tabernae in town life is evident. Through the centuries they have been the dwellings of the proletariat and petty tradesmen. Above all, they were used as stores and workshops. Here old Italian towns of today, the earliest descriptions from Republican Rome, Ostia, the Forma Urbis and the remaining insulae of Imperial Rome show the same system and speak the same language.

Delightful and obviously descriptive of everyday life in Rome is Livy's account of the signs of peace which met Ca-

FIG. 73. Insula with six stories below the Ara Coeli (Arx) in Rome, second century A.D. Reconstruction by I. Gismondi.
Photo Alinari.

14. Livy i. 35, 10; iii. 48, 5; ix. 40, 16; xxvi. 27, 2; Plautus *Curculio* 480. For Ostia see Giancarla Girri and Kleberg, *op. cit.*, in note 11.

millus in the streets of Tusculum: open shops with wares displayed, craftsmen at their work, and the humming of voices from the schools (vi. 25, 9). Not less amusing is Martial, describing the busy life of the tabernae and the noise that drove him away to the arid Nomentanum and "*lar villae sordidus*": the schoolmasters, the early-rising bakers, the day-long pounding of the coppersmiths' hammers and the rattle of the moneychangers (xii. 57).

Riots and inundations of the Tiber were serious dangers for the thousands who lived and worked in the tabernae along the streets (Tacitus *Hist*. i. 86). Varro made it clear that they were dwellings of the poor, "*pauperum tabernae*," as Horace said (*Odes* i. 4), stating that at funerals the heralds (*praecones*) used the expression *ex aedibus* ("from independent houses") even for those who were carried out from tabernae ("*etiam eos, qui ex tabernis efferentur*," *L.L.* 5. 160). In their function of workshops they characterized the town without factories, where production was distributed among independent master craftsmen. We can still see in our own towns the last remnants of this tradition represented by the few remaining individual craftsmen. As in Egyptian towns, known to us from Hellenistic-Roman papyri, and as in Athens and in medieval towns, craftsmen of the same profession were often grouped together along the same street: for instance the scythe-makers (Cicero *Cat*. i. 8), the dealers in incense and perfume at the Vicus Tuscus, the moneychangers and bankers in the Tabernae Argentariae at the Forum Romanum.

We should visualize these tabernae as the typical environment of the artisans of every craft, and of the dealers, booksellers, schoolmasters, and scribes—in endless rows as we see them at Ostia and in the Forma Urbis.[15] "*Quinque tabernae quadraginta parant*," Juvenal tells us (i. 105). Our sources give us vivid descriptions of how cooks, astrologers, and prostitutes occupied tabernae such as those that we can still see in the outer arcade of the Circus Maximus and around

FIG. 74. The shops in the bottom story of the Mercato di Traiano along the Via Biberatica. Cf. Figs. 41 and 68. Photo B. Wahlgren 1956.

15. For references Platner Ashby s.v. Vicus Tuscus, Basilica Aemilia, Tabernae argentariae, etc. For medieval times in Italy see Braunfels, *op. cit.*, pp. 122 f.

the theater of Ostia.[16] Martial (vii. 61) depicted the wine flagons chained to the columns of the porticoes and business spreading out over the thoroughfares until Domitian's wise restrictions changed the life of the streets: ". . . *tonsor, copo, cocus, lanius sua limina servant. / Nunc Roma est. Nuper magna taberna fuit.*" We must remember that this was the life of the great majority. In spite of Martial's criticism, part of the charm of every old Italian town and even of the older quarters of Rome, Naples, and Milan is that along all the streets there are still many of these tabernae, bustling with activity. The plans of such quarters exhibit the closest affinity to the streets bordered with tabernae that we see in Ostia and on the Forma Urbis.

Such streets were found in ancient towns all over the Mediterranean world from the Hellenistic age onward. It was typical for the Romans of Republican times to build high many-storied tenement houses above the tabernae; to start

FIG. 75. Typical row of tabernae in the ground floor of a second-century Roman insula. Casa di Diana, Ostia. Cf. Fig. 85.
Photo E. Nash. Fototeca Unione.

16.   Fig. 88. Dion. H. iii. 68, 4. Juvenal iii. 65. Platner-Ashby s.v. G. Lugli, *Roma antica. Il centro monumentale*, pp. 509 ff., especially p. 603.

FIG. 76. Row of barrel-vaulted tabernae with windows in the attic and
counters, as in the insulae of Imperial
Age. At the Via del Proconsule, Florence, on an eighteenth-century en-
graving. Cf. Figs. 73 ff.

with, this was done in a most unsafe and unsatisfactory way. In our sources high tenement houses are generally considered to be unusual in other parts of the Mediterranean world. They were found, however, in Parabas in Phoenicia, in Arados in Syria, and in Tyre.[17] Arthur D. Nock is certainly right in translating Libanius' *Antiochicus* 270: ". . . as for the city 'Constantinople' which surpasses Antioch in house walls." Probably, Libanius here is contrasting Constantinople's high tenement houses in the style of the Roman insulae with the low Hellenistic towns.[18] If we compare the bazaar street (the *sukh*) of Dura and the cardo of Ostia, there seems at first to be a striking resemblance. But on closer examination we find in Dura a bazaar street with tabernae (*ergastēria*) only, whereas in Ostia tenement houses with upper stories were built on top of the tabernae.[19]

In speaking of the lofty houses of Tyre, Strabo directly compared that town to Rome, but we should remember that even when there were houses of many stories the whole structural system of towns outside Italy seems to have been different from the Roman insulae with their tabernae lining the streets all over the town. In the Hellenistic towns, shops and workshops seem to have been concentrated in the old bazaar quarters. It is most interesting to compare Karanis and the village of Soknopaiou Nesos in Egypt, where we find archaeological evidence of normal modest habitations in the East.

In Karanis the houses often had three stories and an inner court for cattle, donkeys, and camels, but the lowest floors of such houses were enclosed, as they are today in Egyptian towns. They had no tabernae and were obviously intended for private use. Although we know very little else about the

17. Pomponius Mela ii. 7 (103). Strabo xvi, 2. 13 and 23.
18. A. D. Nock, "The Praises of Antioch," *J.E.A.*, XL (1954), 80 (Libanius writes *toichous*, not *teiche*, city walls). Cf. also in Cicero's *De lege agraria* ii. 35 (96) the contrast between Rome with its high and crowded habitations and the Campanian towns. Cf. Libanius 225.
19. Cf. *Excavations at Dura-Europos*, v (New Haven, 1934), pp. 73 ff., Pls. 2 and 9; and M. Rostovtzeff, *Dura-Europos and Its Art* (Oxford, 1938), pp. 47 ff., Figs. 6, 21.

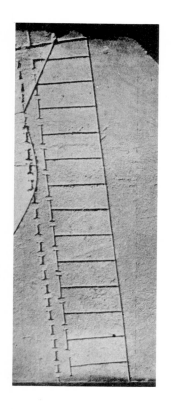

FIG. 77. To the left fragments of the marble plan of Rome from about 200 A.D., the so-called Forma Urbis. To the right ruins of Ostia: above, a row of shops at the Cardo and a corresponding plan on the Forma Urbis (Type I); below, on the Forma Urbis and along the decumanus of Ostia a ground floor of an insula consisting of rows of tabernae, built back to back (Type II).

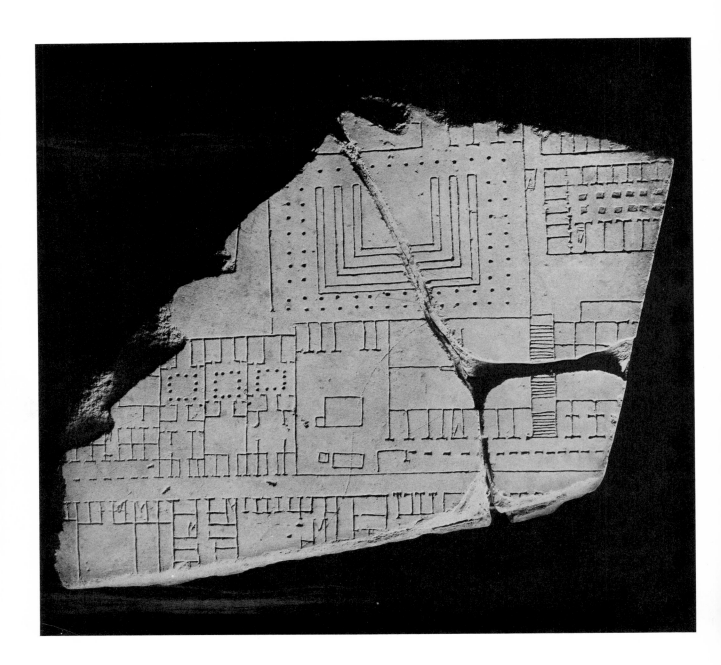

FIG. 78. Fragment of the Forma Urbis.
Along the upper side of the street from
left to right a porticoed house of "type
II," three old-fashioned atrium and peristyle houses and, after an open place,
two houses of "type I" with porticoes
along the street.
Courtesy of the Archivio fotografico delle
antichità e belle arti.

tall tenement houses of the Hellenistic world there is nothing to indicate that they were built above rows of *ergastēria* as they were in Ostia and as they are shown on the Forma Urbis.[20] In the case of Rome, both Cicero (especially in *De leg. agr.* ii. 96) and Vitruvius (ii. 8. 17) make it clear that the high tenement houses were a local phenomenon resulting from a special condition: the overflowing population of Rome at the peak of that national strength which made her conqueror of Italy and founder of an empire. It is also typical of Rome that the erection of tenement houses with shops along the façade helped to spread trade and production all over the town (as in old Italian towns today). Thus, a city like Rome functioned quite differently from towns that had separate residential and bazaar quarters such as we see in the Orient,

20.   Through the courtesy of Dr. Enoch E. Peterson I have had the privilege of studying the material from Karanis in the Kelsey Museum of Archaeology at the University of Michigan, Ann Arbor, Michigan. A. E. R. Boak, *Soknopaiou Nesos. The University of Michigan Excavations at Dime in 1931–32* (Ann Arbor, 1935). We have no definitive information about the tenement houses of the Eastern world; however, the small terracotta models and the columns of Axum, which are supposed to reproduce that kind of town architecture in Alexandria, show a different kind of structure without any tabernae. This is perhaps akin to the primitive high houses of Tunisia and Arabia today. Cf. H. Helfritz, *Chicago der Wüste* (Berlin, 1932); *Geographical Journal*, LXXXV (1935), 370 f.; LXXXVIII (1936), 524 ff.; XCII (1938), 1, 107, 289 ff.; XCIII (1939), 1 f. *National Geographic Magazine*, 1937, pp. 360 f., and the excellent photographs of Shibam, *ibid.*, 1957, pp. 240 f. See also C. Rathjens, "Kulturelle Einflüsse in Sydwest Arabien," *J.K.F.*, I (March, 1950), 1 ff. Strabo's description of the high private houses with vaulted rooms in Babylon (xvi. 1, 5) should also be considered in this connection as well as the court houses with at least one upper story in Colophon—see L. Holland, *Hesperia*, XIII (1944), 91 ff.—and the tendency to provide the peristyle houses of Delos with upper stories. Cf. Martin, *L'urbanisme dans la Grèce antique* (cited chapter II, note 20), pp. 211, 232, and 243 ff. We have also to consider what is meant by *pyrgos* in the Demosthenian speech against Euergus (xlvii. 56) and the material discussed by Arif Mufid, *Stockwerkbau der Griechen und Römer* (Berlin-Leipzig, 1932). For the monumental architecture in Babylon, described by Strabo, it is tempting to compare the giant, tunnel-like halls of the sheiks of the marsh dwellers of southern Iraq of today—*National Geographic Magazine*, 1958, 205 ff. Together with this material should now be considered the insula of Roman type with tabernae and upper stories, recently excavated in Ephesus at the main street outside the Scholastica Thermae. See *Deutsch-Türkische Gesellschaft E. V. Mitteilungen*, 26 (1959), 2; *A.J.A.*, LXIV (1960), 67.

and as, in my belief, they already existed in the Greek and Hellenistic world.[21]

This basic architectural type—rows of tabernae—is found in the central parts of old Pompeii; their rubble construction is rather fragile. It seems quite clear that the Romans started to build high tenement houses above such rows of tabernae at an early date, using the *auxilium altitudinis*, to quote Vitruvius' words (ii. 8, 17), or *altitudo tectorum*, as Pliny said (iii. 67). Livy mentioned that a house with three stories existed in 218 B.C. (xxi. 62), and to Cicero high tenement houses were typical of Rome. Vitruvius (ii. 8. 16 f.) gives an idea of the experimentation and the difficulties connected with this form of domestic architecture.

Nothing can better illustrate the development of a system of tall tenement houses built over rows of shops than the attempts at building second stories that we see today above the endless rows of one-story shops and dwellings along the roads of southern Italy and Sicily (Fig. 79). No doubt this is exactly what began to happen in Republican Rome. In addition to the basic facts already discussed, we should add that the tabernae could be provided with small windows above the doors and with garrets which were accessible by indoor wooden stairs or ladders. We see such garrets in the insulae of the Imperial Age. In their perfected form they had barrel vaults below the narrow balconies along the façades (Figs.

21. This is only a working hypothesis and a suggestion for future research which I have ventured to put forward in "Den romerska storstadens hyresarkitektur," *Acta universitatis gotoburgensis*, L (1944:4), p. 67 (English summary); "Roman and Greek Town Architecture," *Acta universitatis gotoburgensis*, LIV (1948:3), 15 ff.; *A.J.P.*, LXIX (1948), 396 f. (review of D. M. Robinson's *Olynthus*, XII). C. Rosier, in *L'urbanisme ou la science de l'agglomeration* (Paris, 1953), has criticized my suggestions, while A. Kriesis (*Acta congressus Madvigiani*, IV, Copenhagen, 1958) confirms them. Most important is Martin's discussion, *op. cit.*, pp. 46, 212, 229, and 235.

See also Aristotle *Politics* ii. 5, 2 (1267 b). Martin rightly emphasizes (see about Priene, p. 235) that the Greek towns concentrated their tabernae (*ergastēria*) in the commercial and civil centers of the towns, but speaking of Olynthus, p. 229, he does not make clear what kind of activity took place in the "ateliers" (workshops) to be found in every house. Were they used only for household activity or also for industrial production?

FIG. 79. A typical Sicilian row of tabernae for trade or habitation and workshops with added upper stories. Alcamo.
Photo A. B. 1954.

42, 68, 73). At the rear walls of these tabernae almost always two or three initial steps of concrete lead up to form a landing for the garret stairs. Maiuri has shown that this stage in the development of the garrets had already been reached in the baths in the Forum of Pompeii at the beginning of the first century B.C.[22] These baths (Fig. 43) were, in my opinion, a provincial imitation of the town architecture of Rome in its most perfect form from the point of view of both planning and building technique (concrete covered by *opus incertum*).

We see today exactly the same kind of tabernae and bars with the same counters and the same garret stairs in the older quarters of many Italian towns (Figs. 80 and 81). The tabernae facing the street and the steep straight stairways leading to the upper stories, and not connected with the shops below, were features of the typical high Roman tenement houses. They derived naturally from the rows of shops with garrets which often had upper floors built over them. Everyone who is familiar with Italy will at once recognize the same house

22.　*Atti del I Congresso nazionale di studi romani* (Rome, 1929), p. 164. A striking description of a tabernacula and its garret (*superius cenaculum*) with a window (*fenestrula*) is given by Apuleius *Metamorph.* ix. 40–42. See also Girri, *op. cit.*

FIG. 80. Ancient "type 1" in modern usage: Vallerano (Latium). Photo A. B. 1933.

plan in the steep stairs, leading directly to upper stories, opening through narrow doorways between the shop fronts. This striking architectural feature has inspired the folk of Assisi and Gubbio to give it the name *"porta del morto"* (Figs. 81 e, 91), offering an entirely unnecessary and unfounded explanation for the most commonplace phenomenon of their lives.

We can follow a gradual improvement in this kind of architecture. It is evident that the material used in the early insulae was most unstable—planks, half-timber work supporting mud brick, wattle and daub, or rubble—that is, concrete (*opus caementicium*) in its experimental stages. Pliny said that roof shingles were used down to the beginning of the third century B.C. (xvi. 36 f.), and it seems probable that they were used on tabernae and tenement houses during this period, although we do know that roof tiles were in use much earlier on temples and monumental buildings.

The descriptions from Republican and early Imperial times of the dangers of the insulae are abundant, and we find them recurring until the beginning of the second century A.D. when, as we shall see, the brick-faced architecture of Imperial Rome appeared. Very characteristic seem the vivid descriptions of the horrors of *Roma vetus*: houses as inflammable as torches, narrow crooked streets, enormous irregular house blocks (Tac. *Ann.* xv. 38), collapsing houses, and great fires (Strabo v. 3. 7). The elder Seneca (54 B.C.–*ca.* 39 A.D.) speaks explicitly of the reckless height of the badly built houses, of fire, collapse, and narrow streets that gave no escape (*Controversiae* ii. 1, 11). The unfortunate philosopher Athenaeus from Seleucia was not the only one to be killed by night in the collapse of the house in which he lived in Augustus' Rome (Strabo xiv. 5, 4). Dio Cassius' description of the Tiber floods in 53 B.C. shows how common the mud-brick houses were (xxxix. 61). When Augustus said he left a town of marble in place of a town of bricks (*latericiam*), he is contrasting, albeit somewhat illogically, his monumental marble architecture (*Res gestae* 19) with the old town of mud-brick quarters and temples of tufa and travertine. Pliny and Juvenal in their time still gave a most distressing picture of the tenement houses in Rome.[23] All these descriptions of the *urbs vetus* before 100 A.D. bear a striking resemblance to what we know about other crowded cities. In New York, for instance, at the beginning of the nineteenth century fire bells clanged all night because its houses burned like tinder, and in 1836 two of the largest commercial buildings collapsed. In ancient Rome and in New York the basic cause of these conditions was the same, namely, a rapid increase in population which created a sudden demand for housing in a restricted area.

The decisive factor in the transition from this unsatisfactory architecture to the *urbs nova* hailed by Tacitus after the Neronian fire (*Ann.* xv. 43) was—here as in all the architecture of western Europe—Roman concrete. This building material was probably first put to extensive use in Rome in the second century B.C., but experimentation may have taken place in the third century and perhaps even earlier.[24] At any rate, Vitruvius (ii. 8, 17) contrasts the fragile house construc-

23. See De Marchi, *op. cit.*; L. Friedländer, *Darstellungen aus der Sittengeschichte Roms* (9th ed.; Leipzig, 1919), pp. 20 f.; Pliny xxxvi. 106; Juvenal *Sat.* iii. 6 f., 193 f.

24. See Chapter II, notes 7–12. Lugli, *Tecnica edilizia*, pp. 363 ff. Important remarks about the prehistory of *opus caementicium* by Blake, *op. cit.*, pp. 308 ff., and Brown, "Cosa I," *M.A.A.R.*, xx (1951), 61–63, 109.

a   *b*

FIG. 81. Tabernae (shops) ancient, medieval, and modern.

a) Casa del Termopolio, Ostia.
Photo R. Svanström 1940.

b) The door of a taberna with counter to the left. Terracotta relief from Isola Sacra. Ostia.

c) Taberna in the portico of the Decumanus in Ostia. Staircase to attic on the rear wall. For exterior with window of the attic and barrel vault see Figs. 68 and 73 ff.
Photo A. B. 1932.

d) Taberna in a portico of the Via dei Tribunali in Naples. Note the staircase to the attic on the rear wall.

e) Medieval taberna. Castel di Sangro.
After Paatz.

f) Medieval miniature.
After Paatz.

tion of older generations with the excellent new tenement houses. They were distinguished from the old by the use of ashlar masonry at the corners. Vitruvius still speaks of wooden floors (*contignationes*), while the tenement houses of the Imperial Age mostly had concrete barrel vaults, but in other respects the new many-storied houses heralded the city architecture of the future with their walls of concrete faced with reticulate work finished off at the top with a layer of burnt brick.[25] These "noble dwelling houses" ("*egregiae habitationes*"), which Vitruvius regards as the final achievement of

25. Vitr. ii. 8, 1 and 17. See in addition my interpretation in the review of Miss Blake, *Art B.*, XXXIII (1951), 136, note 3; E. Wistrand's commentary and translation in *Eranos*, XLI (1943), 124 f. De Marchi, *op. cit.*, p. 261, gives the same interpretation, but does not explain the use of the baked brick (*structuris testaceis*) which Vitruvius mentioned together with walls of concrete (*parietibus caementiciis*). Strangely enough, M. H. Morgan in his masterly translation of Vitruvius (Cambridge, Mass., 1914) suggests "walls of burnt brick and partitions of rubble work." We know now that "walls of burnt brick" were not in common use in Augustan times. In addition, we see clearly what Vitruvius aimed at in his paragraph 17 by his prescription for mud-brick walls in paragraph 18: "On the top of the wall lay a structure of burnt brick under the tiles and projecting like a coping" (Morgan). Miss Gisela Richter reminds me that roofless enclosures made of sun-dried bricks covered with wild thyme or dry branches to keep off the rain may be seen on Greek red-figured vases and in modern usage in Greece, *R.A.*, 1935, pp. 200–204. It is the same precaution which Vitruvius described as used in roofed architecture.

c

e

d

f

the Augustan Age, did not gain such a complete victory as he would have us believe (see Tac. *Ann.* xv. 38) before the latter part of the first century A.D.

To draw still another comparison with New York, there must have been a transitional period in Rome during which the stage of architectural development resembled what we see today in Manhattan: modern well-planned and well-built apartment houses and skyscrapers which are in striking contrast to the untidy and often badly constructed buildings in other sections of the city. Looking at Ostia (which, of course, should be considered part of Rome) one is surprised to see how complete was the victory of the *urbs nova*, but this was not to come until the Flavian Age or even the second century A.D. Concrete architecture was in general use principally in Rome and Italy, although it—together with reticulate (Fig. 12)—also spread to the provinces, even as far as Jericho.[26] It obviously enjoyed general esteem in spite of Vitruvius, who criticized it and did not deem the concrete walls of his time safe for more than eighty years (11. 8, 8).

It should be added that Vitruvius' criticism of reticulate and concrete is by no means unreasonable. This is indicated by later modifications whereby brick-faced walls replaced reticulate work and concrete was greatly improved. The use of baked brick, that is, roof tiles, as a facing for walls was new to him and he would not trust it unless the bricks had been previously used as roof coverings and thus tested by time and weather. Also we must remember that a large-scale manufacture of baked bricks, such as the later brick-faced town demanded, began only in the second half of the first century A.D., and then produced tiles of much finer quality than Vitruvius, in the Augustan Age, could foresee.[27] We must also remember that the technique of building in stone without concrete, which Vitruvius defended, outlived the Roman

26.   See Chapter II, note 61.
27.   Vitr. ii. 8, 9. The dating of bricks with stamps according to Greek practice, in my opinion, went hand in hand with improvement in quality of mass production. See in addition to my suggestions about this in *Eranos*, XXXIX (1941), 152 f. A. Degrassi's remarks in *Doxa*, II (1949), 130; and H. Bloch, *A.J.A.*, LXIII (1959), 235-37.

Empire in Sicily, in Africa, and all over the Hellenistic world. In the West, however, concrete won an almost complete victory in spite of the defense of other methods of construction as we find in Vitruvius. The use of solid ashlar construction in the castrum of Septimius Severus in Albano is probably partly due to the fact that the peperino was available on the spot but may also have been the result of influences from the architecture of Africa and other provinces, where ashlar walls were still preferred.[28]

For the tenement houses Nero still recommended the type of structure described by Vitruvius: corners of square, hewn stones[29] in spite of the rapid progress and industrialization of baked brick in his days. From Pompeii and many other places we have evidence that the insulae, at any rate in the decades after 64 A.D., were partly of brick-covered concrete. Controlled Roman bricks used as a cover mark the final perfection, as far as technique goes.[30]

Together with endeavors to create more solid tenement houses, constant attempts were made to limit the height of houses being built: "*Machinationes tectorum supra tecta surgentium et urbium urbes prementium,*" in Seneca's words (*Epist.* xc, 7). Earlier, Augustus limited the height of the façades toward the street to 70 Roman feet (20.72 m.), thus restricting piled-up, unsafe late Republican tenement houses of which Cicero disapproved.[31] Nero also strongly opposed high houses and party-walls, Trajan reduced the lawful height to 60 feet (17.76 m.), and in the fifth century the struggle against this tendency to build high towering houses was still continued

28.   See J. Ward Perkins, "Severan Art and Architecture at Lepcis Magna," *J.R.S.,* xxxviii (1948), 61 f., and *Proc. Brit. Acad.,* xxxviii (1951), 277.

29.   Tacitus *Ann.* xv. 43: corners of Sabine or Alban Stone instead of half timber work (=*certa sui parte*).

30.   For the various types of brick and reticulate facing see R. Billig, *Acta Rom. Suec.,* x (=*Opus Arch.,* iii, 1944), 124 ff. Lugli, *Tecnica edilizia,* pp. 444–655. M. Blake, *Ancient Roman Construction in Italy,* pp. 227–307; *Roman Construction in Italy from Tiberius Through the Flavians* (Washington, D. C.,1959).

31.   Cicero *De lege agraria* ii. 35 (96). Strabo v. 3, 7.

by Leo I and Zenon in Constantinople.[32] From the Augustan to the Byzantine Age our sources make it clear that the laws did not fix an ideal height, but merely checked uncontrolled private enterprise and its socially noxious but profitable "skyscrapers."[33]

Laws also opposed wooden *maeniana*, balconies, and other attempts to block the streets (Ammianus Marcellinus xxvii. 9, 8). In Ostia, Pompeii, and Rome we see staircases built of concrete and stone gradually succeeding wooden stairs. As to wooden floors (*contignationes*, Figs. 82 and 83), they still occur to a certain extent in Imperial times and may have been preferred in more distinguished houses.[34] It seems further possible that insulae with barrel vaults of concrete in the lower stories may have had wooden floors in the upper stories—a mixed construction known, for instance, from the Circus Maximus (Dionysius of Halicarnassus iii. 68). The garrets of the barrel-vaulted tabernae always had wooden floors. But apart from this a wholly concrete construction for the tenement houses came more and more into use from the later part of the first century A.D., and onward—at least as far as we can judge from the remains in Ostia and Rome.

As Pompeii and Herculaneum show, the age when the final result of this building activity asserted itself by the brick-

32. Tac. *Ann.* xv. 43; M. Voigt, "Die römischen Baugesetze," *Berichte über die Verhandlungen d. K. Sächs. Gesellsch. d. Wissensch. Philol. hist. Kl.,* LV (1903), 190 f. Aurelius Victor *Epitome* xiii. 13. *Cod. Just.* viii. 10, 12. F. Castagnoli, "Roma antica" in Castagnoli, C. Cecchelli, G. Giovannoni, E. Zocca, *Topografia e urbanistica di Roma,* I (Rome, 1958), 62.

33. See De Marchi, *op. cit.,* Voigt, *op. cit.,* and Friedländer, *op. cit.,* p. 5 and *passim.* Typical are Pliny's and Aristides' speculations about the surface area that Rome would occupy if it did not have the high tenement houses (Pliny iii. 67; Aristides *Or.* xxvi. 8). As the limitations of height only applied to the façades toward the street, there is nothing surprising in Tertullian's words about the immense height of the Insula felicles, *Adversus Valentinianos* 7; cf. *Libellus de regionibus urbis Romae, Regio,* IX, p. 88. 11 Nordh.

34. I have discussed the wooden floors in *Art B.,* XXXIII (1951), 136, and in *Studies Presented to D. M. Robinson,* I (St. Louis, Mo., 1951), 443. That wooden ceilings (*contignationes*) were frequent in late republican Rome appears from *De bello alexandrino* 1: "*Incendio fere tuta est Alexandria quod sine contignatione ac materia sunt aedificia.*"

FIG. 82. A typical *contignatio*. Casa delle Muse, Ostia. Wooden floors were always used in the garrets of the tabernae but also in distinguished tenement houses as in Fig. 83.
Photo E. Nash. Fototeca Unione.

covered insulae was the decades before 79 A.D. This is the sturdy architecture found on every square meter of Ostia and wherever excavations have been made in Rome. The Forma Urbis shows exactly the same type (Figs. 77 and 78). No doubt there were still houses from which the mice and spiders fled (Pliny *N.H.* viii. 103), walls with dangerous cracks, and collapsing buildings. Decay caused by periods of economic depression, poverty, or negligent houseowners, does, of course, always occur and affects even the most perfect architecture. We hear about that also in our sources from the second and following centuries. But it is nevertheless evident that the brick-covered insulae of the Flavian age and onward mark a revolution in the history of town building, and it is a

FIG. 83. Caseggiato delle Trifore, Ostia. A tenement house without shops and with wooden floors (as the exterior with the slight distance between the apartments shows).
Photo E. Nash. Fototeca Unione.

serious methodological mistake to take sources concerning the old, most unsatisfactory town before the Neronian fire as referring to the new Rome, the image of which we have in second-century Ostia and in the few preserved brick-covered insulae in Rome.

This new utilitarian architecture with its concrete and brick façades was in western Europe the most outstanding tradition handed over to European towns, in spite of the lack of chimneys, which made cooking a rather primitive affair (Fig. 98); as for heating and sanitation, the arrangements for these were scanty or nonexistent. The Roman tenement houses were, as a matter of fact, parts of a collective system where very much of the social life, entertainments, baths, and a good deal of the food and personal comfort were provided outdoors by the town community. The Roman insulae cannot be fully understood without those appendages, which covered a remarkably large proportion of the essential needs of domestic life. This must be emphasized, since I wish to establish that in medieval times the Roman tenement houses remained the model. But—to my mind—the obvious connection between the medieval houses and their Roman models must not make us forget that the latter were originally conceived as part of a much better-equipped, rich, and generous town life than that of medieval cities.

What Suetonius tells us about Rutilius' speech *De modo aedificiorum* (*Augustus* 89), Augustus' energetic endeavors to support the progressive urban schemes, Vitruvius' discussions and criticism, and Nero's plans (*Nero* 16, cf. Tacitus *Ann.* xv. 40. 43), all help to give us some idea of how the new town of the second century A.D. evolved. Technical progress is accompanied by a surprising uniformity in the exterior of the houses; a certain matter-of-fact beauty in the façades is achieved by a few, always recurrent elements: well-planned rows of windows, restricted but effective decoration of the main entrances, concrete balconies along the façade of the *piano nobile* (Figs. 42, 73 ff.). The terrace of the Thermae of Trajan, the Sallustian villa on the Monte Pincio, and the so-called Praetorio of the Villa of Hadrian below Tivoli show that this architectural motive was used as a decoration even for quite distinguished architecture. To this standardized architecture belong also the tabernae with barrel vaults below the balconies of the façade, their garrets with small square windows above the door and their counters blocking half the entrance (Figs. 74–76, 80, and 81), as I have already pointed out when speaking of the Forum baths of Pompeii in the 70's B.C. These features can be seen both in medieval and later paintings and in houses right down to our own age.

As a most outstanding embellishment of these stern utilitarian houses there occur arcaded or colonnaded porticoes in front of the rows of tabernae (Figs. 81, 84), exactly as in the Via dei Tribunali of Naples or in Bologna and other North Italian towns. Porticoes were an especially important part of the communal comfort, as is testified by many ancient authors; examples are seen in Ostia and in many fragments of Forma Urbis (Figs. 77 and 78). Their history goes back to Republican times, as is shown for instance by Festus' description of the old porticoes below the Maeniana of the Forum

a

b

FIG. 84. Porticoes and tabernae.
a) Portico in front of a row of tabernae
along the Decumanus in Ostia.
Photo A. B. 1930.
b) The same scheme of arrangement,
still common all over Italy, at the Piazza Caricamento in Genoa. 1925.

Romanum. Nero, who in general supported the current improvements in town building and planning, especially fa-
vored porticoes in front of both insulae and domus. The Romans believed that he even aimed at the distinction of being
the champion of a new kind of architecture and a second
founder of Rome. We see him clearly as one of the supporters
of progressive tendencies in town building which we can
follow from late Republican times onward to their victory in
second-century Rome.[35]

The planning of the houses is no less standardized than
the façades. The point of departure is the row of shops with
added upper stories to which direct staircases lead (cf. above).
The main types of planning are surprisingly few. I have ventured to suggest—at least as a provisional clue to Ostia and
the Forma Urbis—the following classification.

Type I (Figs. 77 and 78): one row of tabernae with upper
stories, such as we see on both sides of the cardo in Ostia and
on numerous fragments of the Forma Urbis.[36] This is to my
mind the basic type for insula architecture. As I have pointed
out (see above), it occurs as early as the third century B.C. below the Portico della Mura del Castrum in Ostia. Exactly the
same kind of houses are to be found today in old-fashioned

35.   For Maenania see Festus s.v. Lindsay, pp. 120–21. For Nero see Suet. *Nero*
16 and 38 (*"quasi offensus deformitate veterum aedificiorum flexurisque vicorum"*);
Tac. *Ann.* xv. 40, with my remarks in *Acta Rom. Suec.*, II (=*Corolla Arch.*, 1932),
84 ff.
36.   *Scavi di Ostia*, I, map 8. The Cardo maps 2 and 3.

towns all over Italy (Fig. 80).

Type II (Figs. 77 and 78): two rows of tabernae built back to back, with upper stories. Again Forma Urbis affords a great number of illustrations. In Ostia the type is equally frequent—for instance the tabernae between the palestra of the Terme di Nettuno and the Decumanus.37 As a modern example we might cite the Mercato Nuovo of Venice.

Type III: For the sake of convenience I group together rows of type I or II, which surround an inner courtyard or building, as for instance in the *horrea* of Ostia and Rome.38

Type IV (Figs. 85 and 86): Great house blocks—what Guido Calza used to call "*palazzi di tutti*"—combining the usual façade with tabernae toward the streets and inner courts with peristyles in two or three stories. The luxury of the domus, with peristyles, is thus transferred also to tenement house architecture. I emphasize the fact that the courtyards of type IV adhere to the tradition of the Italianized peristyles of late Republican and early Imperial times with tablina, axiality, etc. They are not to be understood as *directly* adapted from the Hellenistic towns, though, of course, the Roman architects of the Imperial Age could freely use elements from the whole Empire to meet the demands of more developed living conditions. Typical of this combination are the Casa di Diana, the Caserma dei Vigili, the so-called Case delle Muse, del Serapide, degli Aurighi, and the Horrea Epagathiana in Ostia. This is the final achievement of this kind of architecture, typically Roman in its axiality and in that same wish to create solid architectural units which we see at work in the Roman theaters and libraries, such as the Templum Pacis in Rome or the library of Hadrian in Athens.39

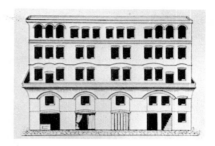

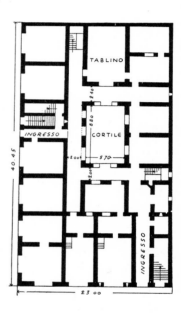

FIG. 85. Façade and plan of the Casa di Diana, Ostia. Cf. Fig. 75.

37. *Scavi di Ostia*, I, map 4.
38. See for type III buildings like those delineated on the fragments of "Forma Urbis" 36, 37 (not Horrea Agrippiana; "Type III" is well described by M. Berucci, *Palladio*, n.s. IV (1954), pp.145 ff.), 169, 176, 179, 184, 191, etc. (Jordan).
39. Calza, "Contributi alla storia della edilizia romana," *Palladio*, V (1941), 1–33. Important are the houses in Volubilis, described by R. Etienne, *Maisons et hydraulique dans le quartier nord-est a Volubilis* (Paris, 1954). Ph. Harsch in an otherwise useful article in *M.A.A.R.*, XII (1935), 9 f., connects these courtyards directly with Hellenistic prototypes without realizing their development in Italy.

FIG. 86. Casa di Diana, Ostia, and a
view of Via dei Tribunali, Naples.
Photo A. B. 1930.

Together with type IV, I group two other mixed types. All over Pompeii and Herculaneum we see atrium houses provided with tabernae on either side of the vestibule of the atrium. Livy's description (xliv. 16, 10) of the house of the Scipiones in the Forum Romanum shows the same combination of atrium and tabernae, obviously due to the dispersion of trade and commerce from the bazaar quarters around the Forum and showing that the owners of the domus wished to make their houses a source of income; competing with the business activity which went on in the rows of tabernae, they took part in the contemporary development of town life in Italy. Connected with these common atrium houses with tabernae there is another type to be found in Herculaneum and in the Ostia of both Republican and Imperial times (Fig. 87); it has, toward the street, a typical insula façade, with tabernae (type I), a staircase to upper stories and a passage to the atrium or peristyle of the interior. Here the domus is protected from the crowded life of the street by means of an insula of type I—a lucrative affair.[40]

A day in Ostia or among the remains of insulae in Rome[41] and a study of the Forma Urbis show that types I and II, that is, large insulae with rows of shops, were the most common. They were the true expression of the prosperity and the commercial and industrial activity in the happy centuries of the Empire. On Ambrogio Lorenzetti's great fresco "Buon Governo" (1338) in the Palazzo Pubblico of Siena we again see open tabernae symbolizing peace and order among the

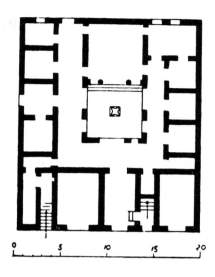

FIG. 87. Casa del Tempio Rotondo, Ostia.

40. For this type I refer to the large Republican atrium house, excavated at the Decumanus of Ostia (*Regio*, IV, *Scavi di Ostia*, I, map 7), to the Domus del Tempio rotondo (*Scavi di Ostia*, I, map 7) and to Forma Urbis, fragment 109 c (Jordan). Typical is Casa del tramezzo di legno in Herculaneum in its final shape (Insula III n. 11). A. Maiuri, *Ercolano. I nuovi scavi* (1927–1958), I (Roma 1958), pp. 207 ff.

41. Most important: the insula incorporated in the Basilica Celimontana dei SS. Giovanni e Paolo. A.M. Colini, "Storia e topografia del Celio nell'antichita," *Mem. Pont.*, VII (1944), 164 ff., Pl. 9 and A. Prandi, *op. cit.*, p. 250; Mercato di Trajano between Trajan's forum and the Via Nazionale; the insula below S. Anastasia and in Via Giulio Romano below Aracoeli. See Lugli, *I monumenti antichi di Roma e suburbio*, I, 61–63; Supplemento, pp. 10 f.; I, 394 ff. and 229 ff.

achievements of good government. Various rather scarce combinations of tabernae different from types I–IV seem to have had but slight importance for future developments.[42] Type I occurs also in a curved version, examples of which can still be seen around the theater of Ostia (Fig. 88) and the Circus Maximus (see also Dion. H. iii. 68, 4). There are also types of obviously distinguished insulae without tabernae, but they—like the domus—belonged to the well-to-do bourgeoisie which vanished with the decline and fall of Rome.[43] These are interesting because they seem to reproduce on the ground floor the usual disposition of the upper stories common to all this architecture, but for the present argument the vast majority, the large insulae with rows of tabernae, are of much greater importance.

The insulae and their shops were often the common property of many owners; their *partes insulae* were, as far as I can see, usually taken as being vertical sections. This most natural development of the proprietary rights no doubt contributed to the rise of a reduced, narrow type of insula, the "strip" or "segment house" (Figs. 89–91), each consisting of only one taberna, and a door to a staircase, or a corridor leading to a court with a staircase, and upper stories each with only two windows. When two such houses were coupled together there resulted a very characteristic façade with two closely connected tabernae in the center and doors at the corners, as we see at the Casa della Capella d'Iside in Ostia.[44] In the upper stories there were probably windows in the center, as in medieval and later architecture of the same kind. These re-

---

42. P. Zicans in a useful essay has catalogued various types of houses on the Forma Urbis, *Acta Rom. Suec.*, v (=*Opus Arch.*, II, 1939), 183 ff.

43. Via del caserma dei vigili, regio II, insula III, Via della Fontana (Fig. 102, *Scavi di Ostia*, I, map 4), Insula dei dipinti, Insula di Bacco Fanciullo at the Via dei dipinti (*Scavi di Ostia*, I, map 3) and above all Via delle trifore (*Scavi di Ostia*, I, map 6) supply especially good specimens of insulae without shops. It is characteristic that the windows of the apartments on the bottom story are placed high up, a feature also found in medieval architecture.

44. Calza-Lugli, "La populazione di Roma antica," *Bull. Comm.*, LXIX (1941), 142–65; G. Lugli, "Il valore topografico e giuridico dell'insula in Roma antica," *Rend. Pont.*, XVIII (1941–42), 191 ff., and "Nuove osservazioni sul valore topo-

FIG. 88. Shops around the theater of Ostia. Cf. Fig. 76.
Photo E. Nash. Fototeca Unione.

grafico e catastale dell' 'insula' in Roma antica," *Rivista del catasto e dei servizi tecnici erariali*, n.s. 1 (1946). See also L. Homo, *Rome imperiale et l'urbanisme dans l'antiquité* (Paris, 1951), pp. 638 ff., and my remarks in *Colloqui del sodalizio*, II (cited note 11).—Casa della Cappella d'Iside: *Scavi di Ostia*, I, map 13.

duced types of insula house do not seem to have been common in Imperial Rome. The large insulae with rows of shops were the true expression of the *pax romana*, as I have already said, but we must not forget that strip houses occur both in Ostia and on the Forma Urbis.[45] In the town that symbolizes Ostia on the Tiber statue in the Louvre (Fig. 92) one of the houses is a typical segment house. Paintings like Bonfigli's representation of Totila's attack upon Perugia (Fig. 93) and all maps and pictures of Rome made in the sixteenth and following centuries show that this type of house became by far the most common in medieval times and onward. It still abounds in old parts of Rome and in old towns all over Italy.[46] It remains an interesting problem to discover when these different types of reduced insulae obtained their immense importance for medieval and later times.

45.   Cf. my notes from Ostia in *Studies Presented to D. M. Robinson*, I, pp. 440 f., and the studies quoted in note 44. For the interpretation of the town on the Louvre basis as a symbol for Ostia see J. Le Gall, *Recherches sur le culte du Tibre* (Paris, 1953), and my remarks, *Gnomon*, XXVIII (1956), 262–63. For the typical strip house in Herculaneum (Insula IV, n. 19–20) called "Casa della Stoffa" see now A. Maiuri, *Ercolano*, I, 425 f.

46.   In Milan, Pavia, and other towns of northern Italy, as also in many "strip houses" in Rome, the entrance door is connected with a corridor to an inner courtyard, where the staircases to the upper stories are to be found. But the façade resembles those of the Roman "segment houses." The segment house at the Semita dei Cippi in Ostia (published by me in *Studies Presented to D. M. Robinson*, I, p. 447, fig. 7) and the fragment 173 of the Forma Urbis (Jordan) have a direct staircase from the street and a corridor like those in Milan and Pavia to an inner court with staircases.

FIG. 89. A "strip house" or "segment" from Herculaneum (Cardo v, 19–20) with a taberna to the right and to the left a wooden staircase to the upper stories. Cf. Figs. 90 ff.
Photo A. B.

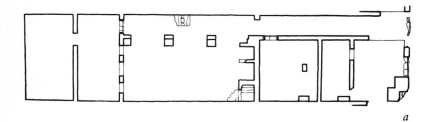

a

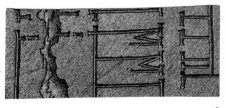

b

FIG. 90.

a) The "strip house" at the Semita dei Cippi. From left: stairs, reservoir, taberna, and corridor to the inner court. Plan by H. Neumüller.

b) A fragment of the Forma Urbis showing "strip houses" with staircases (marked by triangles) and tabernae.

I have repeatedly referred also to other old architectural traditions still alive in Italian towns today (Figs. 76, 79–81, 84, 91)—the rows of tabernae, their garrets, the façade balconies, the direct staircases to the upper stories, the porticoes, the counters, etc.—as obvious and most enlightening parallels to the Roman insulae and their standardized façades. We cannot find better illustrations for the ancient insula façades with or without porticoes than façades in Italian towns from the thirteenth to the twentieth century! To stroll in old parts of Rome also helps us to understand what the narrow streets of Ostia and Rome were like, with their houses of three or more stories and a maximum height of about sixty-five feet (20 m.). And to get a vivid picture of the life in the insulae one may read any description of life in an old Italian tenement house today.[47] All over the towns we find the same vertical division as in Roman "strip houses," the same democracy with shops below, and, independent of them and accessible by the direct and steep flights of stairs, the apartments for better-class folk above them in the same house.

In summarizing my observations I refer to the project of Pope Nicholas V (d. 1455) for the replanning of the Borgo Leontino in Rome—a project known to me through a valuable investigation by Torgil Magnuson.[48] The pope and his architects planned three broad and ample streets. Each of these three streets was to be distinguished from others by the type of dwellings, shops, and workshops which it contained. The upper stories were to be abodes for cardinals and other dignitaries and the three streets were to be decorated with colonnades, constituting six porticoes, two on each street, facing each other.

47. For instance, G. Ceroni's "I vecchi rioni," *L'Urbe*, XVIII (1955), 16 ff.
48. *Studies in Roman Quattrocento Architecture* (Stockholm, 1958), pp. 65 ff.

a

b

A better description of the cardo of second-century Ostia could hardly be found (Fig. 95). One could easily believe that the architects of Nicholas V had made an excavation as did Sigismondo Malatesta in 1448, when, while rebuilding Sena Gallica and renewing the cardo and decumanus, he did actually "*riscoprire li antichi fondazioni della cittade.*"[49] This was not, of course, done by Nicholas V, but the question remains: are these detailed resemblances and the other conformities which I have pointed out as parallels a mere coincidence? To assert as much would, in my opinion, simplify the matter in an unrealistic way, and delude by a seemingly unsophisticated and convenient solution. Indeed, the unsurpassed urbanistic creation which was Imperial Rome is already in itself enough to make us doubt whether such an achievement could be forgotten after being alive in the daily life of Italy and France for more than half a millennium. More enormous catastrophes than those of our medieval age would have been needed to abolish such a legacy, especially in the crowded quarters of common people.

It seems a priori evident that Roman experience and planning as well as technique must have lived on in any case as decaying traditions from the greatest town of the world, the unsurpassed model of town life. It seems almost inevitable

49.   Mario Ortolani, Nereo Alfieri, "Sena Gallica," *Rend. Linc.*, s. 8, VIII (1953), 152 ff., especially 170 f.

FIG. 91. Medieval and later "strip houses" in the Italy of today.
a) Anderson's photograph shop at the Piazza di Spagna in Rome is a taberna of a "strip house" with entrance to the staircase at the left—a type common in Rome and all over Italy.
Photo A. B. 1956.
b) Medieval houses with tabernae and so-called "doors of the dead" (*porta del morto*) at Via S. Francesco in Assisi. Right of the first entrance: two "strip houses" with shops and the narrow doors of the staircases to the upper stories.
Photo A. B. 1957.

that these traditions must have survived in degenerate early medieval architecture. In some cases they were still to be seen in ruins or in use (Fig. 96). These remains probably inspired medieval and Renaissance builders, when in the twelfth century or even earlier they started to overcome the wilderness of their towns, at a period long before Brunelleschi, Alberti, and other Renaissance architects measured the remains of monumental classicistic architecture and long before Sigismondo Malatesta made his excavations to find out the city plan of ancient Sena Gallica and Palladio studied Rome.

Trying to substantiate this working hypothesis we have to distinguish between two things: on the one hand, a conscious and rather learned return to Roman models and, on the other, features without any monumentality, like worn and torn everyday suits. In impoverished towns and times people generally go on building more or less in the same way as did their predecessors—as far as possible and as far as the architectural repertory of happier ages can be adapted to their needs. In the present discussion we must compare the way in which the castrum plan in towns like Florence, Lucca, or even some in Germany remained a decayed but indelible and even inspiring legacy of unbroken urbanistic tradition. We can compare the history of ancient endeavors in widely different fields—for instance the history of Greek perspective. On the one hand, survivals of it in medieval life, as Bernhard

FIG. 92. Base of the Tiber statue in the Louvre with houses symbolizing a town (Ostia or Laurentum?). The second house from the left is a "strip house" with a closed taberna and a staircase. After the fourth house one traces a tower of the walls of the town. Courtesy of the Louvre Museum.

FIG. 93. Bonfigli's painting of Totila's siege of Perugia. In the foreground to the right two "strip houses" with shops and staircases and a house with two shops and staircase.

Schweitzer says in his beautiful book *Vom Sinn der Perspektive*: "Nur noch Bildzeichen . . . ., Erinnerungsfetzen, eine ihres Wesens fast entleerte Hülle . . . ."; on the other hand, the reconstructed and deeply changed perspective of the Renaissance.

To start with let us leave aside the learned Renaissance of monumental architecture and ask how far the available material goes in proving a continuity in utilitarian town architecture from ancient times to the tenement houses of the twelfth and following centuries. The first and last stages are very clear. We have the Roman insulae down to about the sixth century. And Walter Paatz[50] has shown that at least from the twelfth century onward the idea of high tenement houses is present in such Florentine insulae as Palazzo della

50. "Ein antikischer Stadthaustypus im mittelalterlichen Italien," *Römisches Jahrbuch für Kunstgeschichte*, III (1939), 127 f. In addition to these broad insulae, towers with shop and staircase to the upper stories (i.e., typically medieval "segment-houses") should be noted such as Torre degli Amidei (Via Por Sta Maria) and Torre de' Satarelli (Chiasso del Buco; both reconstructed after the war) and others all over Italy. See also P. Tomei, *L'architettura a Roma nel quattrocento* (Roma, 1942), and Chr. Elling, *Rom. Arkitekturens liv fra Bernini til Thorvaldsen* (Copenhagen, 1956), pp. 363 ff.

a

b

d

c

FIG. 94. Staircase, entrance to court, and tabernae, ancient and modern.
a) Pompeii: Forum baths, about 70 B.C. Staircase, entrance to the Thermae, shop.
b) Ostia: Casa di Diana, second century A.D. Shop, entrance to court, and staircase.
c) Entrance and staircase in Ostia, second century A.D.
d) S. Felice (Latium).
Photo A. B. 1930.

FIG. 95. The Cardo of Ostia.

Mercanzia, Palazzo dei Giudici at Piazza Mentana (1333), Palazzo Spini-Feroni (corner of Via Tornabuoni and Lungarno Acciaioli—late thirteenth century) and Palazzo Bezzoli (Piazza dell'Olio, Fig. 97) with its tabernae and cortile. This architecture can be followed back to the twelfth or even eleventh century. Paatz makes it quite clear that these houses stand in a tradition different from that of contemporary Romanesque architecture. He does not hesitate to connect their stern, strictly utilitarian façades with the Roman insulae. In other words, after an interval of some six hundred years we again meet tenement houses often almost exactly like the Roman insulae. They can hardly be explained otherwise than as a renewal of the ancient insula idea which was still alive in utilitarian architecture and in the actual remains of ancient insulae (Fig. 42). Palazzo del Aquila shows that in the hands of a Raphael the legacy could be brought back to the perfection which we see or can reconstruct in the ruins of Ostia and Rome.

In considering the interval of six hundred years between about 600 and 1200 A.D., we are concerned with a problem of great general interest: what legacy can remain in the life of the common people after the downfall of a period of high culture? We meet the same problem (and it deserves a thorough study) in the centuries after 1100 B.C., when we find that the Late Helladic armor, shipbuilding, types of palatial

FIG. 96. One of the tabernae of the Imperial Age at the church of Sta. Anastasia in Rome. The attic is still in use while the taberna below it has gradually been buried by the rising level of the town.
Fototeca Unione.

house (*megaron*), pottery technique, traditional tomb construction, not to mention cults, remained the same, in spite of the fact that all centers of advanced culture were destroyed and the main features of this culture were forgotten, as Homer shows *ad abundantiam*.[51] In studying the domestic architecture we should abandon the strictly formal point of view, try to understand the "unheeded and familiar speech" of poor common life, and make clear that, in the building activity at present under discussion, usefulness and function were the motive forces, not the aesthetic value of the used forms. We have to compare trite, customary ways of the architecture of daily life with quite common features which have remained unchanged from ancient times up to our own or at least our grandfathers' days, such as the commerce on the streets in front of the tabernae, the custom—in certain circumstances—of keeping a lamp burning in the daytime at

51. A model for this kind of research is V. R. Desborough's *Protogeometric Pottery* (Oxford, 1952).

FIG. 97. Palazzo Bezzoli at the Piazza dell'Olio, Florence. A Romanesque window of the third story dates the palace to the thirteenth or even to the twelfth century.
Photo Brita Wikström 1956.

the entrance to the house or the shape of the counters.[52]

We all recognize the survival of Roman traditions in this field when we call to mind the pluvial or cope of the bishop's attire and the monk's hood and habit that are derived from the workers' clothing of ancient times. The pictures carried in medieval and later ecclesiastical processions obviously continue a tradition which stems from the Roman triumphs. Scholars of former times who had close acquaintance with life in Italy both in antiquity and in their own days, Gregorovius for instance, felt this unsophisticated tradition vividly and deeply. It may suffice to note his comparison between the Hercules of Girgenti, whose cheek, according to Cicero, was worn by the kisses of the devotees, and the toe of St. Peter in St. Peter's in Rome. One could also refer to the tenacious tradition of ancient kitchen fireplaces, as we know them from Pompeii, Herculaneum, Ostia, and the tombs of Isola Sacra (Fig. 98). We still recognize them in the stoves of medieval houses and right down to the nineteenth century all over Italy (in spite of the great change when chimneys were added), and we may ask ourselves also about traditional cooking, remembering for instance the *dura farra*, the spelt, which continued in use until recently in the old, crowded parts of Rome and in the Italian countryside under the name of *faricello*.[53]

52. Illuminating are G. Spano's notes "Alcune osservazioni nascenti da una descrizione dell'Anfiteatro di Pompei," *Annali, Istituto Universitario di Magistero, Salerno*, I (1953), and "La illuminazione delle vie di Pompei," *Atti della R. Accademia di archeologia, lettere e belle arti di Napoli*, VII, 2 (1920), 1 ff. An interesting parallel from Greece is offered by A. Kriesis, "Tradition in Evolution: the Persistence of the Classical Greek House," *The Architectural Review*, June 1948, p. 267, and *Acta Congressus Madvigiani* IV, 71, with further references.

53. For the *dura farra* see Ovid *Fasti* vi. 180 and 313; Varro *L.L.* v. 106. For the triumphal processions, see O. Vessberg, "Det romerska triumftåget," *Arkeologiska forskningar och fynd. Studier utgivna med anledning av H.M. Konung Gustaf VI Adolfs sjuttioårsdag*, 1952, p. 132. The pluviale and other items of clerical and monastic attire have always revealed themselves as a legacy from Roman life during the centuries of the persecutions. There workers' dress as well as the apparel of state officials are to be considered, though the latter belongs to the great tradition. See W. Deonna's "De Télesphore au 'moine bourru.' Dieux, genies et demons encapouchonnés," *Collection Latomus*, XXI (1955). The studies of the centunculus of the *Fabula atellana* and the harlequin attire provide us with

Typical of the chain of uninterrupted daily life that I aim to demonstrate is the close resemblance between the Roman workman's tools from a Walbrook site in London and those which are still in use today. As the excavators[54] say, the obvious explanation is "that once a tool had evolved to its most efficient form, it remained unchanged. . . . It is not too much to say that a Roman craftsman, set down in a village workshop of about fifty years ago, would have felt perfectly at home, and could have set to work at once with the equipment which he found there." That is exactly what could be said about the Roman tabernae and the shops or workshops still existing in all old quarters of today. In discussing such trivial examples of continuity, I could also refer to the collections of American furniture, tools, etc., in Sturbridge, Massachusetts, or Mr. Du Pont's Winterthur Museum in Delaware. Over and over again the European background is obvious in quite simple tools and details. They could, of course, have been invented afresh, but it is easy to see (and that is what interests us here as a comparison) that the immigrants had European types in mind. At the start almost nothing changes from what they had brought with them in their minds or in their luggage. In the same way the remains of Roman achievements lived on as a matter of fact.

FIG. 98. Kitchen stove. Fullonica Stephani, Pompeii. Everyone who has seen Italian kitchens with old traditions will recognize this type of fireplace with a receptacle for the fuel below. Photo G. Svanström 1949.

other instances of unbroken Roman legacy in medieval life. See A. Dieterich, *Pulcinella* (Leipzig, 1897), p. 145 and *passim*, and G. Widengren in *Orientalia suecana* (1953). Most illuminating is also the persistence of the ancient wine presses. Cf. A. G. Drachmann, *Ancient Oil Mills and Presses* (Copenhagen, 1932), and my note "The Art of Pressing Wine" in Drachmann's book. Fundamental is Jacono's reconstruction of the wine press in the Villa dei Misteri in Pompeii. The perticae of Taranto seem to be an instance of Roman tradition in town planning, cf. A. Ippel, *M.I.R.*, XLVI (1931), 198, especially pp. 274 ff.

54.   Norman C. Cook and Ralph Merrifield in *I.L.N.*, Oct. 8, 1955, p. 614. Addy in *The Evolution of the English House* (London, 1933) and R. C. Carrington, *Pompeii* (Oxford, 1936), p. 77, have not hesitated to connect the old rows of shops in England—for instance the rows of Chester—with the tabernae of the Roman houses. Referring to Calza's basic contributions I outlined many years ago a study of this kind of tradition in "Appunti sul carattere razionale e sull'importanza dell'architettura domestica di Roma imperiale," *Scritti in onore di B. Nogara* (Città del Vaticano, 1937), pp. 21 ff., and also suggested that a full description of some old street in Rome and its daily life should be made because of their millennial social and architectural heritage.

Much research is required to prove this in the field of architecture, but—as Lavedan has said speaking of buildings in paintings—almost none is done.[55] What is wanted is team-work by students of Roman architecture and law, medievalists, and architects concentrating upon the frail material from the dark centuries, that is, on Italian nonmonumental towns which the painters of later medieval times did not consider worthy representatives of the city (see below)—towns and quarters which still show the commonplace architecture of busy commercial streets and the wilderness of the proletarian quarters of the early Middle Ages. Thus, by painstaking research in the topography of ordinary towns and also, of course, in the archives we may be able to establish the means whereby the heritage from Imperial Rome lived on as a habit, a way of building, which was handy and useful even if it declined in less prosperous ages. Only in this way can the obvious tradition from Imperial Rome which persists in Italian tenement houses from the twelfth century be exactly and definitely proved.

Studying the old medieval towns, before they were systematized by Renaissance activity, we must realize that medieval life not only meant decline and loss from the point of view of Imperial Rome, but that there were also innovations, such as stoves and chimneys, the development of which came partly from the fact that the tenement houses in these towns had lost their connection with the collective system of Imperial times to which they once belonged.

In studying the nature of humble utilitarian buildings we cannot expect much help from medieval paintings unless it be the pictures in illuminated manuscripts. As I shall illustrate below, closed façades evidently came to prevail in the Dark Ages after the sixth century, at least in the finer parts of the towns. When in the twelfth century and later painters abandoned the ideogrammatic way, inherited from ancient art, of making generalized and abstract town pictures, they

55. As far as I know W. Braunfels, *op. cit.*, has established the best program for such research. G. Lugli's study of the segment houses in Rome, cited in note 44, should also be added as an important essay in the direction I advocate.

FIG. 99. Signorelli's S. Sebastiano (detail). In the Pinacoteca Comunale of Città di Castello.
Photo Anderson, Rome.

preferred to paint such streets rather than the renewed insulae or the busy bazaar streets with tabernae which flourished in their own towns and which, in my view, had continued to exist as a more or less decayed architectural survival from the Imperial Age. As a typical example of a common street with closed façades we may look at the lovely painting by Simone Martini, showing the miracles of Beato Agostino Novello in the church of S. Agostino in Siena, or at Signorelli's painting in Città di Castello (Fig. 99) with its marvelous representation of the three great conservers of ancient Roman tradition: ancient remains, ordinary town life, and the Church. In these

FIG. 100. Representation of a town in the Ilias Ambrosiana.
After R. Bianchi Bandinelli, *Hellenistic-Byzantine Miniatures of the Iliad* (1955).

and other paintings from the thirteenth and fourteenth centuries we rarely see a medieval reappearance of the open street of the *pax romana* with its rows of tabernae, even though we know that exactly this modernized utilitarian architecture must have been an important part of town life in the days of the painters! In the same way Vitruvius, in his survey of town architecture in his sixth book, speaks only of atrium houses, peristyles, and Greek megaron-like halls (*oeci*), and omits the tenement houses, which as a matter of fact were already in overwhelming majority in the towns of his days and which he himself discusses in another connection in his second book.

Of course there are exceptions. Miniatures often depict tabernae. As I have already said, Ambrogio Lorenzetti classes open tabernae among the effects of peace and good government. One sees shops in Bonfigli's painting of Perugia (Fig. 93). Lorenzo di Nicolò (or Taddeo Gaddi?) has painted a saddler's workshop and another taberna which might equally well have been seen in Pompeii, Herculaneum, Rome, Ostia, or even in any old-fashioned town of the present age.[56] But that is exceptional. The painters usually did not care for busy streets. And we have also to remember that unsettled

56.   The Prado Museum 2841 and 2842. See F. J. Sanches, *La collection Cambò* (Barcelona). Miss Nicky Mariano has drawn my attention to this instance of exceptional interest for the tabernae.

FIG. 101. The Caserma dei Vigili in Ostia.

times may often have encouraged even poorer people to build houses with closed ground floors, as did the great lords. The streets with tabernae obviously did not dominate the scene as they did in Roman days and only slowly regained their leading role. Already in the Imperial Age we hear about street fighting, which often caused the tabernae of the insulae to be closed in haste and panic—circumstances which herald the end of the predominance of the open business street, even if it, as I maintain, had an inferior afterlife right through medieval times.

For these problems it is important to remember that the closed façades, not less than the tabernae, had an interesting background in the Imperial Age. Already in the Ilias Ambrosiana[57] the towns are represented (Fig. 100) as having only houses with closed façades—exactly as in medieval paintings. The Caserma dei Vigili in Ostia (Fig. 101) gives an excellent specimen of a complex from the second century A.D., fortified in the same way as the medieval houses. It is natural that these barracks were built as a stronghold with closed façade and small windows high up, but it is also interesting to com-

57. R. Bianchi Bandinelli, *Hellenistic-Byzantine Miniatures of the Iliad* (Olten, 1955), Figs. 98–100. Cf. Figs. 103, 104, 106.

pare the streets without shops in Ostia (Fig. 102). Surveying other parts of the Empire one may compare the two- or three-storied houses of the Imperial Age in Egyptian towns, such as Karanis, which show the same type of architecture with closed bottom stories and one main entrance (see note 20).

In a masterly way Swoboda (*op. cit.*, pp. 133 ff.) has shown how, when hard times came, the lowest story of the porticus villas was generally closed. The porticoes were transferred to the second story and, in addition, the house was fortified by towers at the corners. This is shown over and over again on the mosaics from Roman villas in Africa. Reliefs on sarcophagi (Fig. 103) also show many examples of rustic villas with closed lower stories. The great villa ruin—called Mura di Santo Stefano—a little over a kilometer up the road

FIG. 102. Via della Fontana in Ostia shows a street without shops; the windows of the apartments in the bottom story are placed high up.
Photo Anderson.

FIG. 103. Riverside villa in the Vatican Chiaramonti collection (VI-25. Inv. 1280). Cf. Symmachus' delightful description of the villas along the Tiber and the ships with grain from Africa passing by, and, for the architecture, Fig. 104.

Courtesy of the Vatican Museums.

to Anguillara from the Via Clodia, is a fine specimen of this kind of fortified countryside architecture.[58] It affords us one instance among many to compare with medieval villas such as the Palazzo del Lido of Ambrogio Lorenzetti in the Pinacotheca of Siena (Fig. 105). Again, as the open street of the centuries of the *pax romana* contrasts in an almost dramatic way with the closed medieval streets loved by the painters, so the fortified country palaces of the later centuries of the Imperial Age and their medieval descendants stand out in striking contrast to the open porticoes of the villas in the wall paintings from Pompeii and remains of villas from earlier Imperial times.

But to return to the towns. Better than any other monument the great sarcophagus called Traditio legis (Fig. 106) in St. Peter's depicts monumental buildings which, with their closed ground floors, clearly herald the approach of medieval architecture; and there are plenty of other reliefs which show the same kind of architecture more or less as clearly. What a striking contrast to the street of the *pax romana*, the very expression of its rich, peaceful life, its rows of open tabernae all over the town, and the lively commerce in and between them. And how significant it seems that the Renaissance

58.   For instance in the Museo Chiaramonti of the Vatican collections XIX 23, inv. 1501; VI 25, inv. 1280. For the Mura di Santo Stefano see J. Ward Perkins, "Notes on Southern Etruria and the ager veientanus," *P.B.S.R.*, XXIII (1955), 61 and 66. I am much indebted to Dr. Hermine Speier for generous advice about the sarcophagi in the Vatican museums, which illustrate this kind of architecture.

painters concentrate upon the closed architecture and fail to help us detect traditions from ancient shop houses in the popular quarters of medieval towns.

Lavedan (*op. cit.*) has emphasized that painstaking studies of towns and pictures are needed in order to clarify the relations between the towns of the Empire and the Renaissance. To me, after considering the closed architecture of the late Empire, this general consideration is supplemented by the more specialized task of establishing how much remained of open tabernae in the last phase of the Empire and in the succeeding age of unexplored darkness. To what extent did artisans and merchants in late Imperial times transfer their production and trade to closed streets and fortified town houses with windowless magazines on the ground floor?

FIG. 104. Remains of a villa rustica, the so-called Mura di S. Stefano, near the Via Clodia (at the Anguillara road) north of Rome.
Photo E. Nash. Fototeca Unione.

In any case there is no doubt that rows of tabernae lived on, even if they were typical of less conspicuous parts of the town. An apt illustration of them from Rome is found in the words of Ferrante d'Aragona, king of Naples (1458–94).[59] Criticizing the porticoes along the streets of the old untidy city he said to Pope Sixtus IV: "*Disse che esso non era signore di questa terra, et che non gli poteva signoreggiare per amore delli porticali et per le vie strette et per li mignani che vi era. . . . et consiglioli che dovesse fare gittare li mignani et li porticali, et allargare le vie. Et lo papa piglio lo suo consiglio et d'allhora in po quanto sia stato possibile sono gittati li mignani et porticali, et allargate le strade.*"

Here we find Roman porticoes (Fig. 107) regarded as out-of-date, and it is remarkable that the age which advised the abolition of such uncontrolled survivals should simultaneously have initiated a revival of ancient grandeur of the porticoes along the street; the Renaissance of the insulae had started two hundred years earlier in Florence. In this we see together the uninterrupted continuance of decaying traditions side by side with the new growth of the Renaissance.

59.   Braunfels, *op. cit.*, p. 103. We may also note that King Ferrante took exception to the balconies (*mignani*) against which Roman laws had been aimed even in Imperial times.

FIG. 105. Ambrogio Lorenzetti's painting of a palace at the seashore. Accademia di Belle Arti, Siena.

FIG. 106. Roman town architecture of the fourth century. The so-called Traditio legis sarcophagus in St. Peter's. Courtesy Archivio fotografico Gall. Mus. Vaticani.

It is in this muddle of uncontrolled streets and houses, which King Ferrante makes us see in fifteenth-century Rome, that we trace the remains of the unsurpassed urban creation offered by the insulae of Imperial Rome. But, as I have pointed out, we should also remember that Roman insulae were still standing as ruins or were even in use in medieval times (Fig. 96). They may, of course, have inspired builders in the same way as did the ruins of monumental architecture, the laws, or Roman town planning when the *urbs nova* of later medieval times was in the making, with its rows of tabernae resembling those of the *pax romana*. But I am inclined to believe that the traditions inherent in the disorderly commercial architecture were more important for the tenement houses and the revived insulae of the later Middle Ages.

Where did the medieval revival of town architecture first take place? King Ferrante's remarks about the Rome of Sixtus IV seem to prove that Rome was not a creative center before the fifteenth century, although it exhibited any number of remains of Imperial Rome and, no doubt, enshrined many declining traditions from it. *Roma docebat*, in spite of its decay. Gian Giorgio Trissino, for instance, makes young Palladio return three times to Rome to study the ancient monuments. But the new city architecture seems to have been born in the great towns of Tuscany and North Italy, and it is, therefore, of the greatest importance and interest to know if the town builders in these places also had local Roman remains and traditions.

How far did the Roman system of insulae building extend in Imperial times?

I repeat that Vitruvius (ii. 8, 17) and other sources make it clear that the high Roman tenement houses were a typically Roman creation due to special local conditions, the *civium infinita frequentia*, etc. The praise which Vitruvius bestows upon it might easily lead us to assume that this most remarkable achievement of the town life of Imperial Rome was destined to be imitated all over the Empire. But it seems clear that it did not gain predominance in the Hellenistic parts of the Old World. On the other hand, a street like the Strada del Foro in Pompeii (Fig. 108) provides ample evidence that the tenement houses of the capital influenced coun-

FIG. 107. One of the many closed porticoes in Rome. A portico with Ionic columns at the Piazza di S. Cecilia in Rome.
Photo E. Nash. Fototeca Unione.

FIG. 108. Strada del Foro in Pompeii. The tabernae around the late Republican forum baths to the right, to the left the Caseggiato del Portico (Porticus Tulliana), a typical house of Roman type of the Imperial Age (Type I, see Fig. 77).
Photo A. B. 1930.

try towns in South Italy as early as in the seventies B.C. and the last decades before 79 A.D.[60] As far as I can see, we have not yet any material to prove the same thing for Milan and the other great towns of North Italy, or Marseilles, but that seems to be accidental, for in Gaul we again meet with porticoed rows of shops of Roman type with direct staircases from the street to upper stories, though they are built in coursed rubble faced with small square blocks. Such an insula is found next to the "House of the Messii" in Vaison (Vasio Vocontiorum, Fig. 109). The atria, peristyles, etc., of another distinguished house, the "House of the Silver Bust" are fringed by a row of tabernae with a portico in front toward the main street, like the Casa del Tempio Rotondo in Ostia (Fig. 87), which, of course, afforded the proprietor a considerable income. Pierre Grimal, discussing this important evidence, concludes: "*Certains quartiers—les plus populaires—des cités romaines de Gaul resemblaient donc déjà à telle vieille rue de Gênes ou de Nice.*"[61]

Thus, Italy twice produced a town architecture which constituted a revolution in town building and which—in

60. See also the plan of the forum bath, Fig. 43.
61. Grimal, *Les villes romains* (Paris: "Que sais je?" 1954), pp. 112–13. J. Sautel, *Vaison dans l'antiquité* (Avignon, 1926) and *R.E.*, II. 15 (Stuttgart, 1955), pp. 451 ff. (s.v. Vasio). Cf. notes 20 and 38.

FIG. 109. A row of tabernae with a portico (=Roman type 1). Vaison, France. The portico runs along the street (to the right) in front of the tabernae. Photo J. Ward Perkins.

spite of many shortcomings when compared with modern demands—marked a new chapter in the history of town building, and with new and lasting results. First came the tenement houses of Imperial Rome. Then, in the later Middle Ages, there reappeared the typical townhouse with its row of shops along the street, this time destined to spread over the whole western world. Even apart from the question of their historical connection it is evident that in function and planning both are closely related. The old-fashioned houses in Trastevere and on the Campo Marzio with (if I am right) their traditions more than two thousand years old are undoubtedly threatened by modern social demands. Today architects are in full and fervid activity, seeking new solutions to the perennial problem of large towns. No doubt the country towns will gradually follow their lead—as Pompeii started to do before its destruction, and as Vasio Vocontiorum shows. It may be of importance to understand what the old system once meant both as an improvement and a solution not only because of its external forms but also because of its attitude to common problems. Architects, photographers, and students of sociology ought to compile full records of the old tabernae-streets while they are still available for study, and they should try to trace their legacy from ancient Rome through medieval and Renaissance days, not only in architecture but also in daily life.

ADDENDUM

After I had sent the proofs to the press Luigi Crema's "L'architettura romana" appeared in the *Enciclopedia Classica* (III, 12). It is a most valuable work. Here I can only note the numerous points on which we agree and the many contributions he has made to the subject I have ventured to treat.

Some rather revolutionary discoveries and researches make an additional contribution to the discussion of the Iron Age in Italy. Einar Gjerstad has found a layer of "terra riportata" containing Apennine pottery and fragments of huts about the church of S. Omobono south of the Capitoline hill (*Svenska Dagbladet*, Feb. 5, 1960). Somewhere about the Forum Boarium there obviously was an Apennine village dating from about 1500 B.C. It seems clear that this Bronze Age settlement had already started the chain of continuous habitation on or about the Seven Hills. This startling discovery reminds one of the old stories about villages of Arcadians, Pelasgians, or other peoples in Rome before 753 (or 813, 747, or 728) B.C., but above all adds special interest to recent studies which vindicate an earlier date than the eighth century for the beginning of the Villanovan and Early Iron Age cultures in Latium, those, namely, of Hermann M. Karpe ("Beiträge zur Chronologie der Urnfelderzeit nördlich und südlich der Alpen," *Römisch-Germanische Forschungen*, XXII, 1959; "Vom Anfang Roms," R.M. Fünftes Ergänzungsheft 1959; "Sulla cronologia assoluta della tarda età del bronzo e della prima età del ferro in Italia nella zona alpina e nella

Germania meridionale," Civiltà del ferro Documenti e studi a cura della deputazione di storia patria per le provincie di Romagna, VI, 1960, 447–60) and Renato Peroni ("Per una nuova cronologia del sepolcreto arcaico del foro," Civiltà del ferro, 463–99, and "Per una definizione dell' aspetto culturale 'subappenninico' come fase cronologica a sè stante," *Mem. Linc.*, s. 8, IX, I, 1950).

It is of greatest importance for my second chapter that F. Castagnoli now maintains that Metapontum, as early as *ca.* 500 B.C., affords us an instance of Greek regular town planning of the same type as Olynthus: "La pianta di Metaponto. Ancora sull'urbanistica ippodamea," *Rend. Linc.*, s. 8, XIV (1959), 49–55. He and Signora P. Zancani-Montuori connect Metapontum with Paestum, Agrigentum, and Selinus and assume an early date for them also. In the latter cases I still maintain some doubts; the pronounced system with main streets meeting at right angles still seems to me to suggest Italic influence and a date around 400 or later. In any case Metapontum, like Marzabotto, seems to give a distant background to later towns, planned *per strigas*, such as Olynthus, Rhodes, Miletus, Naples, Pompeii, Capua, etc. See Chapter II, note 44.

In a great survey, "Nouveaux livres sur l'art romain," in the *Mededelingen van het nederlands historisch instituut te Rome*, s. 3, X (1959), 185–89, C. C. van Essen has rejected H. P. L'Orange's ideas about the *praecipua cenatio* of Nero and Ferris' interpretation of *Roma quadrata*, rightly emphasizing that *quadratus* never can mean *quadripartitus* (p. 186, note 1). See Chapter II, note 17. In an excellent study ("La Domus Aurea: nuovi problemi architettonici," *Bollettino del centro studi per la storia dell' architettura*, 12, 1958, 47–64) Giuseppe Zander presents a survey (with bibliography) of recent excavations. He reconstructs for the first time a hall with a nymphaeum on the east side of the peristyle of the western wing of the palace and also makes a number of very valuable observations about the alterations of the Domus Aurea after Nero's death and about the aesthetic values and differing architectural aims traceable in the first period. Crema (*op. cit.*) describes the Domus Aurea (pp. 312–14) and discusses an obviously Neronian nymphaeum construction with rectangular niches and apses along the eastern side of the Caelius, discovered by A. M. Colini, *Mem. Pont.*, s. 3, VII (1944), 137 ff.

In a fascinating book *Paradisus terestris, myt, bild och verklighet* (*Acta societatis scientiarum fennicae*, n.s. C., 1, No. 1. Helsingfors, 1958) Professor Lars-Ivar Ringbom (Åbo) tries to connect medieval ideas about the mountain of paradise with Shiz (Gandjak, Takht i Sulayman) in Parthia, described in A. U. Pope's "Preliminary Report on Takht-i-Sulayman I, The Significance of the Site," *Bull. Amer. Instit. Iranian Art*, V (1937), 75 ff. He tries to reconstruct the palace, temple, and golden throne (Takht-i-taqdis), interpreting the pillar, which Eriksson explains as the base of Chosroe's statue (*op. cit.*, p. 111), as the altar of Atur Gushnaps (p. 318), and discussing the oldest constructions as well as the palace and temple of Chosroe and Abaka Khan at the lake on the summit of the supposed paradise mountain Shiz. Ringbom mentions that Iranian, German, and Swedish archaeologists are planning a joint excavation of the site. See Chapter III, note 38.

In an article "Vicus cornicularius," *Arch. Cl.*, X (1958), 231–34, Luigi Moretti suggests that a street of the *corniculari* should be added to the other known specialized streets of different crafts, such as the *vicus lorarius*, the *vicus sandaliarius*, the *vicus materiarius*, and so on. See Chapter IV.

In an article about "Le 'tabernae' a Roma a traverso la 'Forma Urbis'," *Rend. Linc.*, s. 8, XIV (1959), 56–66, R. A. Staccioli starts a most desirable classification of the "tabernae" of the Forma Urbis, explaining them with the help of the tabernae of Ostia and rightly emphasizing that Ostia in Imperial times (after the construction of the harbors) was only a suburb of Rome—with a special character, not as a port town but as a dormitory for port workers, ship chandlers, etc., with exactly the same architecture as the capital. He also takes up the opinion, expressed by me and others, that the tabernae were used for the habitation of the proletariat as well as for crafts and trade. See Chapter IV.

INDEX